Robert Kroetsch:
Essayist, Novelist, Poet

Robert Kroetsch, Photograph by Michael Ondaatje.

Robert Kroetsch:
Essayist, Novelist, Poet

Edited by
David Staines

Reappraisals: Canadian Writers
University of Ottawa Press
2020

 uOttawa

The University of Ottawa Press (UOP) is proud to be the oldest of the francophone university presses in Canada and the oldest bilingual university publisher in North America. Since 1936, UOP has been "enriching intellectual and cultural discourse" by producing peer-reviewed and award-winning books in the humanities and social sciences, in French and in English.

Library and Archives Canada Cataloguing in Publication

Title: Robert Kroetsch : essayist, novelist, poet / edited with an introductory essay by David Staines.
Other titles: Robert Kroetsch (Ottawa, Ont.)
Names: Staines, David, 1946- editor.
Series: Re-appraisals, Canadian writers.
Description: Series statement: Re-appraisals, Canadian writers | Includes bibliographical references.
Identifiers: Canadiana (print) 20200153331 | Canadiana (ebook) 20200153358 | ISBN 9780776631288 (softcover) | ISBN 9780776628875 (hardcover) | ISBN 9780776631295 (PDF) | ISBN 9780776631301 (EPUB) | ISBN 9780776631318 (Kindle)
Subjects: LCSH: Kroetsch, Robert, 1927-2011—Criticism and interpretation.
Classification: LCC PS8521.R7 Z823 2020 | DDC 818/.5409—dc23

Legal Deposit: First Quarter 2020
Library and Archives Canada
© University of Ottawa Press 2020

Copy editing	Michael Waldin
Proofreading	Robbie McCaw
Typesetting	John van der Woude, JVDW Designs
Front cover layout	Steve Kress
Cover design	Bartosz Walczak
Cover image	Vignette tirée de l'ouvrage numérisé « Le Pays des fourrures » (gallica.bnf.fr) provenant du fonds patrimonial Heure Joyeuse, médiathèque Françoise Sagan, Paris.

The University of Ottawa Press gratefully acknowledges the support extended to its publishing list by the Government of Canada, the Canada Council for the Arts, the Ontario Arts Council, the Federation for the Humanities and Social Sciences, and by the University of Ottawa.

Table of Contents

Introduction
    DAVID STAINES   1

Home from Away: Kroetsch's American Decades
    DAVID ESO   5

Gone Indian and New World Myth
    TANJA CVETKOVIĆ   25

"A Sound That Was Almost Human": Non-Speech and the Animal Body in *What the Crow Said*
    ROBERT DAVID STACEY   39

Puppeteers and Collectors, or, Is God a Woman? Godgames in Kroetsch's Writing and Teaching
    MARTIN KUESTER   57

American Borders: Robert Kroetsch, Albert Johnson, and the Northern Frontier
    ALBERT BRAZ   69

Resituating Kroetsch: Georgic, Accident, and Object in Robert Kroetsch's "The Ledger"
    JENNIFER BAKER   83

"Poem for My Dead Sister": Kroetsch's Masterpiece
    PHIL HALL   101

Incomplete Field Notes: Eva Fritsch, Turnstone Press, and the Print Histories of Robert Kroetsch's "Seed Catalogue" and *Seed Catalogue*
    CAMERON ANSTEE   117

"letter as basic form right now": Kroetsch's Epistolary Poetics
    JASON WIENS   137

Kroetsch Abroad: The Travel Poems
DENNIS COOLEY   155

"like when the sun, similarly": Fragmented Fragments
in Robert Kroetsch's Chapbook Poetry
NICOLE MARKOTIĆ   185

Sketches of a Layman
LAURIE RICOU   201

Travelling with Kroetsch: Motion, Commotion, Emotion
WOLFGANG KLOOSS   215

Driving toward Digression
ARITHA VAN HERK   233

Robert Kroetsch: The Author and the Man
RUDY WIEBE   245

Contributors   259

Introduction
DAVID STAINES

Robert Kroetsch: Essayist, Novelist, Poet brings together an international cast of critics, scholars, and writers to examine, to re-examine, and to honour the celebrated essayist, novelist, and poet.

Robert Kroetsch (1927–2011) was a major figure in the development and history of literature in Canada. He won the Governor General's Award for Fiction for *The Studhorse Man* (1969); he was a nominee for the Governor General's Award for Poetry for *The Hornbooks of Rita K.* (2001). He received honorary degrees from the University of Winnipeg (1983) and the University of Alberta (1997). He was an Officer of the Order of Canada. He was the author of nine novels, thirteen books of poetry, and seven non-fiction volumes, not to mention his many articles and essays.

Kroetsch stands as a seminal figure in the Canadian literary landscape. In his early work he introduced postmodern techniques into the mainstream of Canadian fiction. At the same time he co-founded the literary journal *boundary 2*, which charted new paths in the postmodern world, and his editorial work led to his correspondence and meetings with countless postmodern practitioners in the United States, Canada, and Europe. When he returned to Canada in the 1970s, he brought with him his extensive knowledge of the postmodern world. He then moved on to writing poetry while still writing fiction, and he created a new vision for poets across the country; he defined the nature of the poetic experience by searching out the roots of his place in the Canadian landscape. At the same time he wrote countless essays that chart the way to Canadian involvement in the many worlds of contemporary literature.

Robert Kroetsch: Essayist, Novelist, Poet boasts an astonishing array of contributors writing about his major fiction, non-fiction, and poetry. Distinguished fiction writers and poets, professors emeriti, professors, and emerging scholars working towards their doctorates—all these people consider the place of Kroetsch in our cultural lives. They remind us of the immense significance he holds in our twenty-first-century understanding of what it means to be Canadian and as part of our own literary landscape.

The book opens with an absorbing account of Kroetsch's life. Through a careful examination of the Robert Kroetsch archives at the University of Calgary, David Eso uses Kroetsch's own words to "keep the man alive—a poet, novelist, critic, and mentor who raised the national and international profiles of Canadian literature."

The following three essays study Kroetsch's fictional creations. In "*Gone Indian* and New World Myth," Tanja Cvetković examines his remaking of old stories and myth as he turns them into new ones. *What the Crow Said* receives an impassioned reading from Robert David Stacey. And Martin Kuester, whose doctoral dissertation was written under Kroetsch's supervision at the University of Manitoba, studies *Alibi* and *The Puppeteer*, seeing parallels to Kroetsch's teaching methods; he concludes, quoting Dennis Cooley, that Kroetsch "was in a profound way private, at times enigmatic. Reluctant to speak when he was off the podium, he often drew back into memories and ruminations. And he listened."

Kroetsch's movement into the writing of poetry furthered his literary influence. Albert Braz studies Kroetsch's early poem "Poem of Albert Johnson," which was first published in 1975. Jennifer Baker resituates "The Ledger," which was first published in 1975. And Phil Hall considers "Poem for My Dead Sister" to be Kroetsch's masterpiece. Cameron Anstee looks at the print histories of Kroetsch's "Seed Catalogue" and *Seed Catalogue*. Jason Wiens reads "Letters to Salonika" and "Postcards from China" in the tradition of the epistolary poem, while "Letters to Salonika" and "Postcards from China" join "Delphi: Commentary" and "The Frankfurt *Hauptbahnhof*" as the subject of Dennis Cooley's magisterial analysis of Kroetsch's travel poems. And Nicole Markotić reads the final fragments of Kroetsch's uncollected poetry.

The final four essays look retrospectively and longingly at the figure of the man who was Robert Kroetsch. In "Sketches of a Layman,"

Laurie Ricou lets himself, his family, and his students reminisce about the Kroetsch he knew for so many years. Wolfgang Klooss remembers the summer of 1998 when Kroetsch was travelling in Germany, "a journey into the past—a past that resonates in the present." Aritha van Herk remembers driving with Kroetsch around the Battle River country, between Edmonton and Calgary, to Banff, and once between Winnipeg and Gimli, "Driving toward Digression" mirroring his own "endless and incomplete journey." In the concluding essay, "Robert Kroetsch: The Author and the Man," Rudy Wiebe, Kroetsch's best friend, offers a history of their fifty-one-year friendship and the sudden and devastating report of Kroetsch's tragic end.

"Robert Kroetsch was the great force out of the west. He and Rudy Wiebe together were a bolt of energy for the Canadian novel at a time when it really, really needed it. His *Words of My Roaring*, *Badlands*, and *The Studhorse Man* took the novel right out of the parlour, kidnapped it, and re-positioned it in a prairie bar or in open country," comments Michael Ondaatje. "He was the first novelist in our time to insist on being a poet as well. (It usually went the other way.) And he wrote great poems, such as The Ledger and Seed Catalogue. Finally, there was his last wonderful novel *The Man from the Creeks*. Talking with him, a hundred ideas were always generated. He was life-force. I can think of no one else like him."[1]

Robert Kroetsch: Essayist, Novelist, Poet sheds new light on this formidable figure in the Canadian landscape.

Notes

1   Quoted in Sandra Martin, "Author set his books in his native Alberta," *Globe and Mail*, June 25, 2011, S12.

Home from Away: Kroetsch's American Decades

DAVID ESO

> *This goddamned undiscovered country of ours might yet be discovered before it's too late. The horror is that art and love and politics are as necessary as they are futile.*
> — Robert Kroetsch

Born in Heisler, Alberta, Robert Kroetsch (1927–2011) is remembered as an accomplished author of poetry and prose; a distinguished teacher and editor; an Officer of the Order of Canada and winner of the Governor General's Literary Award. Since Kroetsch possessed exilic enthusiasm and post-national patriotism, how might we reconcile his extensive American experience against his literary imagination, widely received as prototypically Canadian? Linda Hutcheon, for example, has called him "Mr. Canadian Postmodern" (160). In considering the scope of his career, I draw on Kroetsch's archived correspondence, published works, and a lecture he delivered in 1996 at Ottawa, titled "Becoming a Writer is Unbecoming: My 20 Years in the U.S.A." The talk focuses on places Kroetsch passed through—Vermont, Iowa, Nevada, South Carolina—rather than Binghamton, New York, the place where he resided from 1961 until the mid-1970s. This errancy of emphasis conforms with the author's habit, when commenting on his biography, of favouring transience. Transience and stability cross-pollinate to generate psycho-geographic complexities negotiated throughout Kroetsch's writing.

A consideration of the author's familiar texts is preceded by a bio-historical sketch, one derived primarily from correspondence and from the "Becoming a Writer" lecture, both resources held in the University of Calgary's Special Collections archive. Researchers from myriad locations travel there to investigate the author's papers. Kroetsch's promotion of world literature and exporting of Canadian writing abroad have supported on-going interest in his work. His co-edited collection of European essays about Canadian literature, *Gaining Ground*, fostered "curiosity about a new literature," extended "an invitation to readers, everywhere, to make new maps of the sprawling and exciting and dangerous ground that is Canadian literature" (Kroetsch 1985, 8). Those words demonstrate the ambassadorial and renegade admixture which explains his dual successes as editor and artist. In part because he "never indulged in the snobbish and enervated withdrawls of those who practice expatriatism as a stance" (van Herk 1986, xiii), he ranks prominently among Canadian writers studied within and without the country.

Upon reaching the age of maturity at the close of the Second World War, Kroetsch left the family farm in the central Alberta region known as Battle River country. He then began a period of wandering that became equivalent in length to his formative years in Heisler. An undergraduate humanities education at the University of Alberta preceded another four years spent acquiring hard-won stakes in the sublime work camps of northern Canada—Fort Smith, Churchill, Mackenzie River, Hudson Bay—and dispensing them, with greater ease, in the urban fleshpots of southern Canada. By the early 1950s, Kroetsch attended Hugh MacLennan's lectures at McGill while experimenting with short fiction. He then accepted a position with the United States Armed Forces as an information and education specialist at the Goose Bay airbase in Labrador. On the periphery of the Korean War, a first novel took shape in his mind: a military satire in the vein of Joseph Heller. Such a fiction never materialized while for two years he oversaw University of Maryland satellite courses and managed the base's mimeographed newspaper and radio station. He wrote of his role on the base for Janice Tyrwhitt of *Maclean's* magazine, calling it "a respectable position if you don't mind going mad" (27, 21.1.5). That Kroetsch first inhabited American territory within Canada's borders seems an apt inauguration for his tenure south of the border. Throughout a twenty-year residence in the United States, Canada's literary and literal landscapes persistently occupied his imagination.

By the time Kroetsch abandoned the idea of spoofing military culture in fiction and quit his job with the Air Force, he had built a comprehensive mental map of American universities. Referring airmen leaving the service to specific academic programs stateside had constituted one of his duties in Labrador. He put that knowledge to work by pursing a master's degree at Middlebury College in Vermont and a doctorate through the Iowa Writers' Workshop. At Middlebury, as the distinguished graduate within his cohort, Kroetsch had the opportunity to dine with Robert Frost. They discussed the charms of rural roadways. At University of Iowa, he struggled not so much as an international student in competition with his American counterparts but more with the seasonal dilemma of whether to join up with the novelists or poets as a member of their softball teams. As usual, this author operates within a constellation of opposing pressures.

This period of wandering (spanning 1945 to 1961) concluded when Kroetsch took a job with Harpur College at Binghamton, New York. Shortly thereafter, the institution officially incorporated with the State University of New York system. Only after he settled in Binghamton did Kroetsch's literary materials solidify. He wrote in 1973 to Patricia Knox of new press about the process whereby retiring from northern, itinerant labour had opened up his comic world of the West: "With my lust for experience behind me (i.e., the lust itself purified, refined, focused) I did in fact begin to *write*" (27, 1.13. 41). As a young man brought up in the age of Hemingway, he had sought adventurous experience, not realizing that the family farm and surrounding villages had already provided the tall-tale narrative approaches and oracular prairie voices that would guide his creative work.

Outside an extensive public appearance schedule in his home country and several writing sabbaticals in England, Kroetsch maintained a permanent address in Binghamton for seventeen years. During that time, he made frequent return visits to Canada: to give readings, meet students, interview with media, and confer with publishers. A key feature to his returns was time spent with family in Alberta, which created an uncanny experience once the world they continued to inhabit had been reconstructed in his art. Kroetsch explains why he missed the chance to meet with novelist Robert Harlow during a 1976 trip to Canada in this way: "I had to do some listening at a family gathering that isn't likely to recur in a long time. Sort of like a gathering of my characters" (334/84.1, 3.11). The same construction appears in a journal entry: "Heisler. My hometown. Like being inside my novel—the extended family, drawn together" (Kroetsch 1980, 42). Trips to Canada fueled Kroetsch's creativity. Alongside reviving personal relationships, they allowed him intimate contact with Canada's burgeoning tribe of postmodern writers, the bevy of small-press publishers he supported with submissions, as well as the upstart editors of emerging literary journals such as *Grain, Salt,* and *Island.*

In 1972, Kroetsch expressed thanks to the editors of *Island*, his hosts on Vancouver Island: "The journey west, the westward visiting, was glorious. The stanching and unstanched flow of beer. The old chinaman bringing fish and chips. The heady talk. The lowering sky. I grieved eastward. May your publication thrive; or flounder on the rocks of its multitudinous success" (27, 2.2.13). A letter from the fall of that year describes *Island* as capturing the eclectic developments in Canadian literature that he keenly followed from afar. That explosive scene united audiences for writers as different as P. K. Page and bpNichol. Contemporaneously, Black Mountain aesthetics had consolidated to the point of monopoly in the American scene he observed from his post in upstate New York:

> The poetry you print is better than much of the shit published in America, the careful copies of each other's poems that poets write nowadays. The strength of your poets is place, place, *place*. They fucking know where they are, they look around, they expose the skin of their hands, of their knees, of their pricks, of their eyeballs to the veritable sand and gravel of this our unbuilt unheavenly city. The magazine itself has a good *feel*. [...] Tomorrow I flee north, into the Laurentians for a few days of being alone, seeking that old winter that drives us into our Canadian visions. (334/84.1, 3.23)

Further to a succinct encapsulation of Kroetsch's view of Canada's fruitfully multiple poetry scene, versus a supposedly homogenous and therefore sterile American one, this passage displays sociability and isolation as key features of his return trips to Canada.

One such visit of the early 1970s combined family bonding, wilderness solitude, and literary research. With his cousins Jerry and Hugh, Kroetsch embarked on a trip down Alberta's Red Deer River in preparation for composing the comic odyssey of William Dawe, featured in

Badlands. A letter to cousin Lorne Kroetsch, not present on the trip, gives a lively account the expedition:

> The downriver trip was an absolutely unique experience [...]. We had enough wine with us so that we might drink same with every meal for two weeks—and somehow ran out in two days. The supply of pot went up in smoke a day later. Fortunately, we broke a propeller and had to spend twenty-four hours in Drumheller waiting for a replacement. I suspect the Drumheller valley will never be quite the same again. From there on we plunged ever south and east, over rapids, over sandbars, over a variety of other bars, mostly in a lost cowboy town called Patricia. The trip yielded up all I had hoped for and more. Now I am stuck with the task of writing the novel.
>
> After the boat trip I borrowed Pat's car, drove back into the badlands alone, and hiked for a couple of days—a weird and beautiful experience, to be out alone in one of those valleys.
>
> Meanwhile, if you know any good escape routes, please keep them open. And I'll tell you, Kroetsch, never leave the west [...]. It's a beautiful life style. (334/84.1, 3.42)

The character Dawe—who searches for fossils along the same Alberta river during the First World War—receives his characteristic kyphotic curvature from his historical precedent, Canadian dinosaur-bone hunter George Mercer Dawson. The persistence with which Dawe seeks out and avoids the company of others he inherits in part from his creator. Kroetsch figures as affable and lonesome by turns. He rejoiced to share his research expedition with cousins, but he returned to the Badlands alone. Addressing his cousin by family name and not as "Lorne," in the final sentence quoted above, produces an eerie effect. It parallels the mirrored narrators and split consciousnesses that organize books like *Badlands*, *The Studhorse Man*, *Gone Indian*, and *The Hornbooks of Rita K*. The latter work studies the poet Kroetsch might have become if he had been born female and had chosen to "never leave the west."

Beyond providing on-site literary inspiration and enriching familial or professional connections, time in Canada during the 1960s and early 1970s provided relief from the pressures Kroetsch endured in Binghamton: his creative pursuits, academic career, and domestic obligations. "Tomorrow I leave for a week in Ottawa and points north," he wrote to Jerry O'Flanagan in 1972. "I need a breath of that freezing northern air, to clear my head" (27, 1.13.23). Sub-zero temperatures helped relieve the strain of his American situation. The border was perpetually accessible to him, with the Thousand Islands Bridge over the St. Lawrence River less than three hundred kilometers away. Ontario winters paled in comparison with the restorative properties uncovered in "sunny" Alberta. He relates the desire to "'knock the east out my breathing'" (quoted in Cooley 2016, 14); visiting western Canada provides "a tonic [for] the disease of the east [that] eats at my spirit some days" (27, 17.38.22). The concept of a curative west appears once more, with reference to Thomas Mann's classic novel *The Magic Mountain*. Kroetsch spent his summers from 1974 to 1977 (Cooley 2016, 4) at the Saskatchewan Summer School for the Arts, which was previously a tuberculosis sanitorium. Swiss Alp "flatlands" haunt the gentle slopes of Saskatchewan when he invokes Mann's novel, describing the school as "a little touch of the magic mountain, in a valley below the wheat plains" (27, 1.9.73).

Flights outbound from Binghamton led Kroetsch to rural destinations on the prairies as well as to major population centres across Canada, where he encountered a thriving literary industry. A conference at York University in 1970 provoked the following reaction:

> What I learned most about was the genuine hunger for a Canadian literature. [... T]he need for fiction and poetry came blazing through as the students responded, asked questions. [...] Yes, we are into it now, not Canadian lit as something given, inherited, but as something we are making. It's good and terrifying at once. Some people didn't like my using the word "terror." They don't want that possibility to intrude—while in Quebec the army stands guard. Perhaps the strangest thing was to come into the situation and see the people in it treating it as somehow normal. Again, for me, the unreality of reality... (334/84.1, 1.23)

His archive preserves equivalent enthusiasm for an abundance of literary events that Kroetsch attended in major cities and smaller centres: such as Fredericton, Thunder Bay, Cranberry Portage, and Jasper. After returning to Binghamton from Vancouver Island in 1972, he wrote: "I felt that in leaving Nanaimo I was somehow leaving, not a place I had visited, but home itself" (27, 2.2.11). The comment suggests Kroetsch desired to make an expansive home for himself throughout all Canada. Foreign exile may have been proleptic to this sense of belonging on a national scale. After only a short stay on Prince Edward Island, he would list that province among those places where he had "lived" rather than toured (2017, 208).

During sabbaticals from his work in the English Department of Harpur College/SUNY-Binghamton, Kroetsch worked on two novels in England. *But We Are Exiles* was completed largely in Cambridge, circa 1963, and *The Studhorse Man* in Sussex, circa 1967. Letters from these locations belie an enthusiasm for Britain that his American correspondence never admits for America. A compelling triangulation between his home and host countries emerges:

> Living in England made me realize how deeply I am anchored in Canada: from the distance offered by a Sussex village [Cuckfield], my American experience seemed very thin. [...] Or perhaps the trouble is that my American experience has been entirely academic. In England I was once again back in a world where few people were professors; that, along with the village and the fields, along with the excitement of London, liberated me into my own past, so to speak. (334/84.1, 1.23)

In 1968, Kroetsch recalled attendance at British cricket matches as among the "high points in [his] life" (591/96.6, 3.42). I have seen no letters expressing comparable enthusiasm for Major League Baseball's halcyon renditions of battle. For him, America boasted an "unlikely" form of "beaut[y]" conveyed primarily through "politics and heat" (591/96.6, 3.42).

The period of his American residence was marked by foreign war, violent attempts to preserve segregation in the south, and nuclear antagonism with Russia. In a letter to William Spanos, a close Binghamton colleague and fervid iconoclast of American imperialism, Kroetsch reacted to the political situation he encountered in the United States:

> It's so goddamned ridiculous, absolutely lacking in any sort of dignity, that I'm vaguely embarrassed to watch the news and find myself watching seriously. To make of a whole life, a culture, a time, this sort of charade—to let Nixon go on getting away with it—is to recognize that Yeats, Lawrence, Pound—they were right—we're waiting for the end. You imagine a military takeover, Bill. Even that inversion of democratic coherence is gone. One understands that recurring human fantasy of the flood, the fire. One sees why the major writers of our time end up writing parody [...] we are the barbarians as well as those who await them. (591/96.6, 11.63)

Often comic in tone, Kroetsch's creative work displays on its surface an apolitical stance. That should not indicate unconcern with dominant forces, however, as the quoted letter indicates. Rather, the author resisted publicly aligning himself with either side of political binaries, which would compromise his practiced ambiguity. Hutcheon identifies his postmodern "refusal to pick sides, the desire to be on both sides of any border, deriving energy from the continual crossing" (162). Kroetsch viewed institutionalism, the will to govern others, and fixity of opinion as the true enemies of liberty and art. He chose not to position himself on a politicized spectrum. For this reason, his work functions more thoroughly as spoof than satire, ever reliant on anecdote, contemplation, and play.

During his years in Binghamton, Kroetsch committed a phenomenal amount of energy to his department. In 1974, he wrote to Spanos: "I must be on something like 15 committees which is against the rules but necessary" (27, 1.9.47). He focused much of his service work on developing contemporary (as well as creative) course offerings, a key point of recruitment for the English department once Binghamton beat out SUNY's Buffalo and Stony Brook campuses for a contemporary literature specialization (27, 1.11.119). Meanwhile, he co-founded the journal *boundary 2* with Spanos, published a staggering array of his own writings, raised two daughters, and came to feel more Canadian for living at a partial remove from the border. Many of his literary models also developed exilic consciousnesses, explored and exploded through artistic creation: Joyce, Conrad, Homer. Other prominent Canadian writers have participated in the same tradition, such as Bliss Carmen, Mavis Gallant, Margaret Laurence, George Elliott Clarke, Suzette Mayr, and Anne Carson.

Just as the overlay of one country's territory upon another's terrain complicated Kroetsch's American entrance via the Goose Bay airbase, he crossed a ragged boundary when finally returning to Canada. Beginning in 1975, he exited America in stages, not tendering formal resignation from his position at SUNY-Binghamton until the summer of 1978 (591/96.6, 31.4). During the intervening years, he worked first as an itinerant writer-in-residence at the University of Lethbridge and briefly taught at the University of Calgary. Correspondence of the period charts his experience of the "native as visitor." Connections with Canadian writers become articulated in the context of eastern/western or urban/rural differences rather than through Canadian/American differences, which had featured heavily in the missives of an earlier period. One such articulation comes in a letter addressed to Dennis Lee: "A profound home-going (there-being), the native as visitor. [...] I suppose your basic landscape is urban; mine is literally landscape (well, no; add a lot of sky) and I have to ask again how the people fit" (334/84.1, 3.50). Sensing a good "fit," Kroetsch accepted a permanent position in Winnipeg, a city whose state of urban decline bore similarities to entropic Binghamton, that site of former manufacturing industries at the "rain-soaked non-centre of nowhere" (27, 1.13.45). Economic decline made Manitoba's "Gateway to the West" a natural location for him. In Winnipeg, he was finally home (from away) to a city in which he had never resided.

Kroetsch taught for nearly two decades at the University of Manitoba (1978–1995) before relocating to Victoria, British Columbia, where he practiced a fidgety version of retirement in his garden. Initially, he resisted Winnipeg for "not being far enough west." Witness how nimbly Kroetsch overturns that expressed doubt within the same letter:

> I'm a westerner in some profound way, and in some profound way Manitoba isn't far enough west. [...]
>
> Right now: the stabbing prairie sunshine. And, outside the dikes of the city, a flood, the worst in years, maybe the worst of the century. We sit safe on a kind of island. It's grotesque. People, out there, working day and night, sandbagging. Trying to save houses, grain, cattle. Maybe I am west after all: this direct pressure of weather on people. (334/84.1, 3.67)

The locations of his post-American life ranged across Manitoba, Alberta, and British Columbia with much travel intervening. Places of residence in each province remained comparatively stable. The prairies justified the longing to return he had explicated for Donald Cameron as early as 1971, expressing then "the need to confront 'the genius of place.' Those goddamned high plains in my bones" (27, 28.2.6). First to Winnipeg, Manitoba, and finally to Leduc, Alberta: coming home to the region he had imaginatively reconstructed renewed a life-long communion with that land and its presiding inhabitants.

During a 2014 interview that I conducted at Binghamton with Spanos—then age eighty-nine and still teaching his counter-hegemonic literary philosophy—he commented on his colleague's long-awaited return:

Eso: A 1976 letter from Kroetsch to you states, "too much Binghamton will do either of us in" [27, 19.17.8]. Do you know what he meant by that?

Spanos: I have no idea what he meant by that.

Eso: Well, do you think his departure was primarily a matter of Canada calling him home or was there a push out of Binghamton at the same time?

Spanos: I don't think he ever had a strong desire to get out of Binghamton but when the occasion happened, he went. It was not a difficult decision, particularly by that time. He had become involved in a relationship with Smaro Kamboureli [...] they both decided that they would go back to Canada so she could get her PhD at the University of Manitoba. It was at that time that this opportunity for him occurred [to teach] at the University of Manitoba. I think he was very happy to go back to Canada. When I went to visit him, he had all his friends come down. We went out to a restaurant and had beer with Dennis Cooley and four or five other people, colleagues of his. They loved him and he loved them. He really found his "homeland" (quote unquote) when he returned to Canada. He was always friendly with people here at Binghamton but not the way he could talk to his fellow Canadian colleagues.

Eso: They spoke the same language?

Spanos: They were speaking the same Canadian language. Exactly. I remember Dennis Cooley as being very, very Canadian and not only Canadian but western Canadian. I mean by this not only that he saw Canada in opposition to the U.S. of A. but also in opposition to the eastern [i.e., central] Canadian establishment. There was this camaraderie that was not of the kind he felt with his Binghamton colleagues. (Eso 2014)

Readers familiar with Kroetsch interviews—via *Labyrinths of Voice* or *Abundance*, for example—will recognize Spanos as a more direct and forthcoming subject than his co-editor on *boundary 2*. Kroetsch comments frequently but always obliquely on Canadian-American difference. Essays in *The Lovely Treachery of Words* take up this theme, such as "The Moment of the Discovery of America Continues." That essay argues for a distinctive predicament within Canadian identity, one the author diagnoses elsewhere as "the frontier in our selves" (27, 1.13.17) and "a precarious balance between whole worlds" (334/84.1, 3.50). *The Lovely Treachery of Words* figuratively bridges those "whole worlds": the chill of the northern dominion, the overheating empire to its south. Of course, a bridge does not bring land masses any closer together but merely facilitates alternate forms of transit.

Like Kroetsch's essay collection, the novel *Gone Indian* artistically refracts the author's dual Canadian and American experiences. In the novel, it is the pompous, Canadian-born Professor Madham who remains in Binghamton. His unsuccessful student, Manhattanite Jeremy Sadness, makes improbable quest through hairy situations on the bald prairie. Spontaneity and hyperbole hold sway over Sadness' Albertan odyssey. Kroetsch provided an abstract to his editors at new press: "[A] novel about going west; not just my going, no, the going of Columbus from the Old World in search of the New, the going of Tristan in search of a new lay for the old king, the going out of and into that produced Canada, Canadians, the change, the metamorphosis" (27, 1.13.40). Echoes of authorial biography suggest that who leaves and who returns does not divide evenly—not in Kroetsch's experience, conquest history, nor classical literature. *Gone Indian* interprets the author's multiple northern returns from his American, academic setting. The representation is complicated by compounding perplexities designed to keep readers (to keep from) guessing.

The central characters gathered under the title *Gone Indian* are non-Indigenous. They perform against the tripartite background of a non-existent dissertation, a series of audio-cassettes in transit across the American-Canadian border, and a winter festival which draws heavily on First Nations practices and myths. When read bluntly, the novel's title could lead some readers to believe that the author shares with Jeremy Sadness an intention to become another Archibald Belaney, an intention to trespass which the American declares to Canadian border officials:

> "Have you anything to declare?"
> "Nothing."
> "Cigarettes? Liquor?"
> "No sir."

> "Where were you born?"
> "New York, New York."
> "How long will you be staying?"
> "Two days. Maybe three."
> "Purpose of trip?"
> "I want to be Grey Owl."
> "I beg your pardon, sir?"
> "Grey Owl. I want to become—"
> (Kroetsch 1973, 6)

Kroetsch makes absurd the character's unabashed appropriation of First Nations costume, from Sadness's moccasins to his braids. The author's anti-racist work includes presentations of racism's typical manifestations, given to select characters but nowhere endorsed.

Similarly, the white characters in *Badlands* perceive the novel's sole Indigenous figure, Anna Yellowbird, as the fulfillment of European stereotypes: according to her silence, servitude, and primitivism. She hardly speaks, un-reciprocally serves male pleasure, and occupies a teepee constructed of dinosaur bones. Yet, the framing encounter between the novel's two Annas suggests that Yellowbird relates the entire story to Dawe's daughter, who seeks to learn about her father's expedition. The-story-within-the-frame opens and closes with Yellowbird's appearance and disappearance. In between, she remains largely invisible while following the boat's progress down the Red Deer River. Therefore, *Badlands* might be read as twofold parody: as an Indigenous character's narration about the folly of Euro-Western homosocial conquest that also depicts how radically the dinosaur-bone hunters misperceive those they term "Indians."

First Nations figures and myths make repeat appearances throughout Kroetsch's writing because they inform the setting of his agricultural childhood, his primary subject. The Battle River passes through Alberta's Parklands and takes its name from military actions between allied Cree-Assiniboine and Blackfoot Confederacy forces. As an outsider, Kroetsch attributed Indigenous sources within his broader cultural inheritances without re-inscribing colonial stereotypes and erasures. The results will often fall short of contemporary ethical standards. Nevertheless, Kroetsch was once ahead of his time, among newcomers, in appreciating the gravity and complexity of such issues. A 1975 letter discusses an academic seminar on First Nations literature in these terms:

> About [Lionel] Kearns and his grad course on the Indian: among non-Indian writers I'd contrast my own Gone Indian with Rudy Wiebe's beautiful Temptations of Big Bear. And then Arts Canada did that great issue on the shaman. What I would want to get at is the shaman/the drunk/the poet: again, it is the plains Indians I know something about. In my novel that's to come out this fall, Badlands, the Indian girl is setting out a NA Indian version of how you got to the underworld to rescue someone who died. See a fantastic book by [Åke Hultkrantz] on the Orpheus story among Indians. For me, after the shaman identification, comes our search for "new ancestors." It sort of boggles the mind to think they were at home with our landscape for thousands of years before our little time began. Some kind of humility should arise out of that. (27, 2.2.29)

Deference to European critics (Hultkrantz, a Swede), fraught associations between drunkenness and shamanism, romanticizing the shamanistic as a signature of First Nations worldviews—these tropes are anachronous in the era of reconciliation. Even so, Kroetsch achieved degrees of humility when representing First Nations contributions and colonial injustices.

"Stone Hammer Poem" commits an un-staking of European land claims: "This stone maul / was found. // In the field / my grandfather / thought was his // my father thought / was his" (Kroetsch 1981, 14). The poem's speaker imagines various hands the object may have passed through but offers only provisional guesses, speculations made precarious through vast swaths of time the poem takes in. An alternate poetic sequence, "Old Man Stories" comes closer to narrative appropriation. Perhaps for that reason, Kroetsch left "Old Man Stories" out of the various editions of his long poems collected under the title *Field Notes*. The tricked-trickster who animates the author's renditions of Blackfoot narratives has been, appropriately, displaced from the Kroetsch canon. Even so, the shadow of that creator-clown extends across his oeuvre.

Cross-cultural or otherwise political tensions form the bedrock and background for many of Kroetsch's published works. They do not occupy their surfaces and foregrounds. In a rare break of character, he composed an ambiguous opinion piece on Canadian-American relations for inclusion in Al Purdy's 1968 anthology, *The New Romans*. As editor, Purdy seems to have preferred invectives against the United States, despite his subtitle, which promised "candid opinions." Kroetsch's submission did not appear in the collection alongside anti-American statements by Margaret Atwood, George Grant, and Farley Mowat. The collection also includes pro-American statements by Robert Fulford, Irving Layton, and Mordecai Richler. Kroetsch's offering would have contributed uniquely for launching a critique against his own country. He described the situation in a letter to E. D. Blodgett:

> By the way, I am not in The New Romans because—the old story—you didn't fire me, I quit. It was quite apparent that Purdy didn't approve of my unpatriotic attack on conservative shit-eating Canada when I was supposed to attack the conservative USA. But—I had included in my wrath the Liberal Party, and when they did in fact begin to support Trudeau I realized I was completely wrong for two paragraphs out of my small allotment, and I encouraged Purdy to remove my whole essay, which he had, I suspect, already done. [...] But what the hell. (591/96.6, 1.7)

Kroetsch's unpublished essay expressed "wrath," an exceptional moment in a career wherein political positions remain deliberately and obstinately opaque. The essay projects his postmodern philosophy onto the political realm in proposing an ironic, yet violent, solution to the insolvable problem of Canadian lassitude:

> My dear Canadians: Why are you not grateful to your absentee landlords? [...] Why do you not kowtow and grovel as you have been taught? Your absentee landlords, here as in Harlem, will give you poverty and slums and a needed sense of being dispossessed. Out of these virtues will come riots and violence and a growing self-respect. Why do only the Separatists understand this? Why don't you all become Separatists? (27, 27.23.5)

It is characteristic of Kroetsch's evasiveness that he selected a book aimed at the faults of the United States to admonish and mock Canadians.

Kroetsch's fabulist poem "How I Joined the Seal Herd" is more typical of his work than the unpublished *New Romans* opinion piece. The poem stems from a trip to Prince Edward Island, "which is where [he] heard the barking" seals (Kroetsch 2017, 208). Readers aware of biographical contexts may feel tempted to elaborate upon this poem's trans-species fantasy, hearing echoes of the foreignness inherent to a Canadian entering American life, or of a creative writer submerged in academia. The speaker strips off garments, abandons credit and identity cards on the beach. He enters the water, transforms, withdraws. "America was a good lay," the speaker summates (Kroetsch 1976, 232). Whether referring to his academic experience south of the border, the United States proper, or even to land itself, the poem provokes but does not satisfy allegorical responses to the artistic fact of Kroetsch becoming seal.

The author's south- and east-ward migrations out of Alberta enacted a reversal of certain familial inheritances. Movement and alienation are ephemeral family heirlooms. "Perhaps my father, born in Ontario, growing up in Ontario, felt he was an exile in Alberta," Kroetsch wrote (1980, 85). His paternal grandparents migrated to from Bavaria, circa 1830, to Carrick Township, a German-speaking area of Bruce County, Ontario (27, 1.6.13). "The Ledger" investigates that lineage by poeticizing a historical document that preserves financial struggles and successes related to a watermill his ancestors ran on the banks of the Teeswater River. Also reflected in creative works, the author's maternal grandparents relocated to Canada from Minnesota (27, 1.6.13). Kroetsch traced that lineage to a great-aunt, Rose Weller, whose lack of speech by the time of their meeting outside of Minneapolis contrasts with the "Ledger," the poem and the original document which constitutes one object within the author's papers. His visit with Weller only partially recovers the "genetic departure" of a previous generation (1995, 61). In the writerly memoir *A Likely Story*, he writes that "Aunt Rose's mouth was a nest [...] the open flower of her mouth. She had given me the sphinx of her mouth" (63). Her aphasia offers the only response to the unstated question governing the author's quest across generational lines.

Trips home from America provided enduring inspiration for Kroetsch's depictions of the Canadian west, whether historiographic or autobiographically inflected. Many works spring directly from experiences on the Canadian prairie, later recollected amid the metaphoric tranquility of geographic remove. One Binghamton letter depicts a trip to Saskatchewan that helped him conceive the anti-hero protagonist of *The Words of My Roaring*: "I crawled out of my sleeping bag and buck naked faced the rising sun and announced to the West that I had *returned*. Reynolds, looking at the cottonwood fluff on the caked earth we had slept on, said something like, 'Kroetsch, we've got to bring fertility back to this country.' And [Johnny] Backstrom was born" (27, 2.6.61). In this passage, Kroetsch declares and celebrates his return to the West rather than to the North, although he later described the resulting novel to Donald Sutherland as "a metaphor for the whole of

Canada" (27, 1.6.66). The author's sense of remove in New York State revivified that western agricultural world where his sense of community, landscape, and narrative took root. Distancing himself from Alberta also helped generate a romantic attachment to all of Canada, one that his American-born daughters inherited. They saw Canada as "a glorious place where you live in a big hotel, go for walks in a city full of castles, and get to stay up late every night" (27, 2.4.124). This description follows their 1970 journey to Rideau Hall, where they saw their father decorated by the Governor General of what would remain for them a foreign land.

While Kroetsch re-worked details of his visits to Canada at a typewriter in Binghamton, western landscapes would often usurp the place of composition. He describes this experience recurrently. In one letter from the end of 1972, he writes: "[M]y mind begins to slip; too much imaginary tripping down the distant Red Deer, yesterday afternoon I looked up from my typewriter and had to figure out where I was. Good sign, I suppose, and promises a comfortable oldage in looney bin" (334/84.1, 3.37). The following spring, he wrote: "A curious experience recently: some mornings, when writing, the Red Deer River is more real than this dreary Binghamton that surrounds me. I set myself afloat, sail away" (591/96.6, 3.29). The psychic overlay of distant places re-draws political and geographical boundaries. Drumheller invades New York State, just as Washington, DC, had resettled Goose Bay. That is one version of a postmodern "presence of absence." Kroetsch gave that postmodern concept a particular Canadian spin, when discussing it during a radio interview: "[W]e can almost hear CBC with it turned off, can't we?" (Gzowski 1989). He may not have found Canadian characters and voices such compelling material for literary production—just as the Badlands may not have appeared so mysterious—if not for the distance that chosen exile in America offered him.

Kroetsch's co-founding of the American literary journal *boundary 2* could explain why some Canadian nationalists adopt anti-Kroetschean positions. An extreme case is found in Robin Mathews' *Treason of the Intellectuals*, where Canadian postmodernism is merely a proxy for American influence. Yet, "American" does not adequately categorize *boundary 2*, whose international editorial board included Toronto's Eli Mandel and Palestine's Edward Said. Two numbers in the journal's first and third volumes explored marginalized world literatures: special issues on contemporary Greek and Canadian writing. The latter provoked John Robert Colombo to call for a Writers' Union of Canada boycott of the journal. His review finds the *boundary 2* presentation inadequate, in part for its focus on "a horde of 'underground' writers" (27, 1.10.3). While Kroetsch acted as general editor for the issue, he recruited guest editors working in Canada. Atwood, Mandel, and Warren Tallman made the bulk of the issue's selections. Kroetsch arranged the inclusion by Douglas Barbour and made space for his own brief introduction. "The Canadian writer must uninvent the word," it states, continuing, "He must destroy the homonymous American and English languages that keep him from hearing his own tongue" (1974, 1). These words anticipate Lee's famous essay—"Cadence, Country, Silence: Writing in Colonial Space"—that *boundary 2*'s Canadian issue first brought to public attention.

A highlight of the issue for Kroetsch was George Woodcock's essay on Northrop Frye, which documents the influence of that critic on a subsequent generation of creative writers. The essay compares the enduring importance of Frye to the "less durable reputation" of Marshall McLuhan (Woodcock 1974, 185) whose thinking through of cliché and archetype Wilfred Watson charts in a subsequent essay. Kroetsch wrote of "Diana's Priest in the Bush Garden" to Woodcock, its author:

> Your response to Frye and his manifestations are what I was hoping to, groping to, find: you give voice to the kind of community, intellectual, personal, that exits among the major thinkers of the Canadian scene. That community, so different from what I experience in the U.S., somehow needs exploring on a level beyond the performance of the individual. (27, 1.8.71)

Kroetsch's peers gain representation in *boundary 2* well beyond the Canadian issue, with repeat appearances by Dorothy Livesay, Lorna Crozier, and Anne Szumigalski as well as Blodgett, Davey, and Lee. Woodcock on Frye and Watson on McLuhan, however gratifying to him editorially, must have provided only partial compensation for the dreamt-of discussion he failed to arrange between Frye and McLuhan. Whereas his co-editor conducted numerous interviews in the journal, Kroetsch had not planned to participate in the sought-after discussion.

Across their collaboration, Spanos occupied the role of activist-editor, attacking, yet sometimes mimicking, America's victory culture and exceptionalist ethos. Kroetsch performed more as a curatorial editor, one perpetually uncomfortable with the authority inherent in his role. Co-editorship of *boundary 2* placed him among other literary editors in the United States at a time of significant cultural shifts, as signaled by the poetics of Olson/Creeley/Duncan and interpreted through new, peer journals such as *Diacritics* and *Critical Inquiry*. Even so, while exposing his students to American poets such as William Carlos Williams and John Berryman—and while "reading the South Americans like Borges [or] the Italian poet [Salvatore] Quasimodo" (334/84.1, 1.23)—Kroetsch's vital literary connections were with his peers in Canada. These include writers such as James Bacque, Diane Bessai, Daphne Marlatt, Ken Mitchell, Michael Ondaatje, Andrew Suknaski, and Rudy Wiebe.

Kroetsch grounded his postmodern literary experiments in geography and community. His writing explores the symbiosis of geography and community—most insightfully, an Alberta blend of same. His travel book, *Alberta*, studies his home province. "As for the proposition [to write the travel book]—try as I will, I somehow can't resist it," he wrote in 1966. "I want more people to read my novels. I need money. And I especially want to make people, including Albertans, more aware of what Alberta is" (27, 1.5.2). Lesson one: when life gives hail, make ice cream. "'That's an Albertan reaction,'" Kroetsch reports (van Herk 2010, 30), that swift turn "from outburst to austerity […] between risk and security" (Cooley 2016, 9). The poetic sequence "Lonesome Writer Diptych" conveys well the author's uniquely active sense of place (and placelessness):

> To our surprise in the
> parklands, we discover
> that even geography is not
> a certainty on this fickle
> planet. Riding the buck-
> ing bull of plate tectonics,
> we hang on for dear life to
> a floating world.
> (Kroetsch 1995, 116)

Extremity of seasons, of scenery; predilection for exaggeration, for mythos; the dizzying boom-and-bust cycle of the provincial economy; a lusty futurity—these features imprint upon an Albertan's "hesitant, unstoppable" character (Kroetsch 1980, 39). His home province may have helped prepare Kroetsch for many aspects of American life, in that

Alberta sometimes fills the gap between a characteristically Canadian hesitancy and stereotypically American determination.

Experience abroad helped clarify for Kroetsch the Canadian aversion to self-promotional bombast. That averting sensibility fused with his innate, Albertan vigor to produce an "enthusiastic humility," in the words of Roberta Rees (quoted in Cooley 2016, 267). I witnessed that humility in action in June 2011, when Kroetsch gave his final public reading before a packed house, alongside Sid Marty, at the Canmore Miners' Union Hall. After a standing ovation, to which he held his poems aloft in reception and salute, he spent more than hour signing books and meeting readers. Last in line, I asked Kroetsch if he would like to join the night's other performers at the nearby Rose and Crown tavern. After a week that included several long drives, a lifetime achievement award dinner, mentoring "the arrogant young who requisition unto themselves the title poet" (334/84.1, 5.9), and work on his final fiction *The Fence*, this veteran writer may have reasonably chosen rest over one more in a long series of late-night gab fests. But Kroetsch responded heartily, "I died four hours ago [...] I'm up for anything now" (Eso 2011).

Like Kroetsch's books and their readers, those words help keep the man alive. As a poet, novelist, critic, and mentor, he raised the national and international profiles of Canadian literature. This achievement extends from his productive regionalism and from a generative anti-parochialism.

WORKS CITED

Cooley, Dennis. 2016. *The Home Place: Essays on Robert Kroetsch's Poetry*. Edmonton: University of Alberta Press.

Eso, David. In conversation with Robert Kroetsch at Canmore, AB, June 2011; and William Spanos at Binghamton, NY, October 2014.

Gzowski, Peter. 1989. "Morningside Interview with Robert Kroetsch, 6 April": hour 3. 591/96.6, Box 71, File 17 (cassette). *Robert Kroetsch Papers*. University of Calgary Special Collections, Calgary, Alberta.

Hutcheon, Linda. 1988. "Seeing Double: Concluding with Kroetsch." In *The Canadian Postmodern: A Study of Contemporary English-Canadian Fiction*, 160–187. Oxford: Oxford University Press.

Kroetsch, Robert, and William Spanos, eds. 1974. boundary 2 (*The Canadian Issue*) 3 (1): 1–249.

Kroetsch, Robert, et al. 2017. "How Do You Interview a Poet? A Conversation with Robert Kroetsch." In *Robert Kroetsch: Essays on His Works*, edited by Nicole Markotić, 205-22. Toronto: Guernica.

Kroetsch, Robert. 1969. *The Studhorse Man*. Toronto: Macmillan.

———. 1973. *Gone Indian*. Toronto: new press.

———. 1975. *Badlands*. Toronto: new press.

———. 1976. "How I Joined the Seal Herd." *boundary 2* 5 (1): 229-32.

———. 1976. "Old Man Stories." *The Stone Hammer Poems (1960-1975)*. Lantzville, BC: Oolichan Books.

———. 1980. *The Crow Journals*. Edmonton: NeWest.

———. 1981. *Field Notes*. Don Mills, ON: General Publishing.

———. 1985. "A Preface." In *Gaining Ground: European Critics on Canadian Literature*, edited by Robert Kroetsch and Reingard Nischik, 7-8. Edmonton: NeWest.

———. 1989. *The Lovely Treachery of Words: Essays Selected and New*. Oxford: Oxford University Press.

———. 1995. *A Likely Story: The Writing Life*. Red Deer, AB: Red Deer College Press.

———. 1996. "Becoming a Writer is Unbecoming: My Twenty Years in the U.S.A." 775/04.25, Box 30 (VHS). *Robert Kroetsch Papers*. University of Calgary Special Collections, Calgary, Alberta.

———. 2001. *The Hornbooks of Rita K*. Edmonton: University of Alberta Press.

———. Various documents. MsC 27, 334/84.1, and 591/96.6. *Robert Kroetsch Papers*. University of Calgary Special Collections, Calgary, Alberta.

Lent, John, and Robert Kroetsch. 2007. *Abundance*. Vernon, BC: Kalamalka Press.

Mathews, Robin. 1995. *Treason of the Intellectuals*. Prescott, ON: Voyageur.

Neuman, Shirley, and Robert Wilson. 1982. *Labyrinths of Voice: Conversations with Robert Kroetsch*. Edmonton: NeWest Press.

Purdy, Al, ed. 1968. *The New Romans*. Edmonton: Mel Hurtig.

van Herk, Aritha. 1986. "Biocritical Essay." In *The Robert Kroetsch Papers: First Accession*, edited by Jean F. Tener and Apollonia Stelle, ix-xxxix. Calgary: University of Calgary Press.

———. 2010. "Our Odysseus." *Alberta Views* 13 (10): 26-31.

Watson, Wilfred. 1974. "Marshall McLuhan and Multi-Consciousness: The Place Marie Dialogues." *boundary 2* 3 (1): 197-211.

Woodcock, George. 1974. "Diana's Priest in the Bush Garden." *boundary 2* 3 (1): 185-96.

Gone Indian and New World Myth
TANJA CVETKOVIĆ

In the 2009 interview "How do you interview a poet? A conversation with Robert Kroetsch," Robert Kroetsch points to the importance of story both for modernists and postmodernists. While the modernist is still looking for a story as "a unifying narrative" to explain the world, the postmodern says "the master narratives don't hold" (Markotić 215). While we no longer believe in the unified story and the unified self, we still have the need to tell a story, to write a story about something. That's our need to express our own voice, to voice our identity and our story. We produce stories, not just one story. Kroetsch told his postmodern story about lemon and we feel free to meditate and reflect upon his lemon poem and create our own stories. We feel the need to be creative, innovative, productive.

In this paper my intention is to tell my story about *Gone Indian* and view it in relation to Marie Vautier's perspective on her idea of New World Myth. Kroetsch's concluding novel in his "Out West" triptych, *Gone Indian* (1973), the third in the sequence after *The Words of My Roaring* (1966) and the award-winning *The Studhorse Man* (1969), displays his questioning sense of the concept of myth. In this novel Kroetsch uses a couple of his postmodern techniques to explore the significance and the meaning of the northwest frontier in Canada through Jeremy Sadness's quest for identity, based on the play, parody, and irony with different mythical fragments and stories. We can trace the way Kroetsch questions different mythological systems rather than truly exploring the qualities and functions of myth in his texts. By examining how he treats mythical fragments in his fiction, and in this novel in particular, however, we can single out certain procedures and draw conclusions about common characteristics which could be compared to similar discussions of myth.

Kroetsch uses the technique of retelling old stories and mythical fragments in a new way, which anticipates the writer's need for newness and change. Another technique, based on the subversion of the old dominant systems and orders, the use of parody, and the inversion of order, relates this postmodern writer to Bakhtin's carnival theory. Actually, it is polyphony and the multiple meanings of Kroetsch's stories, that is, generativity, that places Kroetsch as a writer closer to the carnival theory. As a writer, he resists the traditional mythical and narrative patterns and ideological systems, and turns to deconstruction and demythologization of such systems and patterns.

Many research studies have been dedicated to the carnivalesque element in Kroetsch's poetics.[1] Kroetsch's technique of de(con)struction and demythologization parallels Bakhtin's conceptions of carnival's inversion of order and the subversion of the dominant culture. According to Bakhtin, the carnival culture is based on the destruction of old systems and hierarchies and on the imposition of a new one. He explains:

> One might say that carnival celebrated temporary liberation from the prevailing truth and from the established order; it marked the suspension of all hierarchical rank, privileges, norms, and prohibitions. Carnival was the true feast of time, the feast of becoming, change, and renewal. It was hostile to all that was immortalized and completed (Bakhtin 1965, 10).

In Bakhtin's carnival world, hierarchies disappear, opposites unite and melt into one another, leaving space for transformation and renewal. Carnival also means the release of the suppressed energy and includes festivity, comic crownings and uncrownings, mocking, and the like. As a matter of fact, it requires the inversion of order.

In the carnivalesque vein of inversion, parody, and de(con)struction in *Gone Indian*, Kroetsch expands the conflict between opposites, such as a father-son relationship, myth and history, linear narrative structure and multilayered narrative structure. The novel is the parody of the quest myth as well as the parody of the traditional way of storytelling, which is based on the different interpretations of the palimpsests scattered around. The text is also the invitation for the reader to participate actively in decoding disguised traces left behind by the two narrators, as the authoritative role of the writer is undermined; it represents Kroetsch's attempt "to shape the story while he de(con)structs it at the same time, to turn myth into a new story while he shatters it, to present the truth while he insists on the multiplicity" of meanings (Cvetković 2010, 225–26).

Kroetsch's treatment of myth is well described in his interview with Shirley Neuman and Robert Wilson, in *Labyrinths of Voice* (1982), where he points to the important generative possibilities myth can offer in storytelling. Unlike the modernist approach to myth and T. S. Eliot's comment on Joyce's *Ulysses* that mythical method is "a way of controlling, of ordering, of giving a shape and a significance to the immense panorama of futility and anarchy which is contemporary history" (Ellmann and Feidelson 1965, 681), Kroetsch focuses on demythologizing and deconstructing myth, which is not a unifying force of narration any more but rather a powerful means of producing new meanings and creating new stories based on the free combination and play of mythical fragments. Aware of the entrapping powers of myth, he proposes that "a way out is to retell it" (Neuman and Wilson 1982, 96). One of the results of such a retelling is also a feature of New World Myth, as defined by Vautier in *New World Myth: Postmodernism and Postcolonialism in Canadian Fiction* (1998). By comparing Kroetsch's approach to Vautier's treatment of New World Myth, I show that Kroetsch's postmodernism is close to postcolonialism.

Vautier explores various reworkings of myth in six novels from English-speaking Canada and from Quebec, published between 1975 and 1985: Jacques Godbout's *Les Têtes à Papineau,* Rudy Wiebe's *The Scorched-Wood People,* Jovette Marchessault's *Comme une enfant de la terre,* Joy Kogawa's *Obasan,* George Bowering's *Burning Water,* and François Barcelo's *La Tribu.* Through comparative studies of the novels, she illustrates the characteristics of New World Myth as opposed to traditional European-inspired versions of story. The focus on the decentralization and demythologization of the traditional use of myth in the postmodern and postcolonial discourse results in the weakening status of both classical and biblical myth, which paves the way for the presence of New World Myth. By giving an overview of novels in the French and English traditions, Vautier situates New World Myth in the broader context of classical, biblical, historical myths; and in chapter 1 of her book she concludes with a working definition of New World Myth. She asserts that New World Myth in these postmodern works serves as "a cognitive, imaginative tool in the novelistic exploration of a new post-European worldview" more suited to the world in which we live. She adds that New World Myth is "concerned with both epistemological uncertainty and the need to know, and is intent on imaginatively reclaiming the past while flaunting its awareness of the processes involved in this act" (1998, 35). New World Myth becomes rather a paradigm that reveals how myth is created to suit a particular need in a particular time and place. In a like manner, Dennis Cooley explains Kroetsch's postmodernism in the light of postcolonialism when he cites John Thieme and says that Kroetsch's postmodernism is not "'like the post-modernism of Borges and many of his American followers, an essentially asocial stance, but rather a direct response to the sense that a Prairie literature needs to be remade in an image which bears some relationship to the land'; and, he might have added, in some nearness to the histories of human habitation" (Cooley 2016, 247).

With this taken into account, Vautier elaborates on the qualities of New World Myth by starting from her working definition. She expands her definition of the term and explains that it "encourages a renewed interest in reclaiming the past, and yet flaunts its *re-creation*, through story, of the past in the here and now." Its emphasis is on the narrator as the creative teller of "untold tales that wait for their telling" (47), which underlines the flexibility of New World Myth. The narrator's attempt to recreate the very notion of the past reality adds to the imaginative, creative, mythmaking aspect of New World Myth. Another feature of this conception is a delibarete putting aside of classical myths, or "its self-regulated distancing from the dominant Judaeo-Christian worldview" (46), which points to the liberating quality of New World Myth, as it gives individuals freedom to think and imagine for themselves. This is evident in numerous attempts to rewrite and remake old myths in postcolonial discourse.

In Kroetsch's poetics the generative function of myth rests on adapting a story to a new cultural context. For example, in *Gone Indian* the frontier myth is adapted to a new social and cultural context in the Canadian Northwest Territories, where quest and exploration take place; and the story of Jeremy Sadness, related to the Grey Owl story, becomes a new Canadian myth within that framework of narration. In this way, one special feature of myth in Kroetsch's experimental use—newness—comes into being. In the context of Kroetsch's novels and his approaches to myth and mythical fragment, newness does not mean a new knowledge about the already existing concepts and phenomena, but the removal of the inauthentic stories and stereotypes, the breaking down of the already existing mythical patterns, the breaking of myths and stories into fragments, the free combination of which, mostly by way of parody and irony, could produce meanings other than the already given, and codified by different frames and patterns. Regarding the mythical fragments that are part of the novel, *Gone Indian* refers to the different myths and stories which originate from North American, classical, and Nordic mythologies.

Sherrill Grace, in her essay "Kroetsch and the Semiotics of North," points to the three metatexts beneath the text of *Gone Indian*: Frederick Jackson Turner's epigraph from "The Significance of the Frontier in American History," the Grey Owl story, and Jack Shedbolt's 1963 mural "Bush Pilot in the Northern Sky," at the Edmonton airport. The three metatexts have their own significance and meaning: Turner's epigraph—"For a moment, at the frontier, the bonds of custom are broken and unrestraint is triumphant"—is an invisible but existent text; the Grey Owl story, according to Grace, functions as a "textual construction and absent centre"; and Shedbolt's mural mirrors the text in prophetic warning and "counter-telling energy [...] to face our encounter with north" (16). With the discussion of these three metatexts, Grace points to the significance of North as a frontier, and to its shaping influence on art and on personal and national identity.

Kroetsch's interest in hidden texts is explained by his interest in story. In his essay "Disunity as Unity: A Canadian Strategy," he explains the connection between a meta-narrative and culture:

> The shared story—what I prefer to call the assumed story—has traditionally been basic to nationhood. As a writer I'm interested in these assumed stories—what I call meta-narratives. It may be that the writing of particular narratives, within a culture, is dependent on these meta-narratives. (1989, 21)

In the same essay Kroetsch defines a meta-narrative as "a version of archaeology over the traditional versions of history" (24). In the postmodern world we trust archaeology rather than history: "Against [the] *over*riding view, we posit an archaeological sense that every unearthing is problematic, tentative, subject to a story-making act that is itself subject of further change as the 'dig' goes on" (24). He explains in *The Crow*

Journals that the hidden layers of texts, or, "the text beneath the text, as in *Gone Indian*, is at the root of our Canadian writing" (53). Apart from the three metatexts discussed by Grace that are mentioned above, there are other mythical fragments related to classical mythology, such as the myths of Orpheus, Odysseus, and Demeter and Persephone, as well as the Nordic story of Ragnarok, hidden under the surface narrative. The function of these fragments and metatexts is to undermine the surface story through parody and irony.

According to Kroetsch's idea that "the fiction makes us real" (Kroetsch 1970, 63) and that we do not have an identity until somebody tells our story, the metatexts of the novel can be related to two storytellers and the main characters in the novel, Jeremy Sadness and Robert Mark Madham, and their identity problems. Different metatexts in the novel do not deny identity. On the contrary, they give an additional meaning and expand the possibilities of meaning or, as Jeremy concludes about the impact of the northern frontier on human condition, "the diffusion of personality into a complex of possibilities rather than a concluded self" (Kroetsch 1999, 160).

Jeremy and Mark Madham are another pair of opposed characters in Kroetsch's poetics. By trying to order Jeremy's chaotic experience and putting his quest into words, Madham continues a long tradition of creating an ordered coherent story of a man who opposes the closure of a system he inhabits. While Madham, who, like doctor Murdoch in *The Words of My Roaring*, stands for sterile academic institutions and the written word, Jeremy Sadness becomes a representative of the oral tradition, a quester for the open frontier in a physical and psychological sense, the trickster who opposes history and closure, who shows a tendency for the deconstruction of the written word and the already given world view.

Jeremy and Madham's relationship can be viewed as a father-and-son relationship. Mark Madham, who takes on the role of father, is connected to the urban Canada and the past. On the other hand, Jeremy Sadness dreams northwest, acts spontaneously, creates his own identity by deconstructing the academic way of acquiring knowledge. In a letter to Jill, Madham makes the main difference between himself and Jeremy:

> Your Jeremy, growing up in the east, felt compelled to play Indian; I can only assure you I have been Indian enough. I prefer to forget the experience, and yet I do recollect the sense of being—how shall

> I say?—*trapped* in the blank indifference of space and timelessness. And I would insist it was just that—the pressure not of time, but of its absence—that horrified those brave men who stumbled onto the central plateau of Antarctica. Jeremy, in his own confused and piddling way, had strayed into a like circumstance, a like experience. He records as much. (Kroetsch 1999, 131)

For Jeremy, the journey to the northwest of Canada is the possibility to get the original knowledge and to oppose the institutionalized knowledge represented by Madham as his supervisor. For Madham, Jeremy's quest is the worst escape from responsibility to avoid finishing his doctoral dissertation.

Jeremy's journey northwest and Kroetsch's frontier idea do not conform to the American model frontier, which we can find in Turner's "The Significance of the Frontier in American History." Turner explains the western frontier's influence on the development of an essentially American ethos (Thomas 1987, 80–85) that is white, strong, male, self-reliant, and individual. As described by Kroetsch, the Canadian frontier is more part of one's consciousness than a physical frontier where one can prove oneself. It's a place of blizzards and wastes, mysterious disappearance, isolation. Robert Sunderman disappears mysteriously by faking his own death and starts his life anew as professor Mark Madham in Binghamton; Roger Dorck loses consciousness in a fatal leap with his snowmobile; while Jeremy Sadness himself is lost in the snowy night during the winter festival and the snowshoe race. The effect of the Canadian North on an individual confirms Kroetsch's statement that "it remains a true wilderness, a continuing presence. We don't want to conquer it. Sometimes we want it to conquer us" (Kroetsch 1989, 54). Additionally, in Sherrill Grace's view, the Canadian North in *Gone Indian* is dangerous, mysterious, primordial; it is gendered female, and it is mother and virgin, which encompasses its male questers seeking to conquer, name, and discover it for themselves (1996, 15).

The silence, nothingness, and the void that Jeremy encounters in the North is the place where he can free himself from the bonds of custom. Kroetsch carnivalizes the northern frontier by introducing the winter festival, the snowshoe race, and ski-jump competitions, which break down the established order and make Jeremy enter a new world of disorderliness, leading him to the final transformation of Grey Owl; for to go Indian is to "become released or wild in the carnival sense"

(Neuman and Wilson 1982, 36), and find a new self by losing an old self in the North. Before creating himself anew, Jeremy deconstructs his formalized institutionalized self while searching for the knowledge about himself which he identifies with the "blank page" of Canada's North. The vast spaces North allow an endless expanse of personality, where Jeremy looks for a chance to recreate himself. As a matter of fact, he was "looking for nothing. The primal darkness. The purest light. The first word. For the voice that spoke the first word. The inventor of zero" (22). At the end, he and his lover Bea Sunderman escape her apocalyptical home, filled with clocks and artificial time because "someone didn't trust the sun" (33) and flee into the vastness of the northern Arctic prairie. Jeremy is freed from time to a true northern frontier where he faces the unspeakable silence and "the last first." The only thing left behind is the tape recorder with his voice of life in the North which "the old mad Adam [Madham] of the original day" (97) should recreate into another possibility of language producing a copy of reality rather than an original invention. Beginnings and endings remain blurred once again as many times in Kroetsch's fiction.

Jeremy tries to recreate himself by plunging into the unknown, uncertainty, and silence. Preceding the nothingness he finally embraces are his many failed attempts to create: his numerous unfinished dissertations, and his transformations of self. Jeremy dreams west and north of the world to come, his new self, and the freedom from the constraints of time. His tape recorder is a kind of gun that aligns him with the image of the cowboy that once inhabited a western frontier. His New World is Canada, but the cowboy myth, which is American, cannot survive in the Canadian wilderness. Jeremy's quest for the New World is based on the archetypal quest pattern for origins as he joins Christopher Columbus in his quest "for the oldest New World. The darkest gold. The last first" (156). However, the infinite desire to return to the beginning can never be fulfilled and becomes a renewable source of discovery and story. A portion of Jeremy's dissertation refers to Columbus's imaginative quest for India and reads: "Christopher Columbus, not knowing that he had not come to the Indies of his imagination. Imagined that he had come to the Indies" (157). Every quest is imaginative in its nature, and every story about the quest is based on the power of imagination.

Jeremy's quest story voiced on the tape recorder acts as the counter-narrative to the main text. The whole text of the novel stands in the face of the absent story on the tape recorder, for as Jay Gamble claims, "to encounter the other, [...] is to encounter a negativity, a radical alterity" (Markotić 2017, 116). The two texts interweave, interrupt each other, and one story delays the completion of the other. The creation occurs at poignant junctures between presence and absence. The absent text is what Gamble calls "narrative negativity" (123), which becomes generative when it undercuts another narrative. The constant attempt to tell the story, the delay to recover the story, becomes a potential for the story in waiting and allows the author to recognize a mutual interaction between presence and absence (118). The interplay between the present and the absent texts produces a new story that emerges in the process of retelling and rewriting. Other subtexts in the novel either undercut or subvert the dominant narrative.

The many subtexts of the novel are related to Jeremy's identity transformations, which are preceded and followed by his many leaps and falls. The upward and downward movements of the main and other protagonists are reminiscent of the myth of Orpheus and his descent into Hades. The ambiguous title of Jeremy's first unfinished doctoral dissertation is "Going Down with Orpheus." After his first fall into the snow, when he got frostbitten, he is transformed into "a pillar of ice" (43). While beaten up during the snow race, Jeremy explains to Professor Madham: "Every river is the river Styx" (100)—the river that Orpheus had to cross to enter Hades and find his Eurydice. However, during Jeremy's race, nobody crosses the Styx. Jeremy follows the surface of the river. Unlike Orpheus, he doesn't plunge into the depth of the river. The descent is projected horizontally, always into new territories: "Only the river itself offered a way: you must follow its surface with your feet, almost with the tips of your fingers, in order to see" (82–83). Jeremy is not able to descend to the depth of the river, to plunge into the depth of his psyche, to solve the problem and accept his agony the way Orpheus did. Jeremy's leaps and falls are superficial and are repeated several times. His final fall with Bea Sunderman into the abyss and their disappearance point to the fact that he never returned in a proper way. Jeremy's story becomes a parody of Orpheus's descent.

The final fall is preceded by his love relationship with Bea Sunderman. Bea herself personifies the qualities of Demeter, and her character in the novel is firmly connected to earth; her descriptions are described as the smell of earth and crocuses; and Jill is related to Persephone as she maintains a secret love relationship with Jeremy. However, Jill is not one of the women in Kroetsch's work who spring from the underworld and restore the promising and flowering world, as Helene

Tanja Cvetković

Persephone did in *The Words of My Roaring*. Ironically, she doesn't reinstill life into Jeremy's depressed world. It is Bea who reignites his potency and becomes the powerful mother Earth:

> She gave to the whole room the smell of earth; not of flowers only but the dark breathing silence of ferns in crevices of rock. The lichens, orange and yellow, on a rotting limb. The green moss, cool to the sliding mouse. The smell of a northern forest, where the snow melts itself black into the last shade. (Kroetsch 1999, 155)

The physical union with Bea, when Jeremy transcends the power of language, takes him back to silence and to the beginning. He returns to the point of creation. At that point, the clocks in Bea's house started ticking; time started to flow. This is the moment of Jeremy's triumph when he conquers time, and the moment when Bea, as the mighty goddess Earth, heals the main hero. The opposites blur again. Jeremy frees himself from the role of Odysseus in quest, and, ironically enough, he finishes his quest tragically.

Bea's apocalyptic home, "Worlds End," can be associated with the Nordic myth of Ragnarok, which foretells a series of future events that include the battle and the death of gods, followed by the Great Winter, which in the novel could refer to the winter festival; afterwards the world resurfaces anew and fertile, the surviving and returning gods meet, and the world is repopulated by two human survivors. Ragnarok, "the Doom of the Gods" or "the Twilight of the Gods," marks the end of the mythical cycle during which the cosmos is destroyed and subsequently recreated. The myth mirrors Kroetsch's process of writing, where demythologization meets uninvention and recreation. It also reflects Bakhtin's carnival theory, where the old order is replaced by the new one. Eventually, the whole myth is parodied by Kroetsch's text, as Jeremy and Bea mysteriously disappear into nothingness one winter night so that the book doesn't end in the revival and recreation of the main protagonists' identities. It is only words and story about Jeremy's life that remain on the vast white blank page, resembling the North, as a puzzle to be turned into another reality and possibility by the all-knowing narrator or the reader himself.

If we refer to the qualities of New World Myth present in the way mythical fragments are treated in *Gone Indian*, we notice differences and similarities. One of the main differences between Kroetsch's use of myth and New World Myth texts is that Kroetsch maintains an interest in reworking classical forms, whereas the New World texts turn away from classical myth, as Vautier notices. I argue that it is irrelevant what kind of myth is used. The important fact is the emphasis on the reworking and the recreation of mythical fragment. The end product is the creation of a new myth in Kroetsch, and that is what matters. In New World Myth texts, the stress is on "the creative *making* of New World Myth" (48) or the process of mythmaking, which brings us to a conclusion that Kroetsch's poetics is close to New World Myth texts.

Regarding the definition of New World Myth, the story should suit a new place and time. In that sense, Kroetsch's reworking of the frontier myth, for example, is adapted to the needs of the main hero Jeremy Sadness and his search for identity. The frontier is shifted to the Canadian Northwest Territories and is given a new meaning and significance, while Jeremy's story and his destiny in the postmodern world become a new myth. The whole process of adapting the frontier myth to a new Canadian context resounds in Kroetsch's words that the task of the Canadian writer is to be involved in "the radical process of demythologizing the systems that threaten to define [him]" (58), or, more precisely, his task is to "uninvent" the world.

The emphasis on the all-knowing narrator, Mark Madham, and his attempts to recreate the story of the main hero is well evident in the novel. Mark Madham owns only the fragments of Jeremy's life in the Canadian wilderness. The whole story could be reached through Jeremy, too, one of the storytellers, whose fragmental story, scattered throughout the text, is also available, interpreted through his professor, Madham. As we have two interpretations of the same event, the reader himself is actively involved in decoding the truth of Jeremy's life. The story actually arises from the "space between" (Kirtz 209), or from the interaction between the text and the reader who compares different interpretations to what he discovers as truth.

As a conclusion, *Gone Indian* shows a tendency towards displaying New World Myth qualities rather than differentiating from it. Though Kroetsch rewrites classical myths, which, according to Vautier, is not common to New World Myth, Kroetsch also works on the re-making of old stories and myth and turns them into new ones, which is far more important to his treatment of myth and story than the content of myth he works with. This adds to the generative function of myth and story because many subtexts, hidden mythical fragments that undermine the surface story, could be told in a slightly different way. Kroetsch brings different subtexts to life again in his fiction; he changes them and adapts them to a new context where they acquire a new meaning. He says that it is not the content of the story that matters but "the act of telling the story" (120). The very fiction he creates in this way becomes a new reality, a new text, a mythical fragment, which could show up in a different context. Now we can go back to Kroetsch's statement that "the fiction makes us real" (Kroetsch 1970, 63). Does the fiction really make us real? From Kroetsch's point of view the answer is yes. Jeremy jumps from the bridge and disappears into nothingness. The only thing left behind is his life story on the tape recorder; Mark Madham, who tries to produce a story about his life, and we, the readers, who try to determine the truth about his life and who turn his life into the story, thus bringing him back into existence.

Works Cited

Bakhtin, Mikhail. 1965. *Rabelais and His World*. Cambridge, MA.: MIT Press.

Cooley, Dennis. 2016. *The Home Place: Essays on Robert Kroetsch's Poetry*. Edmonton: The University of Alberta Press.

Cvetković, Tanja. 2010. *Izmedju mita i tišine: Kanadska književnost, postmodernizam i Zapadni triptih Roberta Krouča*. Belgrad: Nolit.

Ellmann, Richard, Charles Fiedelson Jr., eds. 1965. *The Modern Tradition: Backgrounds of Modern Literature*. New York: Oxford University Press.

Grace, Sherrill. 1996. "Kroetsch and the Semiotics of North." *Open Letter* 5–6 (Spring–Summer): 13–24.

Kirtz, Mary K. 1994. "Inhabiting the Dangerous Middle of the Space Between: An Intramodernist Reading of Kroetsch's *Gone Indian*." *Great Plains Quarterly* 14 (3): 207–217.

Kroetsch, Robert. 1980. *The Crow Journals*. Edmonton: NeWest Press.

———. 1989. *The Lovely Treachery of Words: Essays Selected and New*. Toronto: Oxford University Press.

———. 1999. *Gone Indian*. Toronto: Stoddart Publishing Co.

———, ed. 1970. *Creation*. Toronto: NewPress. *Creation*. Toronto: NewPress.

Lecker, Robert. 1986. *Robert Kroetsch*. Boston: G. K. Hall.

Markotić, Nicole. 2017. *Robert Kroetsch: Essays on His Works*. Toronto, Buffalo, Lancaster, UK: Guernica.

Neuman, Shirley, and Robert Wilson, eds. 1981. *Labyrinths of Voice: Conversations with Robert Kroetsch*. Edmonton: NeWest Press.

Turner, Frederick Jackson. [1893] 1961. "The Significance of the Frontier in American History." In *Frontier and Section: Selected Essays of Frederick Jackson Turner*, edited by Ray Allen Billington, 37–62. Englewood Cliffs, NJ: Prentice Hall.

Vautier, Marie. 1998. *New World Myth: Postmodernism and Postcolonialism in Canadian Fiction*. Montreal and Kingston: McGill-Queen's University Press.

Notes

1 See, e.g., Robert Kroetsch, "Carnival and Violence: A Meditation," in *The Lovely Treachery of Words: Essays Selected and New* (Toronto: Oxford University Press, 1989); B. Hariharan, *The Carnival World of Robert Kroetsch* (Delhi: Creative Books, 2012); Robert Lecker, *Robert Kroetsch* (Boston: G. K. Hall, 1986); John Clement Ball, "The Carnival of Babel: The Construction of Voice in Robert Kroetsch's Out West Triptych," *Essays on Canadian Writing* 39 (1989): 1–22; Jason Howel, "Kroetsch's Carnivalesque World: A Bakhtinian Reading of *The Words of My Roaring, What the Crow Said*, and *Seed Catalogue*" (master's thesis University of Manitoba, 1992); Dennis Cooley, *The Home Place: Essays on Robert Kroetsch's Poetry* (Edmonton: University of Alberta Press, 2016).

"A Sound That Was Almost Human": Non-Speech and the Animal Body in *What the Crow Said*

Robert David Stacey

> *The voice of the body. There is no voice of the body, only the voice of the body. That isn't what I mean.*
> — Robert Kroetsch, "The Moment of The Discovery of America Continues"

What the Crow Said is a kind of stupid book. It's a kind of stupid book about stupidity, specifically male stupidity. Being about male stupidity, it is necessarily also a book about sex and death—the pursuit of the one, the denial of the other—which are ever and always the principal sources of male stupidity. Kroetsch was fifty when he was writing *What the Crow Said*, a stupid time in a man's life, and a good time to start thinking about death. Having also begun in that period an erotic relationship with a much younger woman, he was probably thinking about sex too.[1] But then again, if anything is going to make a man think about his own mortality, it's an erotic relationship with a younger woman.

Stupidity, sex, and death: serious business, all of it. But given in *What the Crow Said* a comic treatment. *What the Crow Said* is a long, meandering pratfall, a slow-motion slip on a banana peel; it employs all the devices of the novel to extend the time of, to *indulge* in, what would otherwise be a spit-second realization: *I am falling; I can fall.* Being a comic novel about stupidity, sex, and death, *What the Crow Said* has a lot of falling down—one of Kroetsch's great motifs, in any case—but raised in this novel to an operatic level, provided your idea of opera can accommodate the idea of man plummeting fatally into the shit of a church outhouse, as is the fate of poor Joe Lightening. At some point, *all* the men in this novel fall fatally into the shit, even if they only fall in love. Falling in love is stupid; it makes you wish you never realized you were going to die.

Paul de Man discusses Baudelaire's account of a man who slips on the sidewalk and, in that moment of lost control, is simultaneously the man falling and the man who sees himself as the man falling and thinks "how foolish I am." Baudelaire calls the comedy that entails in this complex set of substitutions and displacements—of the other as self and the self as other to itself—*"le comique absolu"*—absolute comedy. It is absolute because it is not a laugh with or against other people, but a laugh at one's own presumption of an advantage over nature. De Man glosses this anecdote as follows:

> As a being that stands upright [...] man comes to believe that he dominates nature, just as he can, at times, dominate others or watch others dominate him. This is, of course, a major mystification. The Fall, in the literal as well as the theological sense, reminds him of the purely instrumental, reified character of his relationship to nature. Nature can at all times treat him as though he were a thing and remind him of his factitiousness, whereas he is quite powerless to convert even the smallest particle of nature into something human. (214)

To experience a fall is to experience one's powerlessness in the face of nature.

But what makes that fall comic, *absolutely* comic, in fact, is the subject's sudden acquisition of a knowledge he should already have known. "In the idea of fall thus conceived," writes de Man,

> a progression in self knowledge is certainly implicit: the man who has fallen is somewhat wiser than the fool who walks around oblivious of the crack in the pavement about to trip him up. And the fallen philosopher reflecting on the discrepancy between the two successive stages is wiser still, but this does not in the least prevent him from

stumbling in his turn. It seems instead his wisdom can be gained only at the cost of such a fall. (214)

De Man is careful to point out that even the philosopher who would draw from a man's tumble an insight into the human predicament must still himself "go down"; without the sudden, vertiginous *experience* of his fallibility, without the fall, his knowledge is abstract—he has thought nature with his head, but not felt it with his ass.

I can let slip part of my argument by saying that Liebhaber, the novel's main character and would-be philosopher, falls repeatedly and eventually acquires a kind of self-knowledge and sympathy for the human condition by coming to know nature—painfully, mortifyingly—with his ass. To talk of asses—and I must insist we do—is to bring in the notion of the carnivalesque in relation to which *What the Crow Said* has been repeatedly interpreted (with Kroetsch's own encouragement[2]) and with great success. Inevitably, the emphasis in these readings is on the "material bodily principle," which, as Beata Gesicka writes in her analysis of *What the Crow Said*, "embraces the rich imagery that represents the material functions of the human body and the sensual aspects of human existence. Thus, excrement and defecation, sexual acts, birth and death, eating and drinking are common elements" (403). To be sure, Kroetsch fills *What the Crow Said* with a veritable "what's what" of bodily effluvia. For example: during a particularly epic piss-up, in which "every white male in the municipality was hell-bent on getting blind drunk" (101), the men are eventually kicked out of the beer parlour for their disorderly conduct. "The dispossessed men," we are told, were "drunk, shouting, farting, whining, hollering, cursing, belching, swearing, puking, [and] spitting" (101). We should keep this notion of the "material bodily principle"—amply demonstrated by the preceding—in mind; it is not unconnected to what de Man calls the "empirical self," which discovers its empiricism, its contingency as a body subject to nature, in the act of falling on its ass.

De Man, however, extends his analysis of Baudelaire's anecdote further still. The experiential dimension is critical, but even more important for his purposes is Baudelaire's suggestion that absolute comedy involves, on the part of the fallen, a kind of *dédoublement*, a temporal and psychic split. The falling subject views himself simultaneously from two distinct angles, each representing a separate episteme: one a "stage of mystified" belief in his sovereignty over nature, the other in which he has gained "knowledge of his mystification" (213). To the extent that the philosopher (or the comedian) is the fallen man who wishes to represent to himself or to others this double consciousness, he is obliged to adopt an ironic language or a language of irony. Irony provides the only form in which he can hold together *in a single figuration* the two-pronged image of an "empirical self that exists in a state of inauthenticity and a self [...] that asserts the knowledge of this inauthenticity" (214). De Man cautions, however, that this "form of language" is no more authentic than the subject's initial state of mystification "for to know inauthenticity is not the same as to be authentic" (214).[3]

For de Man, irony can never function to reinstitute a lost plenitude precisely because it is "a form of language": "[T]he reflective disjunction not only occurs *by means of language* as a privileged category, but it transfers the self out of the empirical world into a world constituted out of, and in, language" (214). As a human technology, language can only reinscribe its user's unnaturalness, even at the moment it asserts his unavoidably empirical, that is to say natural, susceptibility. The cost of knowledge is one's incarceration in "the prison-house of language," a phrase I borrow from Fredric Jameson, who borrows it from Nietzsche, who writes: "We have to cease to think, if we refuse to do it in the prison-house of language."[4]

I am finally in a spot where I can make my move, as it were, and ask a question that neither de Man nor Nietzsche thought to ask, but which I believe Kroetsch is asking in *What the Crow Said*, which is whether there is not a knowledge, a thinking, and indeed a kind of speaking—I say a *kind* of speaking—that would assert rather than deny man's imbrication in the natural processes of the world, that would preserve his own sense of his "empirical self." If such a knowledge and such a speaking were to exist, it would go some way towards resolving the problem with irony, which is fundamentally the problem of man's unhomefulness in or alienation from the natural world because of language. *What the Crow Said* intimates an alternative kind of knowledge, closer to the knowledge of the fool who has no knowledge than to the knowledge of the philosopher who knows himself to be a fool. It comes down to this: Is there a point after he has realized that, as de Man puts it, "he is quite powerless to convert even the smallest particle of nature into something human," that the human being, seeing that the game is rigged, might reverse this procedure so as to not convert nature into a human artefact, but to seek the natural in himself, and himself in nature—to, in a manner of speaking, refuse to "walk upright?"

Talking birds are stupid. What does the crow say? He says "asshole." He says asshole a lot, mostly at Liebhaber, but to the other men as well—only the men, of course. We have on the one hand, as I mentioned earlier, a large camp of critics who read the novel as an expression of the carnivalesque. They like this kind of language because it draws the reader's attention to the novel's prioritization of what Bakhtin calls the "lower bodily stratum." But there's another camp that reads the novel as exemplary of magic realism. For them, what the crow says is less important than the fact that there's a talking crow in the first place because, well, talking crows are magical.[5] So, we have these two main critical camps, and sometimes their arguments overlap and both definitely bring out salient aspects of the novel, but both camps are so fixated on an animal that talks like a human that they overlook the extent to which the novel is rather more interested in humans that talk like animals.

> "Caw," Liebhaber said. He tried to frighten the magpies away by shouting. "Caw."
>
> "Caw caw." O'Holleran added. ...
>
> "Caw caw caw," Droniuk shouted, hoarsely. He tried to smooth down his hair; he brushed at his unshaven face. "Caw caw caw caw caw," he shouted. He felt guilty.
>
> "Caw caw caw caw caw caw caw caw," the men said now, not so much to the waiting magpies, as to each other (89).

Repeatedly throughout the novel, various characters reject or are moved beyond phonetic communicative speech and in its place indulge in non-phonetic emissions of animal noise. These moments oppose rational discourse, particularly written rational discourse, and hint at a thinking outside language and its trap of irony, the thinking of a humanity set within, not outside or against, the natural cycles of birth, life, and death.

If, as David Appelbaum writes, non-linguistic expressions of the body connect or reconnect the subject with a repressed "corporeal intelligence that knows directly of creaturely death with its power to interrupt life at any stroke" (11), then we can approach these animalistic interruptions of properly meaningful address as key moments in the novel's engagement with death, the denial of which manifests in any number of counterproductive and self-destructive projects, notably Skandl's ice tower. You needn't be Jacques Derrida to recognize in the ice tower, which the men desperately build taller and taller, and which Tiddy recognizes immediately as attempt to "get to heaven" (41), a manifestation of logocentric thought. Monolithic, unitary, phallic, idealistic, inorganic, and anti-terrestrial, the ice tower literally becomes a place of retreat for the men of the town, who more or less take up residence there until it collapses around them.

Appelbaum notes that logocentrism in writing has its analogue in phonocentrism in oral discourse. By phonocentrism, he means the tendency to dematerialize speech, to ignore in the act of decoding spoken language the bodily substrate of words as sound. Rather than attending to the vocality of speech, its noisiness, phonocentric discourse suppresses the potentially disruptive presence of bodily expression that operates along with the speaking of words. "Its theme is domination by the cognitive aspect of vocal experience over the kinaesthetic proprioceptive one" (xi). And there's this: phonocentrism, Appelbaum insists, "must be understood in terms of a vocal preoccupation with immortality" (11). A resistance to phonocentrism in the novel might therefore be read as part of a broader strategy to come to terms with the corporeal and therefore mortal dimension of human life, to refuse the ice tower and remain grounded, to speak in such a way that does not reinscribe one's unnaturalness but commits one to nature and the natural outside a lapsarian economy.

A distinction must be made: the orality of *What the Crow* said is widely acknowledged. The novel has a talky sort of narrator, local dialects and personal idiolects are foregrounded in the various exchanges between characters. Kroetsch himself talks in *Labyrinths of Voice* of wanting to assert the primacy of speech over writing in this novel (39, 64, 119). To follow Kroetsch's own lead in "The Moment of the Discovery of America Continues," we can state that the novel stages the displacement of *"langue"* by *"parole"*—which is why the death of Martin *Lang* is the novel's second major event and one that haunts the male characters for most of the narrative.[6] But *"parole"* is itself further divisible into "speech," by which we mean meaningful oral communication dictated by rule and custom—already idealized—and "voice," which is the particular, organic, noisy mouth-and-lung sounding upon which our speaking necessarily depends. Kroetsch himself seems to hint at a similar concept when he speaks of a "voice of the body" that "isn't what I *mean*" (1989b 19; my emphasis), but his reliance on the classic opposition of *langue* and *parole* restricts a fuller elaboration.

The classic opposition between *langue* and *parole*, Appelbaum argues, inevitably "explains away the missing element" of voice (39). When I am giving a lecture to my students, I use words to convey ideas and concepts or to relay information or to describe a situation. The students listen or don't, take notes or don't, but are always more or less oblivious to the material qualities of the sound of my speaking. This is always the case when the context urges an instrumentalist use of words, or when what Steve McCaffery calls a "restricted economy" of language is assumed (202–03).⁷ But if I were to distort my voice to the point where the words become unclear, or if I were to adopt a bizarre and annoying accent, or if I were to insert gibberish between recognizable word-signs, then the students suddenly become aware that their own "proper" listening had all along required the suppression of my "voice" so as to allow an ostensibly more useful meaning to stand forth, unencumbered and transferable. This is precisely what Appelbaum means by "phonocentrism." Along these lines, it is *voice*, not speech, that we hear when Vera's boy, having recently left the family of coyotes who adopted him as an infant, tries to make himself understood: "What astonished people was the way he jabbered on, hardly stopping to listen, in a kind of speech that was half yips and barks, half what his listeners took to be pig Latin" (119). Kroetsch actually renders this as pig Latin in the text: "'The ercilessmay unsay shall urnbay us,' he yipped and barked. 'Be reparedpay.'" (128). But *pig* Latin is merely a device to render his *coyote* speech in its voicy-ness, it being "a language that no one quite understood," because it was less articulated speech than a "kind of buzz in his breathing" (117).⁸

To discuss the orality of *What the Crow Said*, but take into account neither the non-semantic elements of that orality nor its moments of non-verbal but nevertheless oral expression is to risk misapprehending the novel's main goal. To borrow a phrase from Alfonso Lingis, we can understand the narrative as a quest for nothing short of "true discourse," that is to say, "a discourse based on bodily sensations [that] records what individuals have seen and heard, what their body powers can vouch for" ("Carrion," 137). In personal terms, this is a search over and against a social system that is "governed not by biological or psychophysiological, but by rational, logical and scientific laws" (138). In broader terms, for this is also the story of a town, it is the search for a model of community that would allow itself to hear "the glossolalia of non human things—the humming, buzzing, murmuring, crackling and roaring of the world" along with the "stammerings, quaverings, dronings of one another's voices" ("Murmur," 85). "[I]s there not also communication," Lingis asks, "in hearing the noise in one another's voices—the noise of one another's life that accompanies the harkening of a message?" (88).

Yes, there is. The first major event in the novel is the impregnation of Vera Lang by a swarm of bees. (Did someone say "buzzing?")

> The bees had closed her mouth, her ears. The bees found her swollen lips between her thighs; she felt their intrusive weight and spread farther her legs.
> Then she gave her cry (4).

As for the townspeople,

> they heard a sound that was almost human. Far distant to their ears and yet clear too. They could not describe it later, those same men, yet there were surely as many of them, that day, in Big Indian, as there were drones in the swarm of bees. A coyote, one man said; but not at this time of the day, another answered. Terrified and prolonged, but not a cry for help; despairing and ecstatic too. At first it was a cry of joy, a joy inhumanly exquisite; then it released a sorrow beyond all sorrow. (5)

The novel thus begins, not visually, but sonically, with this "fierce and passionate and desperate ululation" (6). Crucially, it is a sound that momentarily confounds the town's ability to separate human vociferation from animal sound. But as the echoes of her cry begin to recede, "They knew then, the men outside in the streets, the women in their houses, it was a human outcry, pain-filled and sweet, beautiful, wild, terrified" (5). The knowledge that the women seem to possess in this book, and the knowledge that the men to their detriment attempt to repress, is that the sound is no less human for being animal; that, in fact, it embodies precisely a knowledge that our linguistic systems work to eradicate, because it is a knowledge that cannot be expressed within them.

During pleasurable sex, Lingis writes, "Our lips loosen, soften, glisten with saliva, lose the train of sentences, our throats issue babble, giggling, moans, sighs" ("Animal," 171). Or, if it's really good, I suppose, a "fierce and passionate and desperate ululation." Even the more prudish Appelbaum tells us that "the desire to speak unreason and illogic is greatest in the throes of passion, inspiration and awe, when *eros*, art and religions conspire to produce the incoherent sounds of our full humanity" (52). Orgasms are stupid. The orgasmic cry signifies nothing but itself; it does not connect up to chain of significations; it can neither describe, nor narrate, nor enable a self-distancing of the subject as in ironic discourse. But it is in such non-semantic animal soundings—the sounds of our voice, not of our speech—that Lingis and Appelbaum argue we can discover "our full humanity."

So I come to the rather embarrassing claim that Liebhaber, along with each of the other male characters, must "find his voice."[9] Early in the text, Liebhaber, the newspaper editor, is fully subservient to written language, to text: "[H]e was himself hardly more than a mere tray of alphabet, awaiting the insistence of an ordering hand" (59). Recalling that the impetus towards logocentrism and phonocentrism originates in a fear of death and a desire for biological and temporal transcendence, we note Liebhaber's own earlier drunken realization that he was "bound [...] to death" by an "intricate knot of language" (46). All creatures are "bound to death," those without speech no less than those in its possession. But in the Western philosophical tradition, it is our ability to constitute ourselves as individual subjects in language that produces our *mortality*. As Martin Heidegger notes: "Mortals are they who can experience death as death. Animals cannot do so. But animals cannot speak either. The essential relation between death and language flashes up before us" (in Agamben, xi). It is Liebhaber's subservience to language that produces in him a feeling of separation from the natural processes to which all living things are subject—and it is within that separation that his mortal dread arises. Liebhaber initially tries to extricate himself from the "knot of language" by abusing the visual signs of writing itself: he "tried, with a twist of his wrist, to turn an M into a W. Failing at that, he turned a T upside down; but he could read it just as easily upside down as upright" (46). Eventually, he composes the word "glot" which is not a word, but something like the spelling of a sound.[10] He begins to play and experiment with the letters, trying even stranger combinations: "He tried again, the simplest changing of the alphabet— and he heard himself making sounds for which he had no signs at all" (60). Ah, now we're getting somewhere, we think. But it takes a long game of schmier—151 days in duration and a real trial of the flesh— before any more progress is made.

What ends, finally, the marathon card session, during which life had gone on, the women doing all the necessary work quite effectively without the men's help (though no less displaced for all that) is the appearance of Martin Lang's ghost in the basement of the church where the game had moved to some days before. This is how the narrator describes their shout of surprise and terror:

> The roar that went up that morning, into the still frozen air over the town of Big Indian, was third only to Vera Lang's immortal cry and the cry that was to come from the air itself, many years later, over Big Indian.
> (Did someone say "roaring"?)
> The roar was an animal roar. Some remembered it, after, as a bull sound, ferocious, out of the dark earth itself, the sound of the darkness itself. Some remembered the horses that drowned when Skandl's lighthouse broke though the ice, the lost and drowning team abandoned by all, trumpeting a perfection of despair. Some thought a pack of wolves was loosed on the town, purely and simply rabies mad, yelping and howling to a final feast. (98)

This "roar," we are told, in words that self-consciously echo the account of Vera's earlier animal cry, is "so perverse an ululation" that "[c]hildren learned stillness. The old experienced the call of death, heard it and welcomed the summons" (98). But the men, unlike the children and the old people—and the women, of course—remain deaf to the knowledge of their own animal voice, and soon embark on a "war against the sky" that kills or maims every one of them.

As if in retaliation against the human groundlings that would usurp its kingdom, the "sky" responds with "a ferociously hot, dry wind" that blows for weeks on end. Resolved to end all hostilities, Joe Lightning, who "believed in the union of the elements" (139), hopes that a parlay with the eagle, lord of the air, will show him the way towards peace. But instead of wrestling the eagle to the ground as he had planned, he is plucked up by his wrists and carried into the sky. He's dropped, or falls, or lets himself fall, and in that moment before the shit hits his fanny, he releases another of those sounds that punctuates the novel and underscores the theme I have been attempting to elucidate: "It was a simple laugh of pleasure and yet it was a kind of scream too, a scream of release" (141). "Some people, years later, believed they heard from the sky a version of prayer, a kind of holy laugh. Others, when insanely drunk, or on their deathbeds, admitted to hearing a laugh of such absolute obscenity they'd refused, for a whole lifetime, to acknowledge it" (142). The narrator's comments recapitulate the pattern that began with his survey of the various responses to Vera's own "scream of release": the experience of the sound is significant, even life-changing for the subject (in this case, it is also life-ending) and for those who hear it, but it defies memory and narrativization after the fact. Appelbaum tells us that the animal voice, as opposed to speech, is essentially unrepeatable; beyond grammar and semantic accountability, and embedded in corporeal experience, the voice is "process rather than production" (77).

If de Man's account of irony fails to acknowledge the possibility of there being a joy in falling, an ecstasy in surrendering oneself to the empirical fact of nature, it is perhaps because his falling man makes no sound, not a peep. As the silent object of a verbal reconstruction, de Man's falling man can only ever fall into language, when he might otherwise have fallen into shit. His exploration of irony, wonderfully penetrating in its way, is still the way of Descarte's "I am," which, as Derrida notes in *The Animal that Therefore I Am*, "must suspend, or rather detach, precisely as detachable, all reference to life, to the life of the body, and to animal life" (72). This is so because thought makes no sound, has no voice. As Appelbaum says, "mental space is pristine, angelic, soulful, and unperturturbed by bodily upheavals" (5). Joe's laughing scream, Vera's orgasmic cry, her boy's yipping coyote talk, work to reattach being and thought to "life…the life of the body… [and] animal life." And because sound is given, moves outward from the body to meet the bodies of others, the effect is that of a perturbation in and of the social conversation.

At the very same moment that Joe falls into the church outhouse, Liebhaber experiences a release of his own; it is, however, far less jubilant, if no less instructive. His moment comes in a scene that parodies the story of Noah's ark. Trapped under a capsized boat that he had been building in preparation for a flood he had falsely prognosticated some time before, he doesn't know that the water is only a few feet deep. Believing he is going to drown, Liebhaber "beg[ins] to babble and cry, to whimper and scream" (146). He begs the crow who's pecking about on the hull—you see, the animals are outside the ark while man is trapped inside—to go get help, but the crow declines. Eventually realizing that all he has to do to avoid drowning is stand up, Liebhaber "shat himself. At that moment, against the constricting cold of the spring runoff, his sphincter opened; he felt the warm shit ooze softly into his underwear" (147). The crow might have saved for *this* moment his comment: "Well, Lieb, I've got to hand it to you; you are finally a total asshole" (113), but he's flown off by the time Liebhaber effectuates his exit. Two releases here, both degrading, both recuperative: first, the man of language and text is reduced to incoherent and unrestrained "babbling, crying, whimpering, and screaming," vociferations Appelbaum aligns collectively with the *vox naturalis*, the voice of nature; second, the man soils himself—this, too, is a call of nature.

At this point, my own analysis converges with that of critics like Neil Randall who approach the novel in terms of its employment of carnivalesque tropes and ideas. Randall argues that Liebhaber's defecation "is his most important act in the book" (n.p.) because it announces his final capitulation to the organic processes against which he had set himself for most of the story. Along these lines, we should recognize that his blubbering constitutes a similar sort of breakdown or breakthrough insofar as meaningful speech, unlike babble, depends on "retentiveness" and control (Appelbaum, 36) whereby the body is disciplined, made into an instrument to serve an organizing intelligence. Apiece with his literal incontinence, Liebhaber's vocal incontinence marks the final blow to his anti-terrestrial aspirations and his accession to "full humanity."

At the end of the novel, no longer seeking to dominate nature, or to control Tiddy or her gaggle of excessively fertile daughters and grand-daughters, Liebhaber has attained the happiness for which he had been searching throughout the novel. He lies with his love in a post-coital embrace, listening through the window to the sounds of the crow's ordinary cackling and Gladys's ball bouncing against the house. He dies in that moment, unafraid, not even bothering to wake Tiddy, letting her sleep rather wake her for something so trivial: "After all," he reasons, "he is only dying" (195).

Endings are stupid, too.

I have so far avoided using the term "postmodern." Despite Kroetsch's own popularization of the term, I'm not convinced it's an especially useful tool for thinking about this book, except in one way. Before it became the property of Linda Hutcheon and was turned into a template for metafiction, postmodernism in Canada designated a broader ethos that could take multiple forms across the genres. One source of this earlier view is Frank Davey's *From There to Here*, published in 1974. In the introduction to that book, Davey writes: "The modernists sought to control both their world and their art; the postmodernists seek to participate in anarchic cooperation with the elements of [their] environment" (20). He goes on to say, "Most of the new Canadian writing of the sixties and seventies has taken process, discontinuity, and organic shape as its values" (21) and he notes that the emphasis of these works is "phenomenological," marking a "triumph of particularity" (22) over dematerialized, de-corporealized systems of instrumentalist reason. It seems to me that Kroetsch's interest in the animal body and non-phonetic voice in *What the Crow Said* aligns that novel with that different kind of postmodernism, the postmodernism of *process* Davey describes. It also aligns the novel with other explorations of voice in Canada, such as we see in the sound poetry of bill bissett, Penn Kemp, and bpNichol, with their shared emphasis on embodied experience and proprioceptive models for communicating that experience. Ironically, because Kroetsch is so often read as postmodern in one way (dare I mention the epithet "Mr. Canadian Postmodern"?) he is too seldom read as postmodern in the way that might facilitate a productive dialogue with the work of other writers, especially poets, whose primary interest is in sound rather than writing, metafictional or otherwise. It is my hope that the preceding has made some progress in that direction.

Works Cited

Agamben, Giorgio. 2006. *Language and Death: The Place of Negativity.* Translated by Karen Pinkus and Michael Hardt. Minneapolis: University of Minnesota Press.

Aldea, Eva. 2011. *Magic Realism and Deleuze: The Indiscernibility of Difference in Postcolonial Literature.* London: Continuum.

Andrews, Jennifer. 1999. "Rethinking the Relevance of Magic Realism for English-Canadian Literature: Reading Ann-Marie MacDonald's Fall on Your Knees." *Studies in Canadian Literature* 24 (1): 1–19.

Appelbaum, David. 1990. *Voice.* Albany: State University of New York Press.

Bondar, Alana. 2011. "Let the Crow Speak: Magic Realism and Indigenous Knowledge as Beak(ons) of Light in Robert Kroetsch's Ecological Gothic Text *What the Crow Said*." In *Eyes Deep with Unfathomable Histories: The Politics and Poetics of Magic Realism Today and in the Past*, edited by Liliana Sikorska, 65–84. Poznan: Peter Lang.

de Man, Paul. 1983. "The Rhetoric of Temporality." *Blindness and Insight: Essays in the Rhetoric of Contemporary Criticism.* 2nd ed. 187–228. Minneapolis: Universiy of Minnesota Press.

Derrida, Jacques. 2008. *The Animal That Therefore I Am*. Translated by David Wills. New York: Fordham University Press.

Davey, Frank. 1974. *From the There to Here: A Guide to English-Canadian Literature Since 1960*. Erin, ON: Porcepic.

Gesicka, Beata. 2003. "On the Carnivalesque in Magical Realism: Reflexions on Robert Kroetsch's *What the Crow Said*." *Canadian Review of Comparative Literature* 30 (2): 393–409.

Jameson, Fredric. 1972. *The Prison-House of Language: A Critical Account of Structuralism and Russian Formalism*. Princeton: Princeton University Press.

Kroetsch, Robert. 1980. *The Crow Journals*. Edmonton: NeWest Press.

———.1988. *What the Crow Said*. Orig. 1978. Edmonton: University of Alberta Press.

———. 1989a. "Carnival and Violence: A Meditation." In *The Lovely Treachery of Words: Essays Selected and New*, 95–107. Toronto: Oxford University Press.

———. 1989b."The Moment of the Discovery of America Continues." In *The Lovely Treachery of Words: Essays Selected and New*, 1–20. Toronto: Oxford University Press.

Lee, Dennis. 1998. "Cadence, Country, Silence: Writing in Colonial Space." In *Body Music: Essays*, 3–26. Toronto: Anansi.

Lingis, Alfonso. 1994. "Carrion Body, Carrion Utterance." In *The Community of Those Who Have Nothing in Common*, 135–154. Bloomington: Indiana University Press.

———. 1994. "The Murmur of the World." In *The Community of Those Who Have Nothing in Common*, 69–106. Bloomington: University of Indiana Press.

———. 2003. "Animal Body, Inhuman Face." In *Zoontologies: The Question of the Animal*, edited by Cary Wolfe, 165–182. Minneapolis: University of Minnesota Press.

McCaffery, Steve. 2000. "Writing as a General Economy." In *North of Intention, Critical Writings 1973–1986*. Second edition. 201–221. New York: Roof.

Neuman, Shirley, and Robert Wilson, eds. 1982. *Labyrinths of Voice: Conversations with Robert Kroetsch*. Edmonton: NeWest Press.

Randall, Neil. 1989. "Carnival and Intertext: Humour in What the Crow Said and the Studhorse Man." SCL 14.1. https://journals.lib.unb.ca/index.php/scl/article/view/8096/9153.

Slemon, Stephen. 1988. "Magic Realism as Post-Colonial Discourse." *Canadian Literature* 116 (Spring): 9–24.

Notes

1. See Kroetsch's *The Crow Journals* (Edmonton: NeWest Press, 1980), for a somewhat elliptical account of the author's life and concerns during the period of the novel's composition.

2. See, for instance, Kroetsch's essay "Carnival and Violence," which demonstrates a deep familiarity with the mode of carnivalesque as received through Mikhail Bakhtin and Julia Kristeva.

3. The idea of a language that lets you articulate your inauthenticity but not to overcome it; that allows you to express your ironic condition, and even to treat it ironically, but which leaves you trapped in irony nevertheless, is a familiar one in Canadian criticism. Half of everything Margaret Atwood wrote until she discovered theocracy and DNA is about this. Kroetsch himself dwells in and around a similar problematic in a number of the essays that comprise *The Lovely Treachery of Words*. The most articulate expression of the Canadian writer's entrapment within irony may well be Dennis Lee's seminal essay "Cadence, Country, Silence" (1974, revised 1998) in which the author states that in Canada "writing has become a problem to itself" insofar as "to write involves something that makes writing impossible" (10). For Lee, this "something" is language that bespeaks "contradictions in our civil belonging" (10). His proposed solution is that we, as Canadians, fully inhabit our inauthenticity, that we imaginatively occupy the split in our national psyche and make that our point of departure: "The impasse of writing that is problematic to itself is transcended only when the impasse becomes its own subject, when writing accepts and enters and names its own condition as it names the world" (21). Though its concerns are primarily personal and communitarian rather than nationalistic, *What the Crow Said* is no less concerned with a search for a more authentic state of being, but it employs a radically different strategy for accomplishing this goal.

4. Jameson seems to have derived the title of his *The Prison-House of Language: A Critical Account of Structuralism and Russian Formalism* (Princeton: Princeton UP, 1972) from an essay by Erich Heller, "Wittgenstein and Nietzsche," first published in 1963, which uses this particular phrasing. In Walter Kaufman's translation of Nietzsche's *Will to Power* (New York: Vintage, 1968), the sentence is rendered as "We cease to think when we refuse to do so under the constraint of language" (283). The language is less colorful, but the sentiment remains the same.

5. The most influential instance of this approach is undoubtedly Stephen Slemon's "Magic Realism as Post-Colonial Discourse" (1988). Other critics connecting the novel to magic realism are Jennifer Andrews in "Rethinking the Relevance of Magic Realism for English-Canadian Literature" (1999),

Eva Aldea in *Magic Realism and Deleuze* (2011), and Alana Bondar in "Let the Crow Speak: Magic Realism and Indigenous Knowledge as Beak(ons) of Light in Robert Kroetsch's Ecological Gothic Text What the Crow Said" (2012).

6   Kroetsch writes: "There are these two sides to language: *langue* and *parole*. Langue is the great-given, the sum total of words and grammar and literature and concluded speech. *Parole* is what one of us says, the uniqueness of the speaking (writing) person" ("The Moment of The Discovery of America Continues," 19).

7   In "Writing as a General Economy" (2000), McCaffery distinguishes between "restricted" and "general" economies of language. The restricted economy prioritizes idealized meaning and semantic accountability, and achieves this by way of a suppression (at the points of both production and reception) of non-utilizable elements and anarchic "energies" always present in the utterance, whether spoken or written. As for the general economy, it would name a situation that allows those elements and energies to enter into the communicative act by way of the de-suppression of materiality and noise. I am arguing that the animal vociferations of human characters in Kroetsch's novel are analogous to sound poetry, which, McCaffery argues, promotes a "poetics of the general": "Sound poetry shatters meaning at the point where language commits its move to idealization; it sustains the materiality and material effects of the phonematic structures whilst avoiding their traditional semantic purpose. As a poetry of purely phonic outlay, the subject also puts the subject into process, exploding the unitary contours of consciousness and propelling textual experience into a festive economy" (214–15).

8   Vera's boy is not the only character who barks. Martin Straw, having fallen instantly in love with Vera after she lifts her bee veil, chases after her as she drives away: "Like a crazy dog, he leapt, galloped, yapped in pursuit of the vanishing automobile" (109). This instance of a human exhibiting animal behaviour is apiece with many others in the novel. During the horsefly plague, for example, "[a] few citizens of the Municipal District, unable themselves to cope with the flies, fastened makeshift tails to the backs of their trousers or skirts and learned in a matter of minutes to switch them back and forth. Women, especially, took to wearing over their eyes forelocks in the manner of horses. One elderly gentleman figured out how to twitch his ears and the muscles of his thighs" (151).

9   Sounding a bit like a New Age guru himself, Kroetsch intones "Listen to the voice of the blackbird, my dear friends. When you here not one phoneme, not one morpheme—not one smidgen of sound that is familiar: then you will cease to be afraid of your own Voices" ("The Moment of the Discovery of America Continues," 19).

10 It's unlikely that this combination is purely arbitrary. "Glot" brings to mind "glottis" and "glottal," as in "glottal stop," underscoring a latent sonority. "Glot" echoes both "glut" and "clot" as well, suggesting his current linguistic impasse. Thanks to David Eso for the suggestion.

Puppeteers and Collectors, or, Is God a Woman? Godgames in Kroetsch's Writing and Teaching

MARTIN KUESTER

> *Therefore, ladies and gentlemen, just as Greek mytholo-gy came along at one point in the great turning wheel of gods and goddesses through the history of the world as we know it, Christian mythology arrived here on the shores of North America in October of the year 1492. At which point God as a man met God as a woman—for that's where she'd been kept hidden all of this time, as it turns out...*
> —Tomson Highway, *Comparing Mythologies*

Robert Kroetsch was a wonderful teacher and friend and an inspiring influence on my academic career. As I will show in the following pages, his teaching methods, the pedagogical effectiveness of which would sometimes occur to me only in hindsight, are reminiscent of a concept that he addressed—and which he efficiently applied, as I hope to show—in both life and writing: the "godgame" mentioned in my title.

The concept of godgames has been with me for many years, ever since I happened upon it while writing my German *Staatsexamen* thesis on the novels of Robert Kroetsch at the University of Trier, in

Germany, in the early 1980s. I wrote this thesis under the supervision of the late Walter Pache, one of the pioneers and leading representatives of Canadian literature studies in Germany and Europe. Kroetsch used the term "godgame," which was completely new to me then, in conversation with his fellow scholars Shirley Neuman and Robert Rawdon Wilson in the book-length conversation *Labyrinths of Voice*, which offers wide-ranging discussions of many concepts underlying his theory and practice of writing. This intriguing conversation of Neuman, Wilson, and Kroetsch offered a treasure of suggestions for a young student of literature who was still very much under the influence of the structuralist theories that he had been exposed to in the linguistics classes that were a constituent part of the German curriculum for future teachers of English. So for my thesis, I was bent on analyzing the narrative structure of Kroetsch's writing, seeing his novels as literary models offering themselves up to a mainly structuralist analysis (see Kuester 1992 for a summary of the main points). I was, and still am, heavily biased towards binary structures—Saussurian and Barthesian—and what Kroetsch and other poststructuralists and postmodernists did to or with them.

In addition, Robert Rawdon Wilson's seminal essays on godgames—later included in his volume *In Palamedes' Shadow*—that Kroetsch, Neuman, and Wilson refer to several times over in *Labyrinths of Voice*—proved to be guiding and inspiring influences in my future work on anglophone authors, reaching from Geoffrey Chaucer (and his *Pardoner's Tale*) via William Shakespeare (and his Prospero in *The Tempest* and his Duke of Vienna in *Measure for Measure*) through John Milton (and his Attendant Spirit in *Comus* as well as his Father in *Paradise Lost*) to Herman Melville (and his Confidence-Man), John Fowles (and his Magus), and Margaret Atwood. Robert Kroetsch, whom Linda Hutcheon once called "Mr. Canadian Postmodern" (Hutcheon 1989, 160), is certainly one of the leading Canadian writers making use of the ludic as well as critical aspects of postmodernism, and I would claim that the godgames defined and described by Robert Rawdon Wilson are most obviously part of his game playing.

In his discussion about godgames with Shirley Neuman and Robert Rawdon Wilson, Kroetsch says that "I am in a kind of godgame when I write. I get into the godgame when I have to use situation, character and language to make that character experience desire" (Kroetsch in Neuman and Wilson 1982, 67). What is such a godgame exactly? Let me briefly quote Robert Rawdon Wilson:

> In a godgame, one character (or several) is made a victim by another character's superior knowledge and power. Caught in a cunningly constructed web of appearances, the victim, who finds the illusion to be impenetrable, is observed, and his behavior is judged. (Wilson 1990, 123)

Wilson points out that, although named by contemporary British novelist John Fowles in *The Aristos* and used in his novel *The Magus*, the godgame is not a twentieth-century invention but rather "a narrative category that has existed since the tales of ancient mythology" (123). Critics have shown that godgames can serve not only as games to be played to make fun of victim characters but that they can also have a clear educational aspect. Personally, I have tried to show this in the context of, among others, Adam and Eve's education in Milton's *Paradise Lost* and *Comus* (see Kuester 2009) or Shakespeare's *The Tempest* or *Measure for Measure*. In his study of earlier godgames in Kroetsch's writing, for example in *What the Crow Said*, Paul Barrett suggests that "Kroetsch recasts Fowles's godgame under the conditions of postmodernity, removing the all-knowing Magus and leaving only the game" (Barrett 2013, 99). As I would like to claim, this is a view of Kroetsch's godgames that does not apply to the later novels I am interested in here, such as *Alibi* and *The Puppeteer*. There are games in these novels, but these games are not just ludic—they are educational, and there is an educational agent which Barrett was unable to identify in *What the Crow Said*. As for other critics seeing traces of godgames in the later novels, Douglas Glover, for one, writes that "the puppeteer motif brings to mind John Fowles's *The Magus*" (Glover 1993, n.p.).

In *Alibi*, Kroetsch presents a group of characters who seem to be not only in the employ but also under the spell of the rich western Canadian oil millionaire and collector Jack Deemer. Among these characters, there is first of all the collector's agent, William William Dorfendorf, or Dorf for short, who travels all over the world in order to bring together the collections that have caught the eye or, as he is going blind, the desire of Deemer. Then there is the photographer Karen Strike, who seems to be rewriting diary or journal entries that are left behind by Dorf when he disappears after seemingly having caused the death of the minuscule Portuguese doctor De Medeiros; and finally there is the mysteriously attractive Julie Magnuson, who also seems to have died—in a car crash near a Portuguese spa. In Gunilla Florby's words, in *Alibi*

> we are allowed to read the protagonist's journal over his shoulder, as it were—an unadulterated reading experience, if there ever was one. Or so it seems for a while until it dawns upon us that the story—and the reader—is being manipulated in what is in fact a highly self-reflexive process of textual construction... (Florby 1997, 110)

Spas are at the centre of the novel, as Dorf's most recent task in the employ of Deemer is to look for the ideal spa, especially in Britain, Portugal, and Greece, before he finally locates it at Deadman Spring in the Canadian Rockies. And he needs an alibi, as he is a suspect, first of all in the case of Julie's death in Portugal—"What can I do but guess what happened? [...] Did Julie's dwarf, in his jealousy, follow us to the Algarve, there capture Julie, steal her out of her own bed and force her to drive him away in my car?" (Kroetsch 1983, 145)—but Dorf is also a suspect in Dr. De Medeiros's drowning in a lake near Deadman Spring.

In *Alibi*'s sequel, the novel *The Puppeteer*, we meet the same group of people, although Gunilla Florby insists that while "the names reappear [...] the characters behind the names are difficult to recognize" (Florby 1997, 131) so that we are faced with "intertextual incompatibilities" (132).

The core group of characters from *Alibi* is enlarged in *The Puppeteer* to encompass Maggie Wilder, a Vancouver writer who has returned from the United States to Canada, while her husband, an art historian, has gone to Europe to study—and also steal—Greek icons. William William Dorfendorf had disappeared at the end of *Alibi* because he feared that his shooting at—and hitting—Dr. De Medeiros's canoe might have resulted in the doctor's death. Dorf now turns up in Vancouver under the guise of Papa B, a pizza delivery man and puppet player who had been hiding for a time in Greece, on Mount Athos, learning about Greek art as well as puppet plays. Julie Magnuson and Dr. De Medeiros, the first of whom had supposedly died in Portugal and the second of whom had disappeared in a Rocky Mountains lake, also turn up again, and Dorf's guess at what happened—quoted above: "Did Julie's dwarf, in his jealousy, follow us to the Algarve, there capture Julie, steal her out of her own bed and force her to drive him away in my car?" (Kroetsch 1983, 145)—is not that far from the truth, it turns out.

The connection between the two novels, which are set about four years apart, is first of all Maggie's wedding dress. She received it, we may remember, second-hand after it first had been intended for Julie Magnuson's wedding to the mining engineer Fish. Julie, however, suddenly left Fish for Deemer, before she then absconded to Portugal (and later Italy) with De Medeiros. The second connection is once again provided by Maggie. While *Alibi* supposedly consisted of Dorf's notes as transcribed and manipulated by Karen Strike, *The Puppeteer* is supposedly told by Jack Deemer, who is observing—and commenting on—Maggie Wilder's attempts at understanding the story. Or, as Gunilla Florby has it, "Deemer himself proves to be the co-author of the credulity-straining tale" (Florby 1997, 132). Deemer would not be the collector we have come to know, if he himself, adverted by Dorf, were not interested in the collection of icons stolen by Maggie's husband, all the more so as one of these is supposed to show a female version of God.

We might here interpret Deemer as the ultimate puppeteer, playing godgames with the characters of these two Kroetschean novels. Deemer may even be deemed to have pushed Dorf down a cliff after De Medeiros has succeeded in shooting the man (or at least his foot) who had shot at him (and seemingly thus caused his disappearance) at the end of *Alibi*. But Deemer—together with Maggie—then decides to turn Dorf into a saint, and Deemer himself also undergoes important changes: It is finally he himself who decides to wear Maggie's wedding dress, a development mirroring, as I would suggest (following the lead of Barbara Bruce), the icon of a female god by giving us a feminine player of godgames.

Maggie's wedding dress thus plays an important role in *The Puppeteer*: First, it seems to have the magic-realist function of a muse. The first chapter of the novel is a third-person narrative, with Maggie serving as a reflector character (according to Franz Stanzel's narratological system) or focalizer (according to Gérard Genette). When Papa B, the pizza man, first sees her, he is startled by the wedding dress she is wearing, as he probably recognizes it as the one Julie Magnuson had worn four years earlier: "Perhaps he was just as startled as she. She was wearing a wedding dress. She had just that day discovered that when she put on her old wedding dress she could hear the story she intended to tell," and in fact, she claims that she is going to write "the autobiography of a wedding dress" (Kroetsch 1992, 15).

In addition, the wedding dress also mirrors—*en miniature*—the plot of the novel(s) and thus serves as a postmodern *mise en abyme*:

> She was stubbing out the cigarette and absent-mindedly staring at the almost invisible colours in the skirt of her wedding dress when she noticed for the first time, in the intricate embroidery and beadwork

on her lap, the outline in miniature of the dress she was wearing. The dressmaker who had filled the dress with detail had, with the same care, left blank an outline of the dress no larger than a postage stamp. (3–4)

The dressmaker, Josie Pavich, who also plays minor roles in both novels, has thus provided the blank space (or—phenomenologically speaking—the Iserian gap or *Leerstelle*) that both Maggie and the reader have to fill.

This is, however, not the only *mise en abyme* the first chapter offers the readers. On the kitchen walls of Maggie's house in Vancouver, one of the four different calendars—all offering different dates, of course—shows a Japanese print:

In the upper left-hand corner a man read a love letter while behind him his mistress, raising a mirror to cast more light, tried to read over his shoulder while under the verandah a spy read the trailing end of the long letter. (6)

Here we see a mirror image of what is going on in the novel—perhaps reminiscent of the other famous Kroetschean character, Demeter Proudfoot, who sees the world through a mirror: While in *Alibi* there were only Dorf and Karen who struggled for narrative empowerment, here it seems to be Deemer who is trying to read over Maggie's shoulder. But interestingly, Deemer is represented or replaced by a female character. At the beginning of the second chapter, which is written from his first-person perspective but which also sometimes uses Maggie as a focalizer, we may wonder to what extent Deemer really has insight into the views of the woman with whom he later plans to live together on a Greek island—wearing, after all, her wedding dress, which is also the wedding dress of his former wife, Julie Magnuson: "Maggie Wilder is writing this. Reading over her left shoulder, I become a loving supporter, the champion of her need to get the story of her wedding dress down on paper" (17). His words echo those voiced earlier in *Alibi* by Karen Strike, when she comments on her "editing" of Dorf's text: "Now and then I say a few words, joining myself into her train of thought. Sometimes, perhaps just to tease me, she scrambles a few of my words in amongst her own" (17).

The postmodern or poststructuralist context that Kroetsch constructs in his novels is illustrated by the names that his characters bear: Dorf *alias* Papa B is sometimes called "Papa B" and sometimes "Papa

Vasilis" in the pizza delivery service and thus makes Maggie—in the structuralist Saussurian or poststructuralist Derridean fashion—wait "to hear a gap between her naming and the man himself" (Kroetsch 1992, 10). No surface structures can be relied on any more in Kroetsch's universe, neither on the level of linguistic signs nor on that of gender identity.

As for identifying the godlike characters drawing the strings in the background of the novels, the reader is also thrown off track quite regularly. Jack Deemer claims to be the most important narrative voice, and also to be a manipulative narrative voice which "once in a while [...] had to make the rules fit the occasion" (71). In *Alibi*, there is even a reference to "old Jack the almighty" (Kroetsch 1983, 79). Other characters, however, also claim the status of being almost omniscient. There is, for example, Bludgett, the insomniac former lawyer, who "reads everything, even your [i.e., Maggie's] work" (Kroetsch 1992, 11) and who insists on the importance of *obiter dicta*—of incidental remarks—and thus invites us to pay attention to elements in the narrative which do not seem to be of prime importance at first sight and which may lead us into unexpected directions. But in the end, it may well be Deemer who gets exactly what he wants, as Papa B fears: "'Jack Deemer. He wants the dress for the same reason that he wants me. He wants, so to speak, to keep us quiet'" (29). And Deemer really admits at the start of chapter 3 about Dorf that "I wanted him quiet and just a bit more" (30). He feels that it was he himself who had been pulling the strings while others thought they were acting on their own behalf: that "Maggie did her doing for my eyes, not his [i.e., Dorf's]" and that he himself, "the strange presence, gave a permission that poor Papa B, crouched behind his makeshift puppets, could not" (123). While in *Alibi* Dorf still thinks of himself as the narrative (and also somewhat god-like, as Barbara Bruce shows [Bruce 1998, 24]) instance who is able to make the archaeological structure of Deemer's collections cohere, and that it is his "talk that puts [the discontinuity of this scattered world] together" (Kroetsch 1983, 195), he is dead at the end of *The Puppeteer*.

Deemer is an elusive collector, a collector of collections and of people, somebody who wants to store everything in a huge archive without necessarily being too interested in historical connections. But in *Alibi* he had remained unseen. His four warehouses in Calgary are the place for a god-like figure drawing the strings in the background, and this is where Barbara Bruce starts her reading of Kroetsch's novels as godgames, an analysis that obviously developed parallel to and independently of mine and falls back on Robert Wilson's term "shadowy godgame," which he uses in an essay on museums in *Open Letter*:

> The idea of the absent God is of particular importance to my reading of collecting in Kroetsch's work, because it is my intention to show that in the novels *Alibi* and *The Puppeteer* Kroetsch portrays collecting as "a shadowy godgame" (Bruce 1998, 16).

As Bruce puts it, "Dorf, the narrator of the novel, implies on numerous occasions in the text that Deemer *is* the *god* of the godgame, that he is somehow more than human" (19). Bruce also lists quotations from *Alibi* in which Dorf refers to Deemer as a god in the Judaeo-Christian and Deist traditions. She claims that "it is no wonder, then, that Dorf portrays Deemer ... as being a god figure or, at least, having a god complex" (Bruce, 44). This latest qualification may be important, as this god is not always omniscient or omnipotent. There are also items that escape Deemer; for example, "the icon of the face of God" that Dorf had claimed was part of the stolen icons that Maggie Wilder's husband, Henry Ketch, had stolen in Greece and wanted to sell to Deemer for a million. In Bruce's words "to collect 'the face of God' would cement Deemer's position as the god of the godgame" (38).

But Dorf had indicated something else about the icon, perhaps only to stir Deemer's interest: "'That one particular icon—the artist, apparently, saw him as—female. Saw her as female. God. The monks of Mount Athos—You know. Out of the public eye, if possible—Scandalous'" (Kroetsch 1992, 203). God as female? Such a concept would fit the general trend towards gender flexibility in *Alibi* and especially *The Puppeteer*. Richard Lane speaks about "the play of gender transformation throughout *The Puppeteer* and *Alibi*" (Lane 1997, 38). And the master of the godgame, Deemer himself, seems to be going in the same direction, when he settles with Maggie Wilder in a quasi-Edenic garden on a Greek island wearing her wedding dress. As Bruce argues, "If 'the face of God' is a woman's face, then Deemer must become a woman" (1998, 38), and this is what I would argue happens in *The Puppeteer*. Lynette Hunter, who produced a fascinating performance entitled "Can a Man be a Woman?" at the 1994 conference on Kroetsch's work at Niederbronn, in France, also wonders in her chapter on *The Puppeteer* in *Disunified Aesthetics* if there is "the appalling possibility that Deemer is merely appropriating a woman's form because he thinks: maybe, if God is a woman, he had better be on the right side" (Hunter

2014, 43). David Williams, too, comments on "the subversion of gender identity" (Williams 1996, 65) in the novel.

Perhaps Kroetsch himself created in *The Puppeteer* the literature he saw predicated by the critics gathered together in Shirley Neuman and Smaro Kamboureli's 1986 feminist anthology *A Mazing Space: Writing Canadian Women Writing*. He expected to see "a new kind of literature that goes beyond the phallus, or the penis—to become a literature of the heart" (Kroetsch 1989, 201).

As I hope I've shown, godgames play an important role in Kroetsch's work. But I am also tempted to remember Robert Kroetsch as a teacher who may have been playing educational godgames with his students, leading them to make their own discoveries, while he played the role of a Joycean god "paring his fingernails" (Joyce 483), pulling strings in the background without the students always being aware of it. At least that is how I remember pivotal moments during the process of writing my PhD thesis, sitting together with him in the rather awful neon-lighted (or perhaps even enlightened) cafeteria in the bowels of the Fletcher Argue Building of the University of Manitoba. We were having coffee, or what went for coffee there; he would sit back and listen to my ramblings, a surprisingly coherent structure of which suddenly somehow seemed to fall into place. Okay, it's long time ago, and it was in the last millennium, but in hindsight it does sound good.

And what I remember from my grad student days in Winnipeg, which—I have to admit—I may be seeing in a somewhat blurred way, chimes with how Dennis Cooley describes Kroetsch's discourse in *The Home Place*: "He was in a profound way private, at times enigmatic. Reluctant to speak when he was off the podium, he often drew back into memories and ruminations. And he listened" (Cooley 2016, 265). Among other personal reminiscences of Robert Kroetsch's "manipulative" way of speaking and teaching is Kroetsch's talk at the Grainau conference of the German-speaking Canadianists, sometime in the 1980s; in 1989, to be exact. He packed an incredible amount of thoughts on literary influence and literary traces into a wonderful and personal keynote speech dealing with the time he, as a young writer, spent in the Canadian North. His title at Grainau was "Why I Went Up North and What I Found When I Got There"; and this marvellous speech, with the slightly and deliberately changed title "Why I Went Up North and What I Found When He Got There," later became the first chapter of his autobiographical essay collection *A Likely Story: The Writing Life* (Kroetsch 1995, 13-40). But then, with a writer like Kroetsch, we should always be wary of trusting what is given us as autobiography. Quoting Kroetsch's character Maggie Wilder in *The Puppeteer*, Catherine Bates has reminded us that autobiography for Robert Kroetsch is often a decoy (Bates 2017, 148). Some traditionally—or perhaps archetypally—German academics at the Grainau conference obviously were fooled by the surface structure of Kroetsch's autobiographical decoy and later insinuated that storytelling was too easy and not academic enough—it didn't hurt. But his paper and his story were spellbindingly and entertainingly as full of literary theory, of narratology and intertextuality, of blindness and insight, as possible. The magic touch of a teacher. I feel honoured to be among those he taught.

WORKS CITED

Barrett, Paul. 2013. "For Play and Gaming: Robert Kroetsch's Ongoing Godgame." *Studies in Canadian Literature / Études en littérature canadienne* 38 (1): 94–112.

Bates, Catherine. 2017. "Autobiography as Decoy in *The Puppeteer*." In *Robert Kroetsch: Essays on His Works*, edited by Nicole Markotić, 147–61. Toronto: Guernica.

Bruce, Barbara S. 1998. "A Shadowy Godgame: Collectors, Collecting, and Collections in Robert Kroetsch's *Alibi* and *The Puppeteer*." Master's thesis, McMaster University.

Cooley, Dennis. 2016. *The Home Place: Essays on Robert Kroetsch's Poetry*. Edmonton: University of Alberta Press.

Fowles, John. 1981. *The Aristos*. 1964. Rev. ed. London: Triad Granada.

———. 1985. *The Magus*. 1965. Rev. ed. New York: Dell-Laurel.

Florby, Gunilla. 1997. *The Margin Speaks: A Study of Margaret Laurence and Robert Kroetsch from a Post-Colonial Point of View*. Lund: Lund University Press.

Glover, Douglas. 1993. "Shadowplays." Review of *The Puppeteer*. *Books in Canada*. February. 1993. Accessed July 27, 2016. http://www.booksincanada.com/article_view.asp?id=2014.

Highway, Tomson. 2003. *Comparing Mythologies*. Ottawa: University of Ottawa Press.

Hunter Lynette. 2014. *Disunified Aesthetics: Situated Textuality, Performativity, Collaboration*. Montreal: McGill-Queen's University Press.

Hutcheon, Linda. 1988. *The Canadian Postmodern: A Study of Contemporary English-Canadian Fiction*. Toronto: Oxford University Press.

Joyce, James. 1916. *A Portrait of the Artist as a Young Man*. In *The Portable James Joyce*. Ed. Harry Levin. Harmondsworth: Penguin, 1976. 243-526.

Kroetsch, Robert. 1984. *Alibi*. Toronto: General Publishing.

———. 1989. "My Book Is Bigger Than Yours." In *The Lovely Treachery of Words: Essays Selected and New*, 195-202. Toronto: Oxford University Press.

———. 1992. *The Puppeteer*. Toronto: Random House.

———. 1995. *A Likely Story: The Writing Life*. Red Deer, AB: Red Deer College Press.

Kuester, Martin. 1992. "Kroetsch's Fragments: Approaching the Narrative Structure of His Novels." In *Postmodern Fiction in Canada*, edited by Theo D'haen and Hans Bertens, 137-60. Amsterdam: Rodopi; Antwerp: Restant.

———. 2009. "Educational Godgames: A Digression on Another Miltonic Paradigm." In *Milton's Prudent Ambiguities: Words and Signs in His Poetry and Prose*, 119-27. Lanham, MD: University Press of America.

Lane, Richard. 1997. "Pulling Strings: Robert Kroetsch's *The Puppeteer*." *Commonwealth: Essays and Studies* 19 (2): 33-41.

Neuman, Shirley, and Robert Wilson, eds. 1982. *Labyrinths of Voice: Conversations with Robert Kroetsch*. Edmonton: NeWest Press.

Williams, David. 1996. "Cyberwriting and the Borders of Identity: 'What's in a Name' in Kroetsch's *The Puppeteer* and Mistry's *Such a Long Journey*." *Canadian Literature* 149: 55-71.

Wilson, Robert Rawdon. 1990. *In Palamedes' Shadow: Explorations in Play, Game, and Narrative Theory*. Boston: Northeastern University Press.

American Borders: Robert Kroetsch, Albert Johnson, and the Northern Frontier

ALBERT BRAZ

> *The most significant thing about the American frontier is, that it lies at the hither edge of free land.*
> — Frederick Jackson Turner

Canadian representations of the North are often problematic for both national and international reasons. To begin with, Canada has a series of provincial norths, as every province from British Columbia to Newfoundland and Labrador has a north of its own—two, actually, in the latter case. Perhaps even more important, Canadian writers at times allow foreign models to unduly shape their visions of the North. This is certainly true of Robert Kroetsch's depiction of the eponymous subject of his "Poem of Albert Johnson." Kroetsch portrays the so-called Mad Trapper of Rat River as a poet who heroically refuses to speak. For Kroetsch, Johnson is killed not because he considers the North *terra nullius* and fails to respect other people's property but because the Mounted Police and the local trappers cannot abide his silence, notably his refusal to identify himself, and atavistically assault him. That is, Kroetsch transforms an archetypal Canadian story about the Mounties enforcing the law even in one of the most isolated parts of the country—on behalf of Indigenous people against an intrusive white man, no less—into an ahistorical tale about white frontier individualism. The reason Kroetsch is able to construct such an idiosyncratic poetic vision of Johnson is that he frames the Canadian North through a familiar yet foreign national mythology, that of the United States. In the process, he also intimates that he does not perceive Indigenous people as an integral part of his Canada.

The individual who came to be known to history as Albert Johnson rafted into Fort McPherson, a hamlet in the Inuvik region of the Northwest Territories, in the summer of 1931. The following winter a Gwich'in[1] trapper named William Nerysoo reported to the Mounted Police detachment in nearby Aklavik that the newcomer was tampering with his traps. When the Mounties tried to notify Johnson of the complaint, he refused to acknowledge their presence, despite knowing he had been spotted glancing out of his cabin. Then, after the Mounties travelled for fifty kilometres in forty-below temperatures back to Aklavik to get a warrant for his arrest, he responded by shooting one of them, precipitating one of the most famous hunts in Canadian history. By the time it ended, with the death of Johnson on February 17, 1932, he had eluded a posse of police officers, Indigenous and white trappers, and even a First World War ace fighter pilot for forty-eight days in the depths of an Arctic winter. During that period, he wounded two more Mounties, including one fatally.[2] Johnson's seemingly superhuman endurance and craftiness, along with his mysterious identity, have turned him into a legendary figure. He is the subject of numerous novels, poems, songs, television documentaries, and films, most of which extol his individualism, best exemplified by his refusal to name himself. However, no other major Canadian writer has celebrated the Mad Trapper of Rat River as contentiously as Kroetsch.

"Poem of Albert Johnson" was printed in *The Stone Hammer Poems* (1975). While relatively short, at some 270 words and thirty-nine lines, it manages to convey the raw violence of the clash between the purportedly misunderstood Johnson and his barbarous foes. The poet's identification with his protagonist is total, and unequivocal, as one can discern from the two opening stanzas:

> It is his silence   they cannot allow
> offended into a blood reason   the hunters
> surround his cabin   with their loud law

>   he will give no name   to hate or love
>   neither forgive nor blame   the righteous
>   fusillade   no word of hurt or mercy (1975, 48)

The "hunters" are clearly the aggressors, and thus the culprits. Blinded by some primordial vendetta, they incomprehensibly lead an armed attack against the outsider. They are so vexed by his silence that they "bomb-blast" Johnson out of his cabin and into the frigid "Arctic night." In his brave resistance to such unprovoked brutality, the stranger emerges as the "poet or survival / to our suburban pain" (48), underscoring the extent to which the poem is infused with a southern white (and middle-class) perspective.

Kroetsch does complicate matters when he writes that the hunters are not typical outlaws but rather "police and Indians/ together at last" (48), suggesting that their actions may be motivated by legitimate concerns. Still, to the end, he continues to stress that what Johnson's pursuers cannot countenance is his insistence on remaining "the silent man" (49). This is precisely what the speaker-pilgrim admires about the subject, his indomitable ability to preserve

>   his silence   (we stand at his grave in Aklavik
>   mosquitoes swarming at our heads   like the posse
>   that slammed him   out of his last loading)
>
>   the poet of our survival   his hands and feet
>   frozen   no name on his dead mouth
>   no words betraying   either love or hate (49)

In short, Johnson is killed not because of anything he does, including his imperious affirmation of settler-colonial entitlement, but because of who he is, his difference; more specifically, his principled individualism. This is a view that is further highlighted in a footnote that Kroetsch appends to his poem, informing the reader that Johnson was "hunted to death by a small army of men" (49), once again drawing attention to the numeric imbalance in the clash between his hero and his antagonists.

Later in his life, Kroetsch came to reveal some doubts about his poetic interpretation of the Albert Johnson story, aesthetic as much as political. When he assembled his *Completed Field Notes* in 1989, he "omitted" most of *The Stone Hammer Poems*, including "Poem of

Albert Johnson" and his bio/graphs of Wong Toy, F. P. Grove, and Tom Thomson, as well as the Blackfoot-inspired "The Old Stories" (van Herk 1986, x–xii). More significantly, in his curiously titled essay "Why I Went Up North and What I Found When He Got There," Kroetsch writes that while Johnson was a trapper—which is debatable, since there is no evidence that he did any trapping (North 1987, 95, 105)—he was "a white trapper and not a man from the hunting and gathering societies of the North; he was an interloper. He was a transgressor on Indian trapping lines" (Kroetsch 1982, 30). Yet, even then, one senses that Kroetsch's affinities are with the subject of his poem, perhaps since he feels that, like the poet, Johnson had travelled north as a "sympathetic transgressor" (30). Kroetsch, who at the time imagined that he "might one day write a novel about the bush pilots who hunted the mad trapper onto the tundra," goes on to add that "the mad man of Rat River in Wilf Carter's song, the man who shot a Mountie dead, was a hero of my childhood" (14, 30; see also Carter 2007). As he elaborates, "Albert Johnson was both story and artist for me—this, before I went into the North. He wore the silence of the artist like a badge, an indication of his will toward self-destruction. In his transgression he lost his name to the story; he was the death of the author" (Kroetsch 1982, 31). Kroetsch states that when he was working on a riverboat in the North, he "began to hear new versions of the story of Albert Johnson," which he recorded in his 1950 notes and most of which are favourable to the traveller. He adds that some people told him that Johnson "*wasn't a bit insane*" and that a "*greenhorn Mountie made an investigation and got himself shot*" (31).³ Other people claimed that, rather than "springing...traps and hanging them on trees," as Nerysoo alleged (North 1987, 12), Johnson "*thought he was shooting a Hare [K'asho Got'ine] Indian who was robbing his trapline*" (Kroetsch 1982, 31). Still others contended that "*the police shot an unidentified man and called him Johnson just to make the case look good after losing so many men*" (32). Once more, instead of being a transgressor, sympathetic or otherwise, Johnson is really a victim, of either parochial locals or bumbling Mounties, or both.

There are riveting aspects to the story of Albert Johnson, starting with the fact that, as Howard O'Hagan perceptively remarks, "Named, he is nameless" (1993, 68). Rudy Wiebe is among the many writers who are captivated by the elusive identity of the Mad Trapper of Rat River. His experimental short story "The Naming of Albert Johnson" is really a paean to the stranger who is mercilessly chased across a chain of mountains in the borderlands of the Northwest Territories and Yukon by a veritable army of police offers, trappers, and dogs. Structured backwards in time, the story begins with the events leading to the death of the title character on February 17, 1932, and concludes with his identification as Albert Johnson by local people near Fort McPherson on July 7, 1931. Wiebe is transparently partial to Johnson. He portrays the taciturn but seemingly self-sufficient stranger being pursued not only by a posse of humans and canines but also by an infernally noisy airplane, a "beast" assembled from "[s]teel pipes and canvas and wires" that pierces the Arctic silence (1995a, 80, 81). Thus, from the outset, it is impossible to miss the unfairness of the contest. For Wiebe, so heroic are the actions of his protagonist that he becomes "the man" (74–76), the indomitable individual who immortalizes himself in a perhaps hopeless but noble stand against the impersonal forces of the modern world.

Johnson's indeterminate identity calls into question the widely accepted notion that "[b]y naming" people or things, one makes them, altering them "to become/ the sum of shape and name" (Page 1997, 115); this is a position to which O'Hagan himself is partial, writing that when you put a name on something, you "put it on a map, and you've got it. The unnamed—it is the darkness unveiled" (1989, 90). That being said, the uncertainty about his true name is only one of the mysteries about Johnson. For instance, when he was killed, he had a surprising amount of money and other possessions on him, carrying "$2,410 in Canadian bills..., two U.S. $5 bills; [and] a small glass jar containing five pearls valued at $15," among other items (North 1987, 46). Considering that this was the middle of Great Depression, Kroetsch's persecuted hero in reality had "a trapper's small fortune" and "made no secret of it" (O'Hagan 1993, 69, 70), leading people to speculate how he could have acquired it. The suspicion that Johnson may have been involved in some crime, which might explain his silence, is supported by his prowess with firearms. His pursuers not only agreed that he was "a crack shot with a rifle" but also that he was an "expert with a handgun because of the way he handled" his weapons during the first shootout (North 1987, 105). As O'Hagan describes Johnson, in words that contradict Kroetsch's, he was a "born hunter, the man whose rifle has become part of himself and who, in the perception of the moment, aims and fires by reflex" (1993, 82). Needless to say, it was because of the inability of the joint police/trapper force to defeat Johnson that the RCMP felt compelled to engage the services of the ace fighter pilot W. R. "Wop" May, who, besides being able to locate the fugitive's "trail," may have disoriented him with the noise of his airplane (North 1987,

41). Finally, there is the matter of the stranger's mental state. There is a general agreement that Johnson could not have been insane, given his phenomenal achievements and what the RCMP inspector in charge of the chase, A. N. Eames, called his "extremely shrewd" mind (quoted in North 1987, 22). Still, it is possible that Johnson had become bushed, even if that condition does not usually manifest itself in quietude but loquaciousness. "Sane in other respects," expounds O'Hagan, Johnson "may have been insane in the strength of his delusion" (1993, 72). In other words, his very silence can be interpreted in a multitude of ways, beyond a sign of a poetic predisposition.

Parts of the story of Albert Johnson could even be deemed tragic, as well as politically troublesome. In one of his sundry explorations of the Rat River saga, Wiebe muses: "Why are murderers so much remembered?" (1995b, 305), raising the question of why Johnson is more celebrated than his victims. But Johnson is not just a murderer. He is also someone who is murdered by the combined representatives of the community and the government, a detail that may have contributed in no little measure to his widespread popular appeal, and which invites an interrogation of the ethical status of the two acts. If Johnson is vile because he kills another human being, what do we call what the police-trapper force does to him? As the reporter investigating the incident in Thomas York's novel *Trapper* concludes, most people do not really want to read how "Johnson, a madman, had been hunted and killed fifty years ago, and how [Inspector] Eames, a good man, had hunted and killed him" (1981, 9). Most poignantly perhaps, Johnson travels to what he must have thought was the end of the world, north of the Arctic Circle. Yet not only does he find people there, but people who have a claim to the land and who will call on the police to enforce it. Contrary to what US thinkers like Frederick Jackson Turner promise, he discovers that there is no frontier that one can traverse, a place lying "at the hither edge of free land" (Turner 1961, 38), where one would be able to escape society and fashion a new self. Indeed, the essence of Johnson's tragedy would seem to be that there is no northern frontier beyond the reach of the law, both in terms of a police presence and of territorial rights, which is why he finds himself a trespasser on other people's land.

Although probably of Scandinavian origin, Johnson is believed to have lived in the United States mainland before heading north to the Arctic. So it would not be surprising that he would have absorbed some variation of Turner's frontier ideology. More unexpected is that a writer from central Alberta, particularly one who laments that official history "did not account for the world I lived in" (Kroetsch 1983, 70), would also have assimilated such a worldview. It is true that Kroetsch maintains that the Canadian "north is not a typical American frontier, a natural world to be conquered and exploited. Rather, in spite of inroads, it remains a true wilderness, a continuing presence. We don't want to conquer it. Sometimes we want it to conquer us." He further asserts that the Canadian writers he knows exhibit "a peculiar will towards silence," which "on the surface looks like a will towards failure," but really reflects an "impulse towards the natural, the uncreated, if you will," and is "summed up by the north" (1989a, 54). Yet there is considerable evidence in his texts that Kroetsch was deeply influenced by Turner's ideas. Most tellingly, his novel *Gone Indian*, which was published the same year as "Poem of Albert Johnson," bears as its epigraph a quotation from Turner's seminal 1894 essay "The Significance of the Frontier in American History," stating that, "For a moment, at the frontier, the bonds of custom are broken and unrestraint is triumphant" (1973, n.p.; Turner 1961, 61–62). As well, the text informs us that the protagonist, Jeremy Sadness, believes that "his whole life was shaped and governed by some deep American need to seek out the frontier" (Kroetsch 1973, 5), which he ultimately locates in "Edmonton. The last city north. The Gateway" (109, 56). But even in his first novel, *But We Are Exiles*, Kroetsch portrays the crew of the M.V. Nahanni Jane as overtly racialized, between "half-breed crew members" who live along the Mackenzie River and white ones, who fly south to their "stuccoed and mortgaged bungalows and the rented back-rooms and beer-parlours they called home" (1977, 3). Besides, as if drawing a dividing line between the two groups, he engages mainly with the trials and yearnings of the outsiders.

In fact, what is most striking about Kroetsch's "Poem of Albert Johnson" is the utter lack of identification with the local people, something that becomes conspicuously evident when one compares it to Magnus Bourque's "Ballad of Albert J." Written in 1966, when the Gwich'in and Dene Bourque was a high school student in Inuvik, "Ballad of Albert J." leaves little doubt why Johnson is not well-received in the North. To quote the stanza that both opens and closes the poem:

> Out of the Yukon
> Came a broad-shouldered man;
> A man without pity.
> A man without land. (1978, 235, 236)

Thus the reason local people resent Johnson is not only that he does not belong but also that he has not set any traps of his own, and spends the winter "Molesting the Loucheux's trap" (235). It appears to have nothing to do with what Kroetsch represents as his emblematic silence. In light of the Gitksan elder who challenged the British Columbia government's claim to part of the northwest of the province by asking, "If this is your land…where are your stories?" (quoted in Chamberlin 2003, 1), one might feel tempted to query if Johnson refuses to speak, not because he is the poet of silence, but because he realizes that he lacks stories about his presence in the land.

Kroetsch has been praised for his ability to capture the spirit of Alberta like no other writer, being nothing less than "Alberta's Faulkner, Alberta's Dante" (van Herk 2010, 29). But it is not likely that his writings on the North will receive similar accolades. Moreover, this is not because of what Kroetsch terms "the foibles and flaws of story" and the fact "we can't for a moment agree on what the stories are saying" (2010, 17), but because of what his northern texts disclose about his conception of community: that is, who is privileged with a narrative voice, even when electing to be silent, like Johnson.

One unexpected work that sheds considerable light on the ideological orientation of "Poem of Albert Johnson" is Thomas P. Kelley's *Rat River Trapper: The Story of Albert Johnson, the Mad Trapper*. Stylistically, Kroetsch and Kelley are radically different kinds of authors. As befits one of Canada's most successful pulp writers, Kelley is best-known for true-crime books, like the best-selling *The Black Donnellys*, which tend to be action-packed and replete with intrigue. This is also the case of *Rat River Trapper*. In his 1972 novella, Kelley depicts his title character as a "one-man reign of terror" who "single-handed carried out what came to be called the Arctic Circle War" (1972, 2). Such is the havoc caused by Johnson that mothers across the North attempt to "silence their unruly children with 'Hush, or the Rat River Trapper will get you!'" (4; see also 73). Indigenous people have become so terrified that they "*run from [him] with frightened cries*," seeing "*death in [his] eyes*" (6; Kelley italicizes his poetic text). *Rat River Trapper* could, and perhaps should, be dismissed as a potboiler. What makes the novella notable, however, is that Kelley opens each of its twenty chapters with a stanza from a poem called "The Ballad of Albert Johnson," which is written in the subject's own voice. This is a strategy that has impressed even some of his harshest critics. Wiebe, for one, characterizes Kelley's fiction as "sensationalist," failing to make "any distinction between historical fact and hackneyed invention" (1978, 239). Yet he praises Kelley for daring "to tell the story from the Trapper's point of view [in his poem]. That's the kind of risk an artist should take" (239–40). Of course, Kelley's unswerving focus on Johnson is also what makes his poem problematic, and what links it to Kroetsch's.

Like his counterpart in "Poem of Albert Johnson," and Wiebe's own "The Naming of Albert Johnson," the subject of Kelley's ballad dominates not just the text but the world in which the text is situated. The fact Johnson is relatively new to the area, and appears to have no familial or community relation to the land, in no way precludes him from asserting his right to traverse or occupy it as he wishes. He considers himself at "*home*" in his cabin for, as Kelley's narrator notes, to his "way of thinking, possession was not merely nine-tenths of the law. It was ten-tenths" (Kelley 1972, 30, 5). Furthermore, in both Kelley's and Kroetsch's poems, it is Johnson alone who determines what constitutes the law, showing no deference to either the Mounted Police or the region's Indigenous. He is very much an individual shaped by a tradition in which the people who have inhabited the land since time immemorial are constructed "as perpetual nomads" and "Europeans [who find themselves] in a place thousands of miles from home, as settlers" (Chamberlin 2003, 29–30). Or as the Truth and Reconciliation Commission phrases it, they are "colonial settlers," for whom the "mere presence of Indigenous people in these newly colonized lands" has always posed a challenge, since it "block[s] settler access to the land" (2015, 44, 45). Consequently, the question one should ponder is what it says about Canadian culture that two writers as disparate as Kroetsch and Kelley can share the same ideology and be so enthralled by someone like Johnson, particularly since so little is known about him, beginning with his real name.

To this day, there is no consensus on who Albert Johnson was and why he provoked the ire of both northerners and the Mounted Police. Dick North, the most respected scholar on the Rat River incident, points out that Johnson has been "identified as a Swede, a Russian, an American, a Dane, a Finn, a Norwegian, and a Canadian" (1987, 45). Even though North considers the RCMP "the finest all-round police force in the world," he concedes that it is possible that what compelled Johnson to start "springing traps" was that Indigenous people were trapping out of season (102, 125). North also admits that it is equally plausible that Johnson was a veteran of the First World War and had been "shellshocked"; or that he was "an illegal immigrant," which would give him further cause for avoiding the law and being silent about his past (125, 124). Yet the one aspect of the story on which everyone agrees, including Kroetsch, is that the Mounted Police sided with Indigenous people over Johnson. The RCMP has much to atone for when it comes to its treatment of First Nations, considering that it often equates both its enemies and those of "true Canadian manhood" with anyone of non-British descent (Dawson 1998, 37). Nonetheless, the force's role in the Johnson episode suggests that the mythology of Canada as a peaceable kingdom is not all fiction, that there have been critical moments when the Mounted Police has enforced the law on behalf of Indigenous people not only against white people but against someone with "blond hair and pale blue eyes" like Johnson (North 1987, xvii; see also 133).

In an essay on aesthetic representations of Albert Johnson, M. Jeanne Yardley makes the compelling argument that "we need to go beyond a passion for getting the story straight to an understanding of what these narratives are doing in telling it crooked" (1994, 24). In the case of Kroetsch, his "crooked" version of Johnson would seem to demonstrate that Kroetsch is so invested in exploring white settler individualism that he is oblivious to the ways in which settler mobility necessitates the abrogation of Indigenous ownership. Throughout the poem, there is no sense that Kroetsch envisages Johnson's Indigenous foes as potential subjects of their own story. After all, if texts like his prove that Johnson "desires nothing more than to be his own man" (1975, 28), they do so by failing to address how such aims could be reconciled with similar (and more locally grounded) yearnings by the local inhabitants. As Wiebe has Johnson tell William Nerysoo[4] in his novel *The Mad Trapper*, "I never bother anybody.... If they don't bother me" (1992, 53), totally unaware that his very presence in Nerysoo's territory already constitutes a transgression. Kroetsch is not nearly as constructivist as Douglas Barbour, who privileges writing to such a degree that whatever transpired at Rat River purportedly "doesn't/ count. What happend happens now this way. This is the way it happend,/ the way it happens continually, there, in the huge white spaces" (1987, 241).[5] Still, the fact Kroetsch transformed a fabled collaboration between the Mounties and Indigenous people to maintain law and order in the North into a case of antediluvian oppression of a white adventurer suggests that he may not have been as devoid of "ideology" as he sometimes claims (Kroetsch, Neuman, and Wilson 1982, 33). Or to phrase it differently, Kroetsch's depiction of Johnson as a political innocent seems anything but innocent.

One does not have to agree with the historian John Jennings that all novelists and poets who paint Johnson as a hero are "literary jackals" (1985, 87). Yet it is hard to ignore Jennings's contention that there is something troubling about Canadian writers, like Kroetsch, who do not even acknowledge the possibility that when the Mounties first travel to Johnson's cabin, they are "trying to protect the local Indians from the kind of irresponsible pursuit of happiness which had made the American frontier uncontrollable" (1985, 89). Perhaps the best way to illustrate the consequences of such choices is by contrasting Kroetsch's treatment of Johnson with Wiebe's. As noted earlier, in "The Naming of Albert Johnson," Wiebe overtly links his protagonist's adversaries to modern technology, including the invasive airplane as well as the dynamite that they do not hesitate to use to try to drive the besieged outsider out of his cabin (1985a, 85). Eventually, we do learn that the Mounted Police claim they "*have had complaints*" about Johnson and that he will "*need a [trapper's] licence*," since he is in Gwich'in territory (87, 88; emphasis in the original). But the information is provided so late in the text, and in an abstract manner, that it is not likely to reverse the impression that Johnson is a heroic figure who has been vanquished by unnatural forces.

Wiebe, however, frames the conflict rather differently in his subsequent personal essay "On Refusing the Story." The change is apparent from the opening paragraph, as Wiebe presents Johnson, not as a hero, but as "a man who tried to hide in the Arctic" and "should have known better" (1995b, 303). He then reproduces the legend written on Johnson's grave in Aklavik, which reads in part:

> COMPLAINTS OF
> LOCAL TRAPPERS
> BROUGHT THE RCMP
> ON HIM.... (304)

This focus on the local continues when Wiebe explains that he was visiting Old Crow, Yukon, in 1987 to talk to a group of Gwich'in at the community centre about his writings when it was announced that Aklavik had given Dick North permission to have Johnson's body exhumed. The news about the long-dead Mad Trapper generated a lot of interest in the subject, including by one Gwich'in man who thinks it is "all bullshit in all them books!" (308). The same man also asks Wiebe point blank: "Do you know who shot first, that Albert Johnson?" (307). The man insists that it was an Old Crow resident named Johnny Moses, who was one of "three Kutchin men" that served in the police posse that confronted Johnson (314). The man's intervention leads Wiebe to relate his meetings with various indigenous figures connected to the Johnson manhunt, from Nerysoo to Moses's sister and her son. Thanks to those encounters, Wiebe deduces that the very qualities that writers like Kroetsch and he once extolled demonstrate his foreignness, the fact he is not a product of the North. As Wiebe elaborates, the most remarkable thing about Johnson was that, in a place where everyone appears to belong to a community and to be "related to everyone else," he "defended his aloneness with such single-minded and truly horrifying intensity" (318). Moreover, the "non-aloneness" of the people of the Arctic is reflected in the centrality of "the storyteller and the poet/singer" in the region, since the act of storytelling, unlike the written word, entails "a community of listeners" (318–19).

This sort of engagement with northerners, though, is what is missing in Kroetsch's work. The memorialization of an individual who refuses to be part of the community to such an extreme that he will not share his name with those around him, at the very least suggests that he does not think much of them, if he thinks of them at all. Actually, the key to understanding the ideological framework of "Poem of Albert Johnson" may lie in Kroetsch's implied estimation of *The Stone Hammer Poems*. When Kroetsch compiled his *Completed Field Notes*, he excluded most of the poems that comprise his first collection—excising all of them except the title piece, "Stone Hammer Poem," a work that talks about "the/ retreating/the /recreating ice," as well as "the retreating/ buffalo" and "the/ retreating Indians" (1989, 3). Perhaps when Kroetsch was visualizing the conflict between Johnson and the Mounted Police and Indigenous trappers, he could not imagine the last as vital beings, as anything other than "retreating."

Works Cited

Barbour, Douglas. 1978. "The apotheosis of Albert Johnson." In Wiebe, "The Death and Life of Albert Johnson," 240–42.

Bourque, Magnus. 1978. "Ballad of Albert J." In Wiebe, "The Death and Life of Albert Johnson," 235–36.

Carter, Wilf. 2007. "The Capture of Albert Johnson." *The Forestry Forum* (May 18): n.p. Accessed November 19, 2017. http://www.forestryforum.com/board/index.php?topic=25760.0.

Chamberlin, J. Edward. 2003. *If This Is Your Land, Where Are Your Stories? Finding Common Ground.* Toronto: Knopf Canada.

Dawson, Michael. 1998. *The Mountie from Dime Novel to Disney.* Toronto: Between the Lines.

Jennings, John. 1985. "The Mad Trapper in Literature and Film." *Journal of Canadian Studies* 20 (2) (Spring): 80–91.

Kelley, Thomas P. 1972. *Rat River Trapper: The Story of Albert Johnson, the Mad Trapper.* Don Mills, ON: PaperJacks.

Kroetsch, Robert. 1965/1977. *But We Are Exiles.* Toronto: Macmillan.

———. 1989a. "The Canadian Writer and the American Literary Tradition." In *The Lovely Treachery of Words: Essays Selected and New,* 53–57. Toronto: Oxford University Press.

———. 1973/1999. *Gone Indian.* Toronto: Stoddart.

———. 1983. "On Being an Alberta Writer." *Open Letter* 5 (4) (Spring): 69–80.

———. 1975. "Poem of Albert Johnson." In *The Stone Hammer Poems,* 48–49. Nanaimo, BC: Oolichan.

———. 1989b. "Stone Hammer Poem." In *Completed Field Notes,* 1–7. Toronto: McClelland and Stewart.

———. 2010. "What the Kroetsch Said." *Alberta Views* 13 (10) (December): 17–18.

———. 1995. "Why I Went Up North and What I Found When He Got There." In *A Likely Story: The Writing Life,* 13–40. Red Deer, AB: Red Deer College Press.

Kroetsch, Robert, Shirley Neuman, and Robert Wilson. 1992. *Labyrinths of Voice: Conversations with Robert Kroetsch.* Edmonton: NeWest Press.

North, Dick. 1987. *The Mad Trapper of Rat River.* Toronto: Macmillan.

O'Hagan, Howard. 1993. "The Man Who Chose to Die." In *Trees Are Lonely Company,* 67–84. Vancouver: Talonbooks.

O'Hagan, Howard. 1989. *Tay John.* Toronto: McClelland and Stewart.

Page, P. K. 1997. "Cook's Mountains." In *The Hidden Room: Collected Poems,* vol. 2, 115–16. Erin, ON: Porcupine's Quill.

Truth and Reconciliation Commission of Canada. 2015. *Final Report of the Truth and Reconciliation Commission of Canada, Volume One: Summary— Honouring the Truth, Reconciling for the Future.* Toronto: Lorimer.

Turner, Frederick Jackson. 1961. "The Significance of the Frontier in American History." In *Frontier and Section: Selected Essays of Frederick Jackson Turner,* edited by Ray Allen Billington, 37–62. Englewood Cliffs, NJ: Prentice Hall.

van Herk, Aritha. 1986. "Biocritical Essay." In *The Robert Kroetsch Papers, First Accession*, edited by Jean F. Tener and Apollonia Steele, ix–xxxix. Calgary: University of Calgary Press.

———. 2010. "Our Odysseus." *Alberta Views* 13 (10) (December): 27–31.

Wiebe, Rudy. 1978. "The Death and Life of Albert Johnson: Collected Notes on a Possible Legend." In *Figures in a Ground: Canadian Essays on Modern Literature Collected in Honor of Sheila Watson*, edited by Diane Bessai and David Jackel, 219–46. Saskatoon: Western Producer Prairie Books.

———. 1992. *The Mad Trapper*. Toronto: McClelland and Stewart.

———. 1995a. "The Naming of Albert Johnson." In *River of Stone: Fictions and Memories*, 74–91. Toronto: Vintage.

———. 1995b. "On Refusing the Story." In *River of Stone: Fictions and Memories*, 303–20. Toronto: Vintage.

Yardley, M. Jeanne. 1994. "Voyage into Oblivion, Voyage into Legend: The Albert Johnson Narratives." *Canadian Issues/Thèmes Canadiens* 16 (8): 21–31.

York, Thomas. 1981. *Trapper*. Toronto: Doubleday Canada.

Notes

1. At the time of the Albert Johnson incident, the Gwich'in were known in English as the Loucheux. More recently, in addition to Gwich'in, they are also frequently called Kutchin.
2. The historical information in this section is gleaned largely from the opening section of Dick North's *The Mad Trapper of Rat River* (1987, 3–47).
3. Kroetsch's 1950 notes appear in italics in his text.
4. In his novel Wiebe spells the name as Nersyoo (1992, 51), but I have retained the common spelling of Nerysoo for the sake of consistency and to avoid confusion.
5. The unorthodox spelling is Barbour's.

Resituating Kroetsch: Georgic, Accident, and Object in Robert Kroetsch's "The Ledger"

JENNIFER BAKER

Robert Kroetsch's "The Ledger" is a poem primarily concerned with time, object, and accident. Originally published in 1975 by Applegarth Follies, and illustrated with prints of the original ledger documenting the credits and debits of settlers in Bruce County, Ontario, Kroetsch's text functions simultaneously as poem and historical trace of human labour—particularly agrarian labour. But "The Ledger" also participates in a long tradition of situating human labour within a timescale interrupted by the event of the accident. The georgic mode, often subsumed in Canadian literary criticism under the category of the pastoral, concerns itself with such accidents and the ways they disrupt the linear teleology of human agrarian-labour technological progress. While critics like Karen O'Brien have emphasized the imperial and linear time associated with Dryden's eighteenth-century translation of Virgil's *Georgics*, critics like David Fairer and Margaret Rhonda have made a case for the disrupted and disenchanted character of later georgic writing, particularly in the American agrarian tradition. Reading "The Ledger" with some knowledge of both the philosophical history of the accident and of these georgic modalities allows us to see how Kroetsch's accidents disrupt the default teleological model of the imperial georgic, presenting us instead with a model of settlement in provisional time that displaces the human from the centre of the poem's ontological field. In doing so, Kroetsch is really disrupting the ontological lens of settlement in the West: even while he is concerned with human labour's alterations on Canadian landscapes, Kroetsch reminds us that such alterations take place within timescales that stretch well beyond human comprehension of or interventions in their consequences.

The history of the concept of the accident in philosophy is deeply rooted in thinking about objects and time. In *Accident*, Ross Hamilton argues that modern approaches to the concept of the accident as event remains incomplete without its original Aristotelean understanding as a set of secondary characteristics of an object. In Aristotelian thought, the thing can be broken down into "substance" and "accident." Substance, as Aristotle defined it, is the essential quality of the thing—everything that remains inaccessible to us, the "tableness" of the table, for example. Aristotle defines accidental qualities as those secondary qualities of the thing: colour, shape, size, texture, and so on. The long philosophical history of the concept of the accident begins with Aristotle's epistemological struggle to describe the material world even as it changes through time. More accurately, Aristotle's separation of the form of the thing into essential substantial qualities and inessential accidental qualities arises from the attempt to describe how we recognize things as themselves (for example, a table as a table), even as those very things are altered by the passage of time—changing colour or shape either by human intervention or through natural processes of age and decay. As such, the problem of separating substance from accident, Hamilton argues, forms the foundational problem for thinking about the nature of existence.[1] Aristotle's challenge to separate essential qualities from inessential qualities of the thing forms an attempt to describe the thing as it remains recognizable even as its qualities change through time: Aristotle, in seeking to separate these two classes of qualities, implicitly points to the dynamic existence of non-living things and their alterations at a specific point in time.

This is where accident becomes associated with event, and therefore with differing registers of time: the accident signifies the sudden, unexpected alteration of an object's inessential qualities. Hamilton argues that this is the position that philosophers like Alain Badiou take when arguing that the accident represents—if it cannot be explained—a rupture in an already existing system that either forces an explanation and adaptation, or the emergence of a new system.[2] While Badiou treats the accident-as-event as separate from accident-as-quality, Hamilton argues that we can see how both concepts of accident are related, if accidental qualities of objects are unexpected inessential qualities, and accident-as-event represents the sudden alteration of a set of qualities in a system and the emergence of a new system. He argues:

> Although Aristotle's ontological categories opposed substance to accident, over time what we might describe as coordination, symbiosis, or even commingling of his terms blurred or superseded their opposition. Encoded in the accident experience, following it like a shadow, are reformulations of accidental qualities. As a result, moments of conceptual shift function less as breaks than as hinges between one mode of perception and another.[3]

In other words, Hamilton is describing the accident as the ontological bridge between differing systems for understanding the world, and for him, accident and the ability to adapt to and accommodate rapid shifts in ontological positioning is the condition of modernity.

Because "The Ledger" expresses an engagement with the material concerns of agricultural work, narratives of colonization, human engagement with ecological systems, and adaptation and change, re-situating it within the georgic tradition can clarify how the precarious relationship between human beings and non-human objects serves to deconstruct a linear teleological narrative of progressive imperial mastery over nature and other human civilizations. English translations of Virgil's *Georgics* (29 BCE) have long been invested in the processes of change and emerging systems, particularly regarding the social, political, and ecological contexts of agrarian work and in asserting its place in the development of civilizations. Whether or not the georgic mode represents this labour as a linear teleology of progressive mastery over the natural world, or whether that labour is represented as a struggle with the precariousness and contingency of existence depends on the translation; and this makes the georgic a powerful mode in which writers can express the relationship between human and non-human beings and human beings and their social and political organizations.[4] While often mistaken for, or subsumed under the category of pastoral, understanding georgic's history in Canadian literature as a separate modality is important precisely because it is a literary mode that is explicitly concerned with agrarian work and ecological concerns in empire and nation-building narratives. Even while Kroetsch may not have been aware of the historical uses of this mode in Canadian writing, given that the georgic was already being conflated with the pastoral shortly after the beginning of Canadian colonization, in "The Ledger," Kroetsch uses the accident to unravel two distinct modalities that are especially prevalent in Canadian writing that deals with georgic themes of agrarian work and settlement: the "imperial" georgic and what Margaret Rhonda has called the "disenchanted georgic."

Although the imperial and the disenchanted georgic coexisted in the eighteenth century, the imperial georgic expresses the most widely understood characteristics of the mode as we know it. As Karen O'Brien argues[5], the imperial georgic formed a coherent set of conventions from John Dryden's 1697 translation of Virgil's *Georgics*, which began a popular trend in English literature of georgic writing that lasted more than sixty years and coincided with the first wave of English colonization in Canada. Dryden's translation of the *Georgics* expressed a linear teleology of human mastery over nature, emphasized and celebrated technological industry, positioned the empire as the positive source of civilization, and centred the farming family and its work as the engine for successful imperial expansion. These formal characteristics became so deeply engrained in the way writers expressed representations of agricultural work in the eighteenth century that this linear teleology of agricultural settlement came to seem both natural and inevitable, even after the imperial georgic seemed to fall out of popularity by the end of the eighteenth century. Although many critics have recognized these characteristics in canonical texts by such authors as Oliver Goldsmith, Frances Brooke, and Susanna Moodie, they have often been mischaracterized as versions of pastoral. But rather than disappearing into the pastoral, as critics like Raymond Williams have suggested, critics like Margaret Rhonda and David Fairer have both argued that the georgic mode evolved to accommodate concerns with contingency and precariousness, repositioning imperial georgic's preoccupation with the struggle to master and control nature as the human struggle to survive within complex and unpredictable ecological and political systems. Rhonda, as noted, has coined this more nebulous set of conventions the "disenchanted georgic," which include representations of farming that privilege immanence over transcendence and generic mixture over generic coherence.[6]

Reading Kroetsch's "The Ledger" with some knowledge of both the intellectual history of the accident and these two versions of the georgic mode allows us to understand how Kroetsch updates the mode for a postmodern context and how and why the ledger itself, the accident of its discovery, and its accidental qualities come to represent the crux between two differing ontological understandings of agrarian work and its relationship to the natural world. Although Kroetsch has self-identified and has been identified by many Canadian theorists as having been Canada's foremost postmodern theorist and writer, some critics—Alexander MacLeod and Frank Davey among them—see incompatibilities between his regionalist affiliations and his postmodern theory, suggesting that he may be better categorized within the tradition of prairie regionalist writing that is postmodern than within a broader postmodern tradition. In "Canadian Postmodernisms: Misreadings and Non-readings," Davey makes note of Kroetsch's lack of critical attention from international scholars of postmodernism, noting that the only Canadian writer to be mentioned in the context of postmodernism outside Canada is Steve McCaffrey.[7] Pointing to Kroetsch's strong sense of regional pride, Alexander MacLeod points out that "regionalism and post-modernism actually share very little in common. Roberto Maria Dainotto, for example, has suggested that, far from being opposed to each other, regionalism and nationalism should be understood as essentially similar discourses,"[8] and that although regionalist discourses engage with a smaller scale and population, "it offers the same mythical promise of a metaphysical union, a profound but falsely 'naturalized' linkage between the people who occupy a specific cultural geography and between those individual subjects and the objective ensemble of physical geographical facts that produce place."[9] Such a discourse of nationalism runs directly against international postmodernist discourses, which seek instead to critically deconstruct such naturalizing linkages between subjects and place. To the contrary, MacLeod argues that Kroetsch "continuously endorses a more direct, more natural connection to the landscape as the only alternative to the ridiculous textuality of these scholarly pursuits...In every case, Kroetsch's postmodernism endorses, rather than nullifies, the redemptive power of nature, and the author clearly places his support behind a regionalist environmental determinism."[10] But while MacLeod suggests that the answer to this problem of situating Kroetsch's postmodernism may to be to relocate his work in a prairie regionalist context, Kroetsch is better situated in the literary genealogy of Canadian georgics that I have so far drawn out.

Kroetsch, in his attention to work, time, mixture, and digression, presents us with altered extensions of much earlier Canadian

Confederation and Romantic ideas of the georgic cultivation of meaning. While most Canadian literary critics have tended to read Robert Kroetsch's "The Ledger" through the lens of the pastoral, reading this poem through the lens of the georgic foregrounds the ways in which human labour on and within ecological systems reflect differing perceptions of time. Stemming from Dryden's eighteenth-century English translation, Canadian long poems reflecting on georgic concerns have changed in parallel to popular translations of Virgil's *Georgics* over time. For example, early Canadian long poems concerned with Canadian settlement, such as Oliver Goldsmith's *The Rising Village* and Isabella Valancy Crawford's *Malcolm's Katie*, can be read within the imperial georgic mode, which emphasizes a teleological progression from a fallen or disrupted world toward a reclamation of an Edenic ideal, while more contemporary Canadian long poems that explore agrarian work and settlement tend toward what Margaret Rhonda has called the disenchanted georgic: a georgic mode which rather emphasizes the continuing and immanent struggle of labour within, rather than on, the agrarian landscape. Each of these georgic modalities, in turn, privileges a different perception of several different registers of time and scale. While the imperial georgic emphasizes a teleological progression through human agency toward a projected ideal future, the disenchanted georgic emphasizes the mixing of temporal registers to position the farmer—and by extension, the farmer's labour—as the centre of the ontological field and the mirror of the universe.

Importantly, the imperial and disenchanted georgic also present us with different understandings of time and scale. While imperial georgic's linear progression privileges what Paul Huebener has called "Imperial Time"—the projection, in linear narrative, from an imperfect present to an ideal future[11]—the disenchanted georgic privileges what Huebener has called "Provisional Time": a simultaneous mixture of timescales[12] that reflects the farmer's privileged place in the universe as its mirror and centre. It is this mixture that Sarah Mack references when she argues that Virgil's *Georgics* "is built on a movement back and forth through time…one of the effects of Vergil's manipulations is to keep Rome, past present, and (potentially) future, before us."[13] The effect of these multiple temporal registers in the disenchanted georgic is that if Imperial Time is not the only temporal register in the georgic mode, the linear teleology commonly assumed to be an intrinsic part of the georgic is undermined by broader, ecological timescales, like the seasonal and geographical time against which the farmer must constantly contend in his effort to survive in, and even live harmoniously with, ecological systems.

While the poem at first seems to draw a teleological progression from the economical documentation of work in the object to the objects of work themselves to the final objects—the tombstone and the permanent book—the poem itself always interrupts this teleological progression. In doing so, Kroetsch is also interrupting the teleological progression present in the imperial georgic assumption that agrarian work, in particular, represents a processual movement to a reclaimed Edenic ideal. Smaro Kamboureli has argued that

> Kroetsch's long poem decodes the absolutism and dialecticism of the dream and human drama of the Garden of Eden. Although there is in his poetry an abundance of gardens, he does not deal with this archetypal place in traditional dialectical manner. The prelapsarian innocence and guilt consequent to the Fall are continuously reordered....The parodic reversal and its ironic humor [in "The Seed Catalogue"] work against the consoling promise entailed by the dialectical structure of the myth of Eden; the fall is presented as a non-event.[14]

While Kamboureli is addressing "The Seed Catalogue" here, the same analysis can hold true for "The Ledger." Kroetsch does this reordering of the archetypal search for origins by placing the emphasis not on the human actors of the teleology of the imperial georgic, but by emphasizing the tool-objects themselves, and the accumulation of debits and credits that, through accident and error, don't or can't balance. It is the accident of the discovery of the ledger that "The Ledger" is primarily concerned with the accidental qualities of the object not in stasis but as a mutable entity at differing points in non-linear, provisional time. It foregrounds Aristotle's problem with substance and accident by drawing attention to the multiple meanings of the word "ledger" (implying that naming language itself is an accidental quality) while simultaneously focusing on the material object of the found ledger itself and its existence, which is connected to, but stretches beyond, human interventions. The poem opens with the lines:

> the   the ledger survived
> ledger
>   because it was neither
> itself   human nor useful.[15]

Both the arrangement of the lines on the page and their content point to Aristotle's substance-accident problem of the object. The ledger itself survives—despite the pages that are missing, the slippages in meaning represented by the word "ledger," and human interventions in its form and appearance—apart from the scale of a human lifespan. The way the lines are positioned, they can also be read, "the ledger survived itself": the substantive quality of the ledger remains apart from its accidents and accidental qualities. Its "ledgerness" remains: an object identifiable by its intended use but no longer useful.

As Hamilton argues,[16] however, the phenomenon of the accident as event relates directly to the problem of accident as quality. Since the ledger itself is a historical artefact of the agrarian labour of the homesteaders, the missing pages and imbalances of the ledger signify accidents that leave gaps in this flow of historical time, and the poem itself disrupts the ability to create an accurate historical record, provide an origin, or an ending to historical narrative. The first definition Kroetsch gives of the ledger is of a book of final entry, recording the economic processes of the homestead, and includes a list of purchases made by James Darling, which, the poet notes, don't balance. As a possible explanation, the poet observes "some pages torn out (/ by accident) / some pages remaining (/ by accident),"[17] indicating both a passage of time and the disruption of the ledger's usefulness as a marker of the history of Darling's work. The damaged tool is the tool that reveals its former usefulness, and the missing pages—torn away by a human agent that no longer exists. The poem represents itself as an accumulation of these accidental signifiers wrought by traces of labour found in the object, "the poet: by accident / finding in the torn ledger / (IT DOESN'T BALANCE)."[18] But the work of farming moves forward, and the poem accumulates more signifiers, and where the ledger is a broken tool revealing its substantial qualities, it also reveals the past as historical object, wherein the poet's search "is a search for the dead,"[19] echoing the again the ledger's original function as a *book of final entry*."[20] The ledger's failure to record—to balance—historical account begins the process of the slow accumulation of linguistic slippages and signifiers that make up the experiential time of the reader. This idea of experiential time mirrors the processes of homestead building, as the second definition of ledger is the "horizontal piece of timber secured to the uprights / supporting the putlogs in a scaffolding, or the like,"[21] and seems to build from the original economic function of the ledger as a book of final entry for materials purchased.

This unravelling of substance from accident surrounding the ledger as a historical object undercuts the teleological sense of time inherent in the imperial georgic mode, revealing instead the multilateral provisional time of the disenchanted georgic. In this way, the ledger's accidents function as the pivotal point between the imperial and disenchanted georgic ontologies. What is at stake in undercutting this sense of teleological progress is precisely Kamboureli's argument[22] about Kroetsch's resistance to the notion of origin: in an imperial georgic narrative of settlement, Canada originates when homesteaders transform the *terra nullius* into productive landscape, which in turn generates settlement and civilization. Kroetsch's letter upsets this narrative by introducing the unexpected event—the accident—of finding the ledger, of finding its imbalance, and of the loss or destruction of the ledger's historical record in the pages that go missing (or remain) by accident. The fact that the ledger survives mirrors the fact of the ecological landscape and its history of previous civilizations outside human experiential time, as its existence extends beyond human mortality. This revelation of non-human time introduces the contingency of chance into the previously neat teleology of settlement and civilization by widening and complicating the ontological field of the poem to include non-human agencies. The origin in an imperial georgic narrative only exists with human actors; but in the disenchanted georgic, there are no known origins in existence. The origin depends on a point in a single timescale, and so is illusory.

Following the definition of the ledger as the horizontal piece in scaffolding, the poet describes the ecological devastation of the cultivation of the settler community, where "actual settlers"[23] burn and slash, and kill the wildlife to raise barns, grow crops, and raise livestock. But the seemingly neat teleological processes of imperial georgic settlement narratives are again disrupted as we are reminded of the vast timescales of objects and their existence beyond human experiential time. Death unmakes the work of John Darling, who has "No time"[24] and whose "barn is still standing / (the mill, however, is gone) / sound as the day it was raised."[25] The objects of Darling's labour again outlive him, the useful mill is gone with the obsolescence of its task, but the barn, the structure, and, like the ledger, the place where the traces of labour are stored, remain. The third definition for the ledger, "one who is permanently or constantly in a place; a resident. *Obs.*,"[26] further suggests the success of the labour of settlement but notes the decay of the word's valence over time, which reveals both the human place within ecological time—we are mortal—but also the mortality of language. The syntax of the definition suggests not only the obsolescence of the word, but also the obsolescence of the resident. The section makes clear that with each continued arrival—"the sailing ship / arrivals: the axe / arrivals: the almighty dollar"—there are a series of departures, including the "trout stream…passenger-pigeon…the pristine forest"[27] and, tellingly, "the birchbark canoe,"[28] suggesting, also, the absurdity or consistency of residency in a place, the land itself a record of debits and credits. This reference to the already-settled Canadian landscape is also an unmaking of the imperial georgic narrative of settlement: there was no *terra nullius* to make into civilization; there was an existing civilization that colonizers unmade in the name of their own ontological perspectives.

Smaro Kamboureli argues that it is these arrivals and departures that shape Kroetsch's sense of place;[29] the dynamics of unpredictable change within the ecology of place thwart the settlers' attempts to—as in the imperial georgic—recover the Edenic ideal. In this sense, the poet's failure to locate a sense of origin underscores his dislocation, but it is a dislocation not only in place but also in time. She argues:

> The garden is used as a principle for organizing the unstructured space of the prairies. Kroetsch's repetition with difference exemplifies how he appropriates place by overcoding locality: the tonal and syntactic transformations of the same question, the ungrammaticality of his grammar, are an attempt to decode the memory of the original origin, namely that of nature. The grammar of Kroetsch's narrative is one of dislocation, a dislocation enunciating what has become of nature as the "original" origin. By deconstructing the notions of originality and origin, Kroetsch alludes to the underlying ideology that constructed these very myths.[30]

While Kamboureli takes her point of interpretation as Kroetsch's "Seed Catalogue," her argument here is equally applicable to "The Ledger": the long-standing myths of the imperial georgic are the ordering and structuring of the natural world, both syntactically and materially. Kroetsch's poetics work to undermine that sense of order by decentralizing the locus of that narrative via the unintended and unanticipated accidents of existence—placing the emphasis on objects that persist beyond human experiences of them, civilizations that exist despite colonizers' efforts to override them with their own system of order, and overloading the semantic functions for ordering language by pointing to multiple definitions of a single signifier. If the imperial georgic as an ontological category results in the assumption of an ordered, teleological world, Kroetsch broadens the field of existence to include the accidental and unanticipated interruptions of that world.

This idea becomes further highlighted in the section detailing the ledger as "the nether millstone,"[31] which details simultaneously an event in which the draining of a pond leads to an abundance of fish and an accident that crushes a man's arm in the waterwheel of the mill. The poet muses,

you must see	under the turning wheel
the confusion again	the ripened wheat, the
the chaos again	razed forest, the wrung
the original forest	man: the nether stone.[32]

This passage details the process in which the past becomes the foundation for the chaotic present, the collapse of all of the temporal signifiers of the poem—the ledger as book of final entry, the ledger as support beam, the ledger as resident, and the nether stone, have all become historical objects which signify differently in the accident—it is in the accident that all temporal registers collide: the ecological, and the historical explode the syntax of the sentence and the narrative, language signifies simultaneously across several different meanings.

While the nostalgic tone of the poem and its references to obsolete or broken tools certainly evokes the idyll, it is genealogical time that reconnects this poem to georgic concerns. The speaker reveals his connection to the past through this genealogical lineage—the search for ghosts is also a search through family history, and reveals the speaker's relationships not only to the other historicized characters of the poem but also to their objects. The fifth definition of the ledger seems to suggest a kind of finality—"a large flat stone, esp. one laid over a tomb,"[33] but gestures instead toward the thread of genealogical time which ties the poet to place. This section opens with the text of a letter that seems to reply to the poet regarding a genealogical inquiry about his late great-grandmother, describing her appearance and personality while also describing her death. But the genealogical narrative is interrupted several times: the grandmother has lived three marriages, with three different last names, and a list of children who had died—many unnamed, some with unexplained deaths—marks the interruption of any kind of easy teleological narrative of family reproduction:

Jennifer Baker

> Census, 1861
> County of Bruce:
> Deaths in 1860
> (Age and Cause):
>
> 1yr: croup
> blank: born dead
> 5 months: fits
> blank: dysentery
> 16 yrs: hurt
> by sawmill wheel
> 38: I Deth
> Inflammation
>
> Henry's father: dead
> (The doctor had good
> horses).[34]

This list of accidents and the fact that the list itself includes gaps, blanks, and vagaries in its recording suggests more than just the difficulty in recording historical events; the gaps, vague references, and the fact that the poet's grandmother had been married three times, taking three different last names, suggests the difficulty in relying on any simple linear genealogical narrative as a connection to landscape or place, in the sense that the propagation of community and rural culture extend themselves through family farms. The poet's family tree, we discover, is a structure predicated on the maternal line, rather than on a paternal line, which is unknown. The records of the deaths in Bruce County show the prevalence of accidental deaths and deaths caused by illness—acts of nature or of random chaos that disrupt both the genealogical lineage of those families while also disrupting the teleology of agrarian settlement labour, where labourers are taken from the landscape by sudden accident, despite the best human efforts (the doctor's good horses, for example). Yet another collision between timescales that results in the accidental rupture of meaning, narrative, and history.

The last section of the poem has accumulated lines from each of the other sections, bringing the accumulation of past signifiers into a current attempt for a genealogical narrative about the poet's great-grandmother's place in the settlement narrative. The final definition for the ledger—"a book that lies permanently in some place"[35]—similarly suggests permanence and closure, which is unravelled throughout the rest of the poem. "The ledger itself," the poem repeats, "survives,"[36] and in the second repetition of this line in the section, the ledger is "surviving," the tense shifting from the simple present tense to the present progressive tense. This tense shift suggests that the survival is ongoing, an act that remains forever present in the poem itself. The repetition of the phrase, "WHAT DO I OWE YOU"[37] interspersed with the lyrics from the folk song, "Bury Me Not on the Lone Prairie" also suggest the poet's continuing search for the meaning of genealogy in terms of history or origin, a process which is taking place and repeated in the present throughout the poem's accumulation of the historical and material traces of the work of settlement. The poem ends with the missive, "REST IN PEACE / You Must Marry the Terror,"[38] which is both an echo of the previous section of the poem about the poet's great-grandmother and an echo of the definition of the ledger as a grave marker. Read through the lens of the disenchanted georgic's embrace of the accident, however, to "Marry the Terror" is also to embrace the truth of an existence without absolute control or mastery. The terror—the shock, the accident—are integral to the poem's ontology: in a universe comprised of infinite experiences of time and of unknowable qualities and interactions, the accident is not only a point of rupture but is also an expected agent of change. The accident shifts the world; the substance remains.

Kroetsch's "The Ledger" uses both the accident as event and the accident as secondary quality to disrupt the linear teleology of imperial georgic narratives of settlement. In doing so, the object itself—the ledger and its alternative definitions—becomes the nexus point between two opposing ontologies of agrarian work and settlement. On one hand, the imperial georgic mode had functioned since the eighteenth century as the core narrative of colonization: the farmer is the agent of imperial expansion into landscapes presumed to be empty or otherwise "wild," and farm work generates the foundations and supports of civilization—the recovery of the Edenic ideal. On the other hand, the disenchanted mode is one privileging a multilayered and decentralized understanding of the role of agrarian work as work within a complex set of systems both knowable and unknowable to the farmer. Labour, in this case, is relegated to sustainable survival, and the human subject is decentred from the ontological field, which is broadened to include a variety of timescales and an awareness of non-human existences. In other words, it is the accident that opens the space of the imperial georgic and reconfigures it as the disenchanted georgic.

Understanding these shifts in modalities is an important pivotal point in Canadian literature that deals with agrarian work because the imperial and disenchanted georgic modes act as shorthand systems that reveal how Canadian writers understand the relationship between agrarian work and ecological systems. More than ever, an awareness of the deepest logical consequences of our assumptions about human intervention with those ecological systems—and the ways we perpetuate these ontologies through cultural projects—is material and vital to understanding current environmental crises, and they have real-world consequences: imperial georgic ontologies privilege colonization over decolonization, technology over ecology, and human progress over ecological responsibility, evolving into the ontological foundations of the industrial agrarian capitalism responsible for massive ecological damage that some methods of farming are currently perpetuating. In this way, this study of Kroetsch's "The Ledger" is a small part of a much larger project of accurately naming and drawing out the systems of understanding embedded in our cultural depictions of agrarian work and its connections to social, economic, and ecological responsibility. No solution to environmental crisis comes without embracing a shift in ontology: we must marry the terror.

Works Cited

Davey, Frank. 2011. "Canadian Postmodernisms: Misreadings and Non-Readings." In *Re:Reading the Postmodern*, edited by Robert David Stacey, 9–37. Ottawa: University of Ottawa Press.

Hamilton, Ross. 2007. *Accident*. Chicago: University of Chicago Press.

Huebener, Paul. 2015. *Timing Canada: The Shifting Politics of Time in Canadian Literary Culture*. Montreal: McGill-Queen's University Press.

Fairer, David. 2011. "'Where Fuming Trees Refresh the Thirsty Air': The World of Eco-Georgic." In *Studies in Eighteenth-Century Culture* 40: 201–218.

Kamboureli, Smaro. 1991. "Origins without Beginnings: Robert Kroetsch." In *On the Edge of Genre: The Contemporary Canadian Long Poem*. Toronto: University of Toronto Press.

Kroetsch, Robert. 2000. "The Ledger." In *Completed Field Notes: The Long Poems of Robert Kroetsch*. Edmonton: University of Alberta Press.

Mack, Sarah. 1978. *Patterns of Time in Vergil*. Hamden, CT: Archon Books.

MacLeod, Alexander. 2011. "Reconciling Regionalism: Spatial Epistemology, Robert Kroetsch, and the Roots of Canadian Postmodern Fiction." In

Re:Reading the Postmodern, edited by Robert David Stacey, 9–37. Ottawa: University of Ottawa Press.

O'Brien, Karen. 1999. "Imperial Georgic, 1660–1789." In *The Country and the City Revisited: England and the Politics of Culture, 1550–1850*, edited by Gerald MacLean, Donna Landry, and Joseph P. Ward. Cambridge: Cambridge University Press.

Rhonda, Margaret. 2013. "Georgic Disenchantment in American Poetry." *Genre* 46 (1) (Spring): 57–78.

Virgil. 2005. *The Georgics of Virgil*. Translated by David Ferry. New York: Farrar, Strauss, and Groulx.

Notes

1. Ross Hamilton, *Accident* (Chicago: Chicago UP, 2007), 2.
2. Hamilton, *Accident*, 9.
3. Hamilton, *Accident*, 8.
4. In the "First Georgic," for example, Virgil's farmer is confronted with the accidental discovery of the remains of a soldier in his field:

    And someday, in those fields the crooked plow
    Of a farmer laboring there will turn up a spear,
    Almost eaten away with rust, or his heavy hoe
    Will bump against an empty helmet, and
    He'll wonder at the giant bones in that graveyard.

    The Roman world of Virgil's *Georgics* is a cycle of war and conquest, the politics of which extend far beyond the timescales of individual Roman citizens. The farmer must learn to anticipate potential disaster and adapt to the dynamic ecologies on which his labour depends. Survival requires constant attention and work: "Just as one who struggles to row his little / Boat upstream against the powerful current / Should but for a moment relax his arms, the current / Would carry him headlong back downstream."

5. Karen O'Brien, "Imperial Georgic, 1660-1789," in *The Country and the City Revisited: England and the Politics of Culture*, ed. Gerald Maclean, Donna Landry and Joseph P. Ward (Cambridge: Cambridge University Press), 161.

6. Margaret Rhonda coins this term first in her dissertation, "Disenchanted Georgics," from Rutgers University, but distills it in "Georgic Disenchantment in American Poetry." *Genre* 46 (1) (Spring): 57–78. It is important to note here that when I use the term "disenchanted georgic" it already carries with it a sense of modernity, and in particular it is concerned with the

contradictions inhering in agrarian work under the constraints of capitalism. Rhonda writes that the disenchanted georgic

> derives from these Virgilian tendencies but…is substantially reformulated under the historical conditions of capitalist modernization. The disenchanted character of georgic poetry—its attention to the difficulty of labor and the sensory discomforts of mediation—takes on new significance, I argue, with the rise of new forms of agrarian and industrial capitalism that render portrayals of settled agricultural work increasingly fraught. These shifts mark the emergence of a georgic strain specifically responsive to these social and economic upheavals (61).

To this I would add, for the purposes of our current time, environmental crisis. There is an implicit argument to be made here that Kroetsch's nostalgia for the tools of farm labour is not emblematic of a longing for a simpler farm life, but that it serves to amplify these feelings of discomfort within the disenchanted georgic: a georgic under capitalism.

To this I am adding David Fairer's assessment in "Where Fuming Trees Refresh the Thirsty Air: The World of Eco-Georgic," *Studies in Eighteenth-Century Culture* 40 (2011), that "Georgics never underplay the fact that nature imposes a responsibility, and in Virgil and his eighteenth-century imitators, natural forces have a way of getting back at you. Co-operation is a sager bet than human mastery. Ingenuity, effort, vigilance, experience, respect, and above all care in husbandry (Virgil's *curas*), are the principles that will see you through" (205). I see these two definitions of the darker shadings of the georgic mode as related and have combined them under Rhonda's terminology.

7   Frank Davey, "Canadian Postmodernisms: Misreadings and Non-Readings," in *Re:Reading the Postmodern* (Ottawa: U of Ottawa P, 2011), 17.

8   Alexander MacLeod, "Reconciling Regionalism." In *Re:Reading the Postmodern* (Ottawa: U of Ottawa P, 2011), 130.

9   MacLeod, "Reconciling Regionalism," 130.

10 MacLeod, "Reconciling Regionalism, 144.

11 Paul Huebener, *Timing Canada: The Shifting Politics of Time in Canadian Literary Culture* (Montreal: McGill-Queen's UP, 2015), 29.

12 Huebener, *Timing Canada*, 22.

13 Sarah Mack, *Patterns of Time in Vergil* (Hamden, CT: Archon Books, 1978), 4.

14 Smaro Kamboureli, "Origins without Beginnings: Robert Kroetsch," in *On the Edge of Genre: The Contemporary Canadian Long Poem* (Toronto: U of Toronto P, 1991), 113.

15 Robert Kroetsch, "The Ledger," in *Completed Field Notes: The Long Poems of Robert Kroetsch* (Edmonton: U of Alberta P, 2000), 11.
16 Hamilton, *Accident*, iv.
17 Kroetsch, "The Ledger," 11.
18 Kroetsch, "The Ledger," 12.
19 Kroetsch, "The Ledger," 13.
20 Kroetsch, "The Ledger," 13.
21 Kroetsch, "The Ledger," 13.
22 Kambloureli, "Origins Without Beginnings," 106.
23 Kroetsch, "The Ledger," 13.
24 Kroetsch, "The Ledger," 15.
25 Kroetsch, "The Ledger," 15.
26 Kroetsch, "The Ledger," 15.
27 Kroetsch, "The Ledger," 16.
28 Kroetsch, "The Ledger," 17.
29 Kambloureli, "Origins Without Beginnings," 113.
30 Kambloureli, "Origins Without Beginnings," 113.
31 Kroetsch, "The Ledger," 17.
32 Kroetsch, "The Ledger," 20.
33 Kroetsch, "The Ledger," 12.
34 Kroetsch, "The Ledger," 23.
35 Kroetsch, "The Ledger," 27.
36 Kroetsch, "The Ledger," 27.
37 Kroetsch, "The Ledger," 25.
38 Kroetsch, "The Ledger," 28.

"Poem for My Dead Sister": Kroetsch's Masterpiece
Phil Hall

> *I look to words and nothing else for my own redemption.*
> — Robert Creeley

The goal of this paper is to begin to put a great Canadian poem in its theoretical, historical, and experimental contexts so that it can be better appreciated. It is an appeal for further study, rather than a full analysis.

…and here is a story Kroetsch told me. I don't want the details. Here is my sense of it:

> A flock of white birds always migrated in an unexplainably odd flight pattern. None of the experts could figure out why they turned at a certain mountain, then turned again, then turned again, instead of flying straight. They could have flown straight. What was wrong with those birds anyway?

Phil Hall

> in the greenest of comparison, water
> reads our trace against corrodibility
>
> sky is a dark virtue, whisk a word
> rinse a retrieval off the hard map
>
> klee cries, the verb retaliates,
> is isn't not enough to grieve
> (Kroetsch 1995, 157-58)

Robert Kroetsch is of that small tradition of major poets who, during their lifetimes, were recognized and identified, by themselves and the world, as primarily novelists. Thomas Hardy and D. H. Lawrence are of this group. Like Hardy and Lawrence, Kroetsch wrote initially, and often later, from a specific regional perspective: Wessex and Nottinghamshire in England, and our prairies here.

There is an advantage and a detriment to not being primarily seen as a poet: a poetic slyness can grow more uniquely when it is unscrutinized or dismissed, so that the poetry is late to be assessed, and then has to be reassessed for its sophistication and importance; and equally, the ambitions of such a "non-poet's" poetry tend to stay small, close to the occasional. (Witness Lawrence's *Nettles and Pansies.*)

Robert Kroetsch was able to grow within the advantage of not claiming to be primarily a poet, and to avoid the detriment of staying occasional. His ambitions for his poetry were, amid a lot of shucking and denial, grand. *Completed Field Notes*, again despite its denials, and despite its "the Long Poems of"—is a life-poem.

For us today, Kroetsch's poetry is identified with the experimental as well as the regional. His decision to return home from the United States to the Canadian prairies in 1978 is a legendary story now: Kroetsch's move to the University of Manitoba instigated (or coincided with) a revival of prairie literature in Canada.

This story of his return is also the story of a melding of experimental open-field poetics with a renewed dedication to origins—an avant poetics that Kroetsch brought back to Canada with him (from Charles Olson, Robert Creeley, *The New American Poets* anthology, and the like), and had reinforced here by his many Canadian poet friends, such as bpNichol, George Bowering, Fred Wah, and others).

"Poem for My Dead Sister": Kroetsch's Masterpiece

In "Poem for My Dead Sister" there are 168 lines. There are seven sections with subtitles: Morning / Before the Leaves / Petaluma, CA / Saying / Arrangement / Visibility / Figuration.

Notice that after the first three subtitles, the last four turn away from any narrative connection, and instead are about process, about poetics: Saying / Arrangement / Visibility / Figuration.

As a novelist among poet friends, Kroetsch makes a virtue out of not knowing (pretending to not know) what he's doing:

> ?what happened
> I have to / I want
> to know (not know)
> ? WHAT HAPPENED
> (Kroetsch 1989, 4)

As if Kroetsch wasn't already then a Governor General's Award winner for fiction, a professor at the State University of New York (Binghamton), and an editor of *boundary 2*, one of the best postmodernist American academic journals of the 1970s—where, for instance, a special issue on Charles Olson was produced in fall 1973/winter 1974, with Kroetsch as joint editor. (In 1978, the year Kroetsch left Binghamton, the spring/fall *boundary 2* is a double Robert Creeley issue, and Kroetsch is still listed as the poetry and fiction editor of the journal.)

Kroetsch is constantly saying, "I am no poet!" while discovering (or insisting on) the freedom to try anything, like a precocious kid taking a writing workshop, or a Sunday painter who doesn't know what he can't do. The novelist is on holiday, just goofing around. As *Completed Field Notes* proceeds, the goofing becomes more somber. He is also like Frank O'Hara in this regard, another unpoet-like poet. Kroetsch could start at dumb zero, at still-life exercises, a stone hammer, a family ledger…

He was the farmhand who did not own the field. But he could do the wider thing; he could go into language as well as place, and delve the unchiseled connections, be unpredictable, blunt, innocent/sly, or even cowboy theoretical.

Phil Hall

> the wilted snow obliterate
> as obligation feeds exiguous
>
> hurray is ha, is haw
> or hem the lucifer of light
>
> leaves will be green, if green
> tumescence riddles
> (Kroetsch 1995, 159)

Then some expert was looking at ancient glacier patterns in those mountains, and when she laid the flight migration of those white birds over the old glacier patterns, it became clear that the birds were instinctively tracking a way that had not been a way for eons.

Think of D. H. Lawrence, on a ship, coughing and angry between novels, or of O'Hara on his lunch break from MOMA, or of Hardy in his local graveyard after having sent off *The Mayor of Casterbridge*—all three discovered themselves to be serious poets. They took themselves seriously inside their poems.

This innocence of a poet's discovery is part of the charm of *Completed Field Notes*; its missteps and indulgences are elements of its honesty. If we read it as one long poem, unevenness is an element of what adheres.

A *note* is from the land of incompleteness. Like a painter's field-board, a note's beauty is in its off-handedness, the blatant try, untouched-up. The moment caught, and let stand.

In this, *Completed Field Notes* anticipates "Poem for My Dead Sister" in which the *blatant try* by grief's tongue, if heard outright for the triumph over anguish it is, can seem excruciating and equally embarrassing in its field-boardedness.

In "Poem for My Dead Sister" we are overhearing a song of devastation (of *Trojan Women* proportions) being made up out loud at hand by someone who doesn't know anyone is listening, and (maybe for the first time) doesn't care. (Of course, *appearing* to not know anyone is listening is another convention.)

Completed Field Notes is an apprenticeship to poetry as well as to place. But if it began as a legitimately innocent enthusiasm, it quickly attracted a set of personae as well. The fox, the trickster, the crow: these totem creatures are appropriated costumes.

And when, in "Poem for My Dead Sister," the personae drop, are burnt off by loss and age—what is left? Within "the illumined catastrophe" we hear only "the stalwart crow said, caw."

But then, in "Poem for My Dead Sister," everything is speaking out in its true tongue—even the crocuses, as they open, "cry." A stark Romanticism is upon the land.

> tropic having lost itself in posse
> jarred in the penumbra
>
> or preternatural permutation
> illusory as allusion gifted
>
> carbon insufficiencies surmounted
> as sun is sun as is
> (Kroetsch 1995, 161)

Some say the white birds were flying faithfully an absent map. *They are writing sonnets. That is the way they have always gone. It gets them there.*

Others say that the route they took each year amounted to an unreadable, instinctual form. *An enacted cadenza, a marrow compass.*

The Stone Hammer Poems (1975) is prosy with Blackfoot Old Man tales. Kroetsch says: "My daring to steal these tales is an act appropriate to the tales themselves." That may seem like a dodge now, but Kroetsch had found one of his personae.

"Stone Hammer Poem" is chiseled very much as if by someone taking that iconic poetry-writing workshop for the first time, and learning, as we all did, to pare down. "The poem / is the stone / chipped and hammered / until it is shaped…" This is about folk art, but it leads to a *Well-Wrought Urn* from an imagist set of dictums.

By the very next sequence, *The Ledger* (1975), the workshop trimness is blown. (The not-knowing, and the pretending-not-to-know, both stay.) *The Ledger* "doesn't balance," accident is here now, the stone is "singing." "You Must Marry the Terror" says a tombstone. We are being tricked into wising up.

In the book designs of the first editions of *The Ledger* and *The Seed Catalogue,* the grid rulings and the advertisement blocking of the original artifacts were recreated. When the grids and ads fall away in the later editions that are *Completed Field Notes*, we effectively have Olson's field and his ranging groups of text that use the page more fully than in traditional imagism. Form is a matter of energy zones now.

Kroetsch got to this Olson field by way of a loyalty to the accounting (and accounting for) of home artefacts, ledgers, catalogues. And in *Completed Field Notes* he is rehearsing techniques that will arrive perfected in "Poem for My Dead Sister." For instance, allusions to the language of British nursery rhymes ("How do you a garden grow?"), the use of regular stanza-braces to try to hold down the difficulty of saying anything straight or epigraphical, and an emphasis on the tiny bridge-words (and, but, so, the, if, of, or).

> wilderment (be) (ac)cretaceous, else
> the mendicant (a dreamer) recollect
>
> (mined full) or heir (the waste) of solitaire
> greet gratefully green (or sun as yet unseen)
>
> (across the riding bridge the ridded plain)
> sock in the weather and (arouse) the rain
> (Kroetsch 1995, 163)

Kroetsch's growing tendency to silence, and to a recognition of the death of meaning, throughout *Completed Field Notes*, can also be read as presaging and foreshadowing the work he will come to in "Poem for My Dead Sister."

In "Seed Catalogue": "the absence of" "the absence of" "the absence of"… (1977, 23, 25).

In "Letters to Salonika": "The world is ending, but / the world does not end"; "the despair of the poet on meeting reality" or "By meaning we mean something that means / but, in the process, means its opposite" (1983, 138).

In "Sonnet #5": "nothing / but / nothing / but / darkness / outside my / window // nothing / but / darkness // outside / my window / nothing but / darkness // the shape of water" (1989, 213).

Over these early poems, this is the same bare voice, facing meaninglessness, that we will hear when the poet's sister dies. He is practising how to voice it.

"Poem for My Dead Sister": Kroetsch's Masterpiece

One of the other things that is happening over the years of Kroetsch's poetic development is a bonfire of the male vanities, a burning off of the "studhorse man" persona. Kroetsch, in poetry, found ways to be less of a cocksman. By poetry he earned a welcoming humility.

At the end of *Completed Field Notes*, Kroetsch says, "My life erases everything I write." The poet is fighting with silence. He is Silence's mouthpiece (1989, 254).

When Kroetsch says: "And finally, the book, in its incompleteness, is for my two daughters, Meg and Laura, a tenuous suggestion of the ways of a father's love," the field is now clear for exploration of a brother's love (1989, 270).

> melothy of mixedness, the crane
> chimney the crane, the craw, caw crow
>
> call the caller (not), the guessed gone
> livery of wanting, the goshawk, going, gone
>
> the bird is (not), the birds sings, trill, coo
> the trail is (not), walking, the toe
> (Kroetsch 1995, 165)

It is a long way over a short and busy time (twenty years), between "Stone Hammer Poem" (written in 1972) and "Poem for My Dead Sister" (1990). As a poet, Kroetsch grew quickly away from the poem of aimed detail into a wide, unpredictable experimental poet. This growth is why today there is an experimental poetry award in Kroetsch's name. He may have played the hayseed, but he was devoted to risk-poetics.

And when Kroetsch wrote "Poem for My Dead Sister" two years after *Completed Field Notes* came out, the raw dexterity of this late poem—its almost-inarticulate cadenzas, its sputtering yet sure form—here was a Kroetsch poem not playing at its playing-at anymore. A deadly serious, intricate, desperate, child-like, blubbery, and funny-because-it-is-true, sad poem.

Shocking—after the playful, sly regionalism that preceded it—is this poem's uncompromising postmodernist surety, its use of sophisticated flap-doodle.

Phil Hall

The first word in "Poem for My Dead Sister," its first subtitle, is "morning"—a word-play, a homonym for "mourning."

Each section of the poem consists of four parts. In each part there are three couplets. So each section contains 2 x 3 x 4 = 24 lines. So, 24 x 7 sections = 168 lines. There are no capital letters, and no periods. This is what Kroetsch calls "a grammar of the intolerable."

Kroetsch at first tucked the poem into the back of a book of essays about growing up and becoming a writer. In *A Likely Story* (1995), "Poem for My Dead Sister" is prefaced by a brief introduction that presents its biographical coordinates, in keeping with the other essays around it, December 1990.

"Poem for My Dead Sister"—such a title imposes a narrative reading, a preemptive narrative reading, on a poem that doesn't reflect its title in any obvious narrative ways. The only possessive pronoun ("My") appears in the title; there are no personal pronouns in the poem.

That one-paragraph introduction to the poem (the story of his sister's dying) has been dropped by the time the poem reappears in *The Snowbird Poems* (2004). Obviously, the introduction was a way to *tie in* the poem with the rest of *A Likely Story*, and a way to justify its inclusion there. The poem lingers over none of the details of its origins overtly. It can barely get its mouth around the season or the time of day.

> sigh the dumb wick burnt
> arrowed as of to ever spent
>
> willow and wine a look annealed
> flight to the roused nothing, once and was
>
> the truce presented, now a now be were
> the track annihilate, choke the bear bare
> (Kroetsch 1995, 167)

This late long poem is the culmination of all of Kroetsch's experiments in *Completed Field Notes*. It is a poem equally about the betrayals and salvations of language as it is about personal history or loss—it is a language poem, not a memoir.

Considering this, I think that Kroetsch the Trickster, Kroetsch the Fox, Kroetsch the Crow, Kroetsch the Old Man—knowing the power of, and the newness of, his poem—or not wanting to know—tucked away its importance from us and himself by first hiding it in plain view. Then, realizing the poem had been smothered, he included it in *The Snowbird Poems*, among weaker poems.

Julie Beddoes, in reviewing *A Likely Story* in the *NeWest Review* in 1996, mentions "Poem for My Dead Sister." Pamela Butling and Susan Rudy, in *Poets Talk* (2005), interview Kroetsch for a few pages about the poem. And Dennis Cooley, in his book *The Home Place: Essays on Robert Kroetsch's Poetry* (2016), writes one paragraph in his back notes about it.

Beddoes says that "Poem for My Dead Sister" is of a "grief beyond anecdote." She sees that it was "written with a need to cope," and that it achieves "an entangling which deflects the sorrow." She is reading the poem presaged by the introduction that came with it; she is reading the narrative that isn't quite there.

In "For Play and Entrance: The Contemporary Canadian Long Poem," Kroetsch reminds us that his term "field notes" came from archeology: "the finding man who is essentially lost" (Kroetsch 1989b, 129). (From the novel *Badlands*, this: "We are a people raised not on love letters or lyric poems or even cries of rebellion or ecstasy or pain or regret, but rather old hordes of field notes" [Kroetsch 1975, 2]).

Kroetsch also reminds us that Gertrude Stein is one of his heroes, but that he doesn't "go as far as, say, Susan Howe." He's reading her. He says: "Grammar won't say what I have to say" (Butling 2005, 14).

To comment, in that interview, on the couplet form of his poem, Kroetsch speaks of "an iambic trance," of the poem being an elegy, and of its use of Anglo-Saxon alliteration.

When asked if he was conscious of paralleling the L=A=N=G=U=A=G=E poets, the poet says simply: Yes.

He says that in his poems he is "arguing with the Canadian poetic establishment, which I see as incredibly dull."

He admits that using a visually regular form was a way to "contain my grief," but at the same time the poem's word-play humour and use of bad puns was so rampant that "even Dennis Cooley was offended!"

Butling & Rudy: You're interrogating literature at the level of sound and word, instead of discourse.

K: Yes that's right (Butling 2005, 17).

White birds—without a Latin genus. What good are details—if there is no telling? Details are just sound. *Inside* a story there is no story. It is all *likely*. A vowel is not white, it is an opening of shape and sound above the white landscape. A spoken V above a traversed O.

Finished with poetry, Kroetsch says, by the end of *Completed Field Notes*, he had "run out of ways to subvert myself." And finally, Kroetsch tells us that this poem was the first one he ever wrote on a computer. "I had never used a computer…I was playing.…"

Dennis Cooley, in his footnote on the poem, calls it "almost metaphysical," "a retreat into high modernism," and "a lapse into a kind of poetry Kroetsch seemed to have left behind." He points to the poem's "Latinate dictions," its "near refusal of semantic sense," and its "tight" "crabbed" "neologisms" (2016).

In "Poem for My Dead Sister," there are notably no baseball metaphors, no hockey metaphors, no homestead talismans; refreshingly so.

Kroetsch is not talking to George Bowering, or bpNicol, or any of his other poet friends. In this sense, the poetry has ceased to be occasional. The poet is no longer saying, "Hey, look what I've done." He is now saying, "Behold."

He is not talking to Canadian Literature (there are no buried references to "a double hook" for instance). He is not strutting. He is not even talking to his dead sister. The poem is talking to *itself*, finally, as a poem should, especially at moments like the one that is this poem's moment…

By proprioception the internal mytosis sings.

> the lost life, we ewe ourselves
> she we, astound the crittered riverbed
>
> the wasn't us is all we are and sleep
> the harpooned angel, and the crypt accuse
>
> accost the apple and across the bow
> home the hunter is, and well the crow
> (Kroetsch 1995, 169)

This is what Kroetsch told us. Kroetsch would honour what tugged at him—by resisting it. Into song. As we all might hope to.

To crawl free of the regional, to crawl free of grammar, one must constantly pay backward to regionalism and grammar, homages, offerings—so that we will not be in offense of the monster Tradition, or the monster Family, or the monster Syntax—and be eaten up by them for a lack of understandability.

Only after years of being an acolyte to realism can one perhaps go past noun-verb-subject completely and remain whole—by discovering new song.

If you insist, this is what "Poem for My Dead Sister" is "about."

There is something in the daily bread of this poem that encourages counting.

There is no set number of words per line, but without counting it feels as if there is: we find an upper limit of nine small words, and a lower limit of one ("run"), but the usual number of words per line is from five to seven.

The poem's numbers seem insistent, consistent. Maybe this comes from the echoes of Chaucer, that cramped courtliness; or its seasonal echoes of Spenser's *The Shepheardes Calender*; or its echo of Robert Louis Stevenson's epitaph poem ("Requiem") "home is the sailor home from the sea" that is alluded to in the line "home the hunter is," that formal bend to the phrases; or its echoes of Thomas Hardy's dated Georgian landscapes; or the many echoes of nursery babble and nursery rhyme that are in it as well.

Maybe one suspects Kroetsch of counting syllables because the structure seems so carefully made. But, counting, we find that, no, these are not syllabics, but that something of an "iambic trance" (as Kroetsch says in the already mentioned interview) is here anyway. Maybe, as Olson used to argue about the typewriter, Kroetsch's first encounter with the shaping procedures of a computer is a factor in all of this as well.

As Kroetsch says also, in the Butling and Rudy interview, this is "an anti-lyric." It is also an absorber of traditions. I have mentioned Chaucer, and Spenser, the Romantics, the Georgians. The poem is very consciously in the English tradition of elegy—Milton's "Lycidas," Tennyson's "Break, Break, Break." I hear Zukofsky's *80 Flowers*. And James Joyce (consider the word "melothy," how it contains "melody," "mouthy," and "melty" for starters). And Gertude Stein, as acknowledged.

In Canada, Kroetsch has a strong affinity with Wilfred Watson, whose "number-grid verse" uses numbers overtly to inter-shuffle *visual* space with *auditory* space. Each number, each margin, is a different voice talking interactively (as the margins in *The Ledger* can be). Ray Ellenwood, when reviewing Watson's *Poems: Collected/Unpublished/New* in BRICK magazine, in 1988, describes Watson's work in a way that could also be a description of Kroetsch's work, especially "Poem for My Dead Sister": "[T]he poems are often games, gifts to friends, publicly private, very self-consciously artificial and witty, as riddles have always been—aware of their part in ancient tradition" (Ellenwood 1988, 54–58).

James Reaney, also, is a precursor to this tone of child's voice play at deadly games in stark farm settings that we encounter in this late poem of Kroetsch's. As is Dennis Lee contiguous, in his children's poems, as well as his more recent small word-jamming poems in *Un* and *Yes/No*. And bp, of course bp. And all of Kroetsch's close influences, his wide reading …

In Kroetsch's essay on the long poem in Canada, *For Play and Entrance* (there's the studhorse man, again, in that title's sexual pun), he shows us who he's reading, who he's talking to while writing *Completed Field Notes*. The essay opens with a quote from bp. Kroetsch is reading *The Martyrology*, he is reading Phyllis Webb's *Naked Poems*, he is reading Daphne Marlatt, and Robin Blaser, and Fred Wah, and George Bowering, and Roy Kiyooka, and many others. All of that input has come to bear, and to focus; so that eventually nothing is beneath or above his sister poem ("glod" is not "glikely"). Even rhyme fits, cliché bends, deterioration is paused for, grinned at.

Let it all fit. And fly. The long poem can take it. *Saying / Arrangement / Visibility / Figuration.*

"Poem for My Dead Sister" does tell a thin story. The subtitles carry a direction (*Morning, Petaluma, CA*) as well a process ("trope the jeered corral"). The movement is from winter prairie to California and back again to "fallow the stubble field," and to "the wasn't us is all we are and sleep." Beyond this arc, the poem does what an open-field poetics does best, it enacts from the inside rather than describe from the outside, it inculcates expressionism, not portraiture.

But it is not unfriendly in its lack of a storyteller, or in its denial of a story while telling one, or in its denial of syntactic comfort, or in its denial of outright seriousness. It is what it says it is: a poem for a dead sister. *Sheila*. Say her name.

"Poem for My Dead Sister": Kroetsch's Masterpiece

There is a strong sense in which some of the musical slants and processionals of this poem contain an enactment of the shared childhood that Kroetsch knew with his sister, early secrets and sayings, in-jokes:

> beelzebub and flibberjab
> one of is insect, one is gab
>
> one is mote in moter's aye
> one is how to say good-bye
>
> one a will is, one enough
> cow and cat at water trough
> (Kroetsch 1995, 165–6)

There is even a sense that if one could hear the poem read out, it would have a magical, incantatory, divination quality. Could it heal? Transport by structured wild-and-traditional sounds: "melothy of mixedness"—as with Macbeth's witches—"wind and winter weave a tone / wind and winter weave a bone" (Kroetsch 1995, 165–6).

Then when Kroetsch won the Order of Canada, we took him to the Lumsden pub to celebrate. Our young waitress found out what the occasion was, so she brought a bar napkin to the table and asked Kroetsch to sign it. He was happy to.

I swear—looking across that table—seeing upside down—as I witnessed what Kroetsch scrawled as his name on that napkin—for a moment his signature was the exact migration pattern of those white birds.

Robert Kroetsch achieved in this late poem something that he was striving for in all of his *Completed Field Notes*. By dropping his personae, his ah-shucks deflectiveness, his male aggressiveness-in-prose tendencies, and his occasional verse dialogue with many poets and friends—he was able to write at last an unapologetic postmodernist poem, fully realized. A masterpiece.

He was able to orchestrate for us at last the tentative masquerade of all pronouncement.

And because of this poem, plus *The Hornbooks of Rita K*, plus the *Completed Field Notes*, Kroetsch's poetry (like that of Thomas Hardy and D. H. Lawrence) has come to be as much read, or more read, than his fiction.

These days, many of us think of the "non-poet" Robert Kroetsch as one our finest poets.

> delay, descending day, apostrophe
> approve the call, the cliff of solitude
>
> appearance peer, onto the glaze of what
> is is or muted mood, the naked pot
>
> tip down, and clock unwind the winter tree
> and sky and mallard fly the winter free
> (Kroetsch 1995, 170)

WORKS CITED

Beddoes, Julie. 1996. "Can One, in the Nineties, Be a Love Poet?" *NeWest Review* 21 (3): 30.

Butling, Pauline, and Susan Rudy. 2005. *Poets Talk, Daphne Marlatt, Erin Mouré, Dionne Brand, Marie Annharte Baker, Jeff Derksen, and Fred Wah*. Edmonton: University of Alberta Press.

Cooley, Dennis. 2016. *The Home Place, Essays on Robert Kroetsch's Poetry*. Edmonton: University of Alberta Press.

Ellenwood, Ray. 1988. "games, gifts, and riddles." BRICK 33 (Spring): 54–58.

Kroetsch, Robert. 1975. *Badlands*. Toronto: General Publishing.

———. 1975. *Stone Hammer Poem*, Lantzville, BC: Oolichan Press.

———. 1977. "Seed Catalogue," 23, 25. Winnipeg: Turnstone Press.

———. 1983. *Letters to Salonika*. Toronto: Grand Union Press.

———. 1985. "Sounding the Name," in *Advice to My Friends*. Toronto: Stoddart.

———. 1986. "Spending the Morning on the Beach," in *Seed Catalogue*. Winnipeg: Turnstone Press.

———. 1989. *Completed Field Notes: The Long Poems of Robert Kroetsch*. Toronto: McClelland and Stewart.

———. 1989. *The Lovely Treachery of Words: Essays Selected and New*. Toronto: Oxford University Press.

———. 1995. *A Likely Story: The Writing Life*. Red Deer, AB: Red Deer College Press.

———. 1995. "Poem for My Dead Sister." In *A Likely Story*, 157–170. Red Deer, AB: Red Deer College Press.

———. 2000. *Completed Field Notes: The Long Poems of Robert Kroetsch*. Introduction by Fred Wah. Toronto: McClelland and Stewart.

Lawrence, D. H. 1964. *The Complete Poems*. Edited by Vivian de Solo Pinto and Warren Roberts. London: Penguin Books.

Newlove, John. 1974. *The Fat Man: Selected Poems 1964–1974*. Toronto: McClelland and Stewart.

Watson, Wilfred. 1986. *Poems: Collected/Unpublished/New*. Edited by Shirley Neuman. Edmonton: Longspoon, NeWest.

Incomplete Field Notes: Eva Fritsch, Turnstone Press, and the Print Histories of Robert Kroetsch's "Seed Catalogue" and *Seed Catalogue*

CAMERON ANSTEE

> Into the dark of January
> the seed catalogue bloomed
>
> a winter proposition, if
> spring should come, then,
>
> with illustrations:
>
> —Robert Kroetsch, *Seed Catalogue*

> *The poem spreads and proliferates in its various guises.*
> —Dennis Cooley, "On Robert Kroetsch and Turnstone"

Robert Kroetsch's "Seed Catalogue" is, according to Aritha van Herk, "one of the most-studied long poems in Canadian literature."[1] When discussing it, however, we must distinguish between "Seed Catalogue" the poem and *Seed Catalogue* the book. Through four distinct editions of the book, the poem's republication in Kroetsch's *Field Notes: The Collected Poetry of Robert Kroetsch* (1981), the 1989 and 2000 editions of *Completed Field Notes: The Long Poems of Robert Kroetsch*, and innumerable anthology appearances—perhaps most notably in Coach House's influential *The Long Poem Anthology* (1979)—the print histories of both poem and book have become obscured.[2] Moreover, given the distinctive characteristics of the design and production of the first edition of the book, this print history is a notable absence in existing scholarship. Published by Turnstone Press in 1977 as number seven in their Poetry Series One, the first edition was designed by Eva Fritsch and included screen reproductions of historical seed catalogues beneath the text of Kroetsch's poem, emphasizing the already intertextual nature of the work. Fritsch's design underscored the complex relations of the poem to the seed catalogue as an historical document by rendering the catalogue present in the visual codes of the book. The particular successes of her design have never been reproduced, and this is to the detriment of our ability to read the poem.

 Robert Bringhurst argues for the role of the book designer as "interpreter"—"[t]he printed page is a surface where things inside the book and things outside the book intersect."[3] This paper examines Fritsch's design against subsequent printings of both poem and book in order to explore how book design can support and extend the meaning of a text by engaging *things outside the book*. "Seed Catalogue" is a particularly productive text for such a study given what Kroetsch described as the poem's concern with "the way we read the page and hear its implications,"[4] as well as its ubiquity in the field of Canadian literature. *Seed Catalogue* is inescapable and yet, despite the book's generous first edition of 1,000 copies, all too rarely encountered in its original form. Its conspicuous presence in the field renders it an ideal case study for the history of small-press book design in Canada, and of the ways that institutional demand for affordable, large-scale reprints can degrade and obscure the original paratextual apparatus of a text, eroding possible meanings in the process.

 In the absence of direct archival documents concerning the design and production of the first edition—for example, there is no correspondence in the Turnstone archives from Fritsch, Turnstone, or Kroetsch on these matters—I am instead going to draw on Kroetsch's own discussion of "Seed Catalogue" and of long poems in general, as well as on critical readings of the text. I am building here on Julia Moss's consideration of the design of Kroetsch's earlier collection in her 1998 article "The Particulars of Space: Looking at Robert Kroetsch's *The Ledger*." Moss traces the complex relationships between editions of *The Ledger*, examining typographic and layout changes that altered the symbolic contents of the book. Moss refers to the "creative complicity" of the publishers of the book, Applegarth Follies (Michael Niederman and Hilary Bates), in constructing the meanings of *The Ledger*: "[The publisher's] presence is conspicuously evident throughout the text, to the extent that they have had an impact on the semantic effect of the poem."[5] It is such complicity and semantic effect on the part of Fritsch and Turnstone that I want to trace here.

"Seed Catalogue," the poem, does not live in isolation, but rather exists in direct relation to the rest of Kroetsch's "continuing poem," that is, the works collected in *Field Notes* and *Completed Field Notes*, as well in relation to Kroetsch's source materials. Manina Jones characterizes these relations: "*The Ledger*, like Kroetsch's *Seed Catalogue*, is both part of the collected poem *Field Notes* and is itself a 'collected poem,' since its constituent elements are collected from elsewhere."[6] In *On the Edge of Genre* (1991), Smaro Kamboureli argues that each piece of the total work can be read "individually as long as they remain independently published," but that their collection in *Field Notes* and *Completed Field Notes* "manifest[s] the plurality of Kroetsch's sense of place."[7] Starting from Kamboureli's discussion of the collected context of Kroetsch's continuing poem, material and visual considerations must be introduced into how "Seed Catalogue" is read in different individual contexts. Reading each poem in these later collections must not be conflated with reading the poems in their various individual states at semantic, visual, or book-historical levels.

Discussing the composition of the poem in an oft-quoted passage from *The Long Poem Anthology*, Kroetsch writes:

> The seed catalogue is a shared book in our society. We have few literary texts approaching that condition. I wanted to write a poetic equivalent of the "speech" of a seed catalogue. The way we read the page and hear its implications. Spring. The plowing, the digging, of the garden. The mapping of the blank, cool earth. The exact placing of the explosive seed.[8]

The seed is both potential and burden. It is the responsibility of the present to history and to the shared documents that connect the two. This concern with origins is common in Kroetsch's books. He is constantly excavating history and its source texts. He works with fragments, anecdotes, primary documents, tall tales, memories, and innumerable other forms of written and oral communication. We see this worked out in "Seed Catalogue" as the poet-speaker wrestles with how to be a poet in the prairies (*"How do you grow / a poet?"*).[9] In the poem, Kroetsch is self-conscious about placing his writing in relation to other types of writing and storytelling, and about how stories are told in different environments under different conditions. The poem's arrangement on the page reflects this. The text of the poem refuses the stability and clarity of the left margin and instead occupies different spaces depending on the type of material being presented. Direct quotes from catalogues, for example, always occupy the left margin, while the parts of the poem original to Kroetsch move across the page. It is a narrative poem with no single through line and a fragmented text built of multiple voices, including Kroetsch's original words, children's rhymes, the advertising copy from seed catalogues, and letters of attestation from satisfied customers. These multiple sources speak to the greater intertextual and lived environment of historical seed catalogues, Kroetsch's "Seed Catalogue," and *Seed Catalogue*.

Eva Fritsch's design of the first edition is sensitive and responsive to these ideas. Fritsch was born in Sweden in 1949, moved to Canada in 1958, and was a student of fine arts at the University of Manitoba from 1973 to 1976 where and when she crossed paths with Turnstone Press (founded by David Arnason, John Beaver, Dennis Cooley, Robert Enright, and Daniel Lenoski in the Montcalm pub near the University of Manitoba in 1976). She designed dozens of projects for the press between 1976 and 1981, including titles by Miriam Waddington, Douglas Barbour, and Ralph Gustafson. She also worked for *cv2* and *Arts Manitoba* during those years, and is currently a painter.

The original wraps and dust jacket are restrained and minimalist, with only the title, Kroetsch's name, and a simple green and blue line design on a cream stock. Nothing on this cover prepares the reader for what is encountered on the inside. The book designer, in Robert Bringhurst's terms, "[draws] meaning to the surface where its shape can be revealed."[10] This is echoed in Fritsch's own description of her process: "My designs all had to be in response to the poetry and after a good read of the manuscript I would come up with a design [...], with Bob's manuscript I wanted to get a hold of an old seed catalogue."[11] In the first edition, Kroetsch's poem is printed with the pages of an actual seed catalogue beneath his lines. However, it should be noted that the screen prints are not from the original 1917 catalogue Kroetsch claims he responded to in the poem, but nonetheless catalogues from the same company and approximately the same years. The colophon tells us the "screens are reproductions of pages from two McKenzie's Seeds catalogues, dated 1916 and 1922. We wish to thank Mr. William A. Moore of McKenzie Steele Briggs Seeds at Brandon for supplying them."[12]

"Seed Catalogue" was already a highly visual poem in its purely textual form, and these concerns were extended in the design of the first edition of the book. Laurie Ricou, reviewing the book in *Arts Manitoba* in 1978, describes its appearance:

> The design of the book, lovingly created by Eva Fritsch, creates another poem, or expands the possibilities of the poem. [...] The poem is printed in dark green on light, sky-blue paper. On each page, under the text of the poem, are beige silkscreens of pages from McKenzie's Seed Catalogues.[13]

Dennis Cooley described the catalogue images as printed "lightly in gold,"[14] not beige.[15] The ink has faded in the four decades since publication and we can now only imagine—or remember—how the colours once looked. However, this loss of visual information through the gradual degradation of the printed book feels aligned philosophically with many of the concerns of the poem.

Fritsch's choice to screen-print seed-catalogue pages beneath the poem is a visual *and* textual intervention in Kroetsch's work. It is comparable to some of the design work done at Coach House in the late 1960s and early 1970s, and most closely resembles Frank Davey's *Weeds* (1970) in its aesthetics. *Weeds* uses a large format page—7" wide by 10.75" tall—printed in brown ink on green paper, with images of weeds printed beneath the text in green. However, in Davey's book, the intervention is purely visual. Fritsch's design for *Seed Catalogue* prints not only images from the seed catalogues, but also the advertising copy. There is more text than image in the reproductions, and this creates the possibility for Fritsch's design to intervene more aggressively in the text if the reader is interested in engaging with the design of the page.

In Fritsch's design for the first edition, the poems appear only on the recto pages while the images of the seed catalogue occupy recto and verso, taking on greater visual importance than Kroetsch's poem. The catalogue pages occupy more surface area of the page and thus more of the reader's visual field. Each part of the poem also begins on a new page—section 2 is not placed directly under the end of section 1, for example, but instead begins one-and-a-half pages later. This is a luxurious decision on the part of Fritsch, and a decision only made for "Seed Catalogue." There are poems in addition to "Seed Catalogue" in the book, and these are printed without the images and on both recto and verso. Throughout the "Seed Catalogue" section, Fritsch also supplies page numbers only on the verso pages, but supplies them on recto and verso in the other sections of the book. In subsequent reprintings, including in editions of *Seed Catalogue* as a discrete book, the elements of the poem are compressed and constricted, making it in a more claustrophobic poem, whereas the first edition has a lovely patience and the poem itself has room to breathe. Space, the largeness of the prairies, is important in the poem. Fred Wah, introducing the 2000 edition of *Completed Field Notes*, writes:

> It ["Delphi: Commentary"] is, as are many of the poems in this book, about the imagination of place. And space. It is through poems like "Seed Catalogue," "The Sad Phoenician," "Mile Zero," and "Delphi: Commentary" that we can witness those invisible manoeuvres of our imagination over such large space, prairie space, sea-to-shining-sea space, frozen norths and frozen rinks, vastness. Imagine. Space with enough time to be lost.[16]

Fritsch's design embraces such conceptions of space. Her design uses a larger page than any of the later editions—the first edition is 7.5" wide by 10" tall. The 1979 second edition is smaller, measuring 6" wide by 8.5" tall, while the current in-print 1997 edition, and the one most often seen in classrooms, is smaller still, measuring 5.25" wide by 7.75" tall. The different editions of *Field Notes* run through various sizes as well—5" wide by 8.75" tall (1977), 5" wide by 8.25" tall (1989), and 6" wide by 9" tall (2000).

Section 5 of the poem—the section containing Kroetsch's "I don't give a damn if I do die die do die do die" stanza[17]—illustrates the effect of this choice. The section contains only twelve lines, and occupies less than half of a single recto page in the first edition. Comparing the space on the page this section has, and thus the emphasis it is given, in Fritsch's design, with its appearance and arrangement in later printings, reveals a radically altered reading experience. In *Field Notes* (1981), section 5 is positioned at the bottom of the recto page, towered over by the scale of the list of "absences" in section 4. In *Completed Field Notes* (1989), it is in the middle of the verso page, wedged between the end of

Section 4 and the beginning of Section 6. The effect is even more dramatic when one looks at anthologies. In *15 Canadian Poets x3* (2001), for example, the "do die do die do die" stanza is orphaned at the top of an entirely new page. The practical effect of these differences in later reprintings of the poem is a more claustrophobic and rushed reading experience—the poem on every page of these editions fills the margins to their limits on all four sides, with no space between sections.

"Seed Catalogue" exists in different contexts within its various editions in other ways too. In the first edition, "Seed Catalogue" comprises the first of three sections. It is followed by a second section of thirteen individual poems:

> There is a World
> Alberta Haiku (Failed)
> Snowfall
> Getting Up to Find an Aspirin
> Conservative Streak
> Abandon Ship
> Anthem
> Historia Animalium
> Native
> Highway One
> Jealousy
> My Tree Poem
> Identification Question

The book concludes with section 3: "How I Joined the Seal Herd." This poem is included in *Field Notes* and both editions of *Completed Field Notes*, establishing it as part of the "continuing poem," but the other thirteen poems are not collected in these later books and are actually changed in subsequent editions of *Seed Catalogue* from Turnstone. The 1979 edition makes the slight adjustment of moving "Jealousy" to the end of the section, and includes minor housekeeping, described by Dennis Cooley as follows:

> Kroetsch writes to Marilyn Morton at Turnstone on October 30: how about cleaning up the typos in a reprint? Everyone agrees something bright and shiny is called for. On February 8 Kroetsch sends a jocular letter mocking the editors and lobbying for a sexier more sellable version. We get it out soon.[18]

The 1979 edition was redesigned without the seed-catalogue reproductions, and with a new cover—the first iteration of the now-recognizable red cover with a yellow sheaf of wheat. The 1986 edition does not include "How I Joined the Seal Herd," but does include a different second section of poems under the title "Spending the Morning at the Beach":

> Fiji
> Brisbane
> Noosa Heads 1
> Noosa Heads 2
> Geelong, Victoria
> Sydney
> Wellington, New Zealand
> Rotorua
> North of Auckland, Parry Kauri Park
> The Hibiscus Coast

This set of poems is included in the two editions of *Completed Field Notes*.[19]

The poem is obsessed with the possibilities of growth, generation, and explosion contained in the idea of the seed. As Wanda Campbell writes, "[t]he image of the seed is especially attractive to Kroetsch because of its dual potential for upward and downward movement."[20] Campbell argues that the "energy" of the poem derives from the tension "between the seed full of explosive potential and the careful containment of the catalogue."[21] These forces are present on the page in the images from the two catalogues; the language and the images that sold those possibilities are visible. The poem is also anxious about different kinds of language—think of the speaker's desire to be a "postman" delivering "real words / to real people."[22] The catalogue—a shared text—is a metaphor and an actual document; it holds and presents "real words" that are also acts of imagination. Semantically and visually, the catalogue presents the vocabulary of growth, survival, and nourishment that the poem dwells on and grow from. Dennis Cooley, in *The Home Place: Essays on Robert Kroetsch's Poetry*, identifies the relationship between advertising copy, settlement, and colonization, and false promises that run through the seed catalogues and thus the poem:

> It seems right to wonder: to what extent does the embellishment [of language] derive from the propaganda that once lured settlers to the

West? In it the prairies were invented as a veritable outburst of seed and blossom. The myth captivated with its promised lushness and plenitude. Superlatives and wonderfully creative language abounded.[23]

Catalogues contributed to these processes of selling the idea of settling the West. Indeed, in a 1980 interview with Flemming Brahms, Kroetsch speculates that in "Canadian literature I'm sure you can do a thesis on the mail-order catalogue as a sub-text in terms of fantasy, of hope, of education—and depiction."[24]

These ideas are manifest in the promises contained within the seed catalogue that are rendered visible by Fritsch's design through her use of the catalogue descriptions, the letters of attestation to the quality and success of the various seeds, and in the images of perfectly formed fruits and vegetables. In Fritsch's design, each section of the poem exists in dialogue with a carefully selected background image, creating a distinctively meaningful reading experience that can only be accessed in the first edition. In some cases, these images underscore existing and pronounced ideas from the text. In others, the images highlight less overt concerns of Kroetsch. In still others, Fritsch's choices introduce perhaps new ideas, or at least the potential for them.

Section 1, with a description of "Copenhagen Market Cabbage," is printed over top of ads for different varieties of cabbage. Prominent in the middle of the page is the claim "All Head Early," underscoring the uncertainty between seasons and cycles of growth, decay, and regeneration that is prominent in this section of the poem: "Then it was spring. Or, no: / then winter was ending."[25] In a poem obsessed with growth and its difficulties, Fritsch's choice identifies these themes early and foreshadows the manipulation of nature and natural processes to come in the pages that follow. In some sections, Fritsch makes more literal choices that follow the text directly. In section 2, beneath Kroetsch's story of the speaker's father, the badger, and the potato patch, Fritsch selects an ad for seed potatoes with an image of potatoes spilling out of a basket in a representation of plenty. Section 5 prints ads for melons beneath Kroetsch writing about melons. Section 6 prints ads for cauliflower beneath a catalogue description of cauliflower. In section 7, Kroetsch introduces the reader to Brome Grass, his metaphor for how one grows a poet in the prairies:

Brome Grass (Bromus Inermis): "No amount of cold will kill it. It withstands the summer suns. Water may stand on it for several weeks without apparent injury. The roots push through the soil, throwing up new plants continually. It starts quicker than other grasses in the spring. Remains green longer in the fall. Flourishes under absolute neglect."[26]

Here, Fritsch selects an ad for "Three Great Grasses of the West," with Brome first on the list.

Other sections, however, engage with Kroetsch's text in more symbolic and expansive ways. Section 3, with a description of Hubbard squash, is printed over different pages for squash. Section 3 also, however, presents images of "Seed Wheat" beneath Kroetsch's descriptions of *"playing dirty"*[27] in the granary, an image that plays on the many puns on the title throughout the poem, but more specifically on the sexual connotations of this particular section. In section 4, Kroetsch's long catalogue of absences is printed on top of full spreads from the seed catalogue, boasting "Western Canada's Greatest Seed House," emphasizing plenty, abundance, and promise in contrast to the many absences of Kroetsch's text on these pages. Section 8, containing "THE LAST WILL AND TESTAMENT / OF ME, HENRY L. KROETSCH,"[28] returns to the earlier full catalogue spreads. This choice reminds the reader of Kroetsch insisting that the seed catalogue is a "shared book in our society," and implies that the seed catalogue is one item that is passed between generations. The seed, from Kroetsch's poem and from the advertising copy contained in Fritsch's design, is a connection between past, present, and future, an object of commerce, of growth, of nourishment, and of textual significance.

Section 9, concerning the cousin "shot down while bombing the city that was his maternal great-grandmother's birthplace,"[29] is printed over top of ads for the chemical weapons of agriculture ("FARMOGERM," "CUTWORM KILLER") as well as ads for farm machinery that emphasize the ease of completing tasks with new, increasingly mechanized technology. This is an ironic echo of the similar application of advances in mechanization put to use in bombing runs during the Second World War. Section 9 in particular emphasizes the uneasy relationships within the poem between technology, growth, and destruction. The image of bundled hay in Fritsch's design evokes the shape of an exploding bomb, and can prompt consideration of Kroetsch's play on "explosion" in the book ("a bomb/exploding / in the earth / [...] It was a strange / planting").[30]

My discussion above has leaned more heavily on Fritsch's design than on Kroetsch's poem. I intend this as a corrective to the sheer volume of work done on the poem already; it is an attempt to establish a sense of balance between Kroetsch's poem and the particular ways it was presented by Eva Fritsch and Turnstone Press in 1977. Kroetsch was himself thrilled with the design, and his many comments on books and bookmaking in the 1970s demonstrate a remarkable openness to collaboration that give the reader licence to see Fritsch as a collaborator in the meaning of the poem in its first edition. If we look to some of what Kroetsch said about the book, about long poems in Canada, and about the books that were being made by small-presses in the 1970s, our failure to wrestle with these issues comes into starker contrast. In "For Play and Entrance: The Contemporary Canadian Long Poem" (1983), Kroetsch describes a "kind of madness in the recording" of Canadian long poems owing to the tension between "a) the temptation of the documentary, [and] b) the skepticism about history," and the liberal use of "photographs, collages, analysis, protests of accuracy and source, [and] afterwords" in such books.[31] In Kroetsch's poem, the letters of attestation and the catalogue descriptions perform this function, and in the first edition, Fritsch's design extends the existing expression of the same. Kroetsch writes that such works "[challenge] the authenticity of history by saying there can be no joined story, only abrupt guesswork, juxtaposition, flashes of insight."[32] The interest of such poets—and Kroetsch includes himself in their number—"is in, not story, but the *act* of telling the story,"[33] and he argues that these poets produce books that "replace language with image."[34] He declares that the poet should be understood not "as maker, but [rather as a] bookmaker," and emphasizes "the book-ness of the book."[35]

In "On Being an Alberta Writer" (1983), Kroetsch refers to the 1917 *McKenzie's Seed Catalogue* that he discovered in the Glenbow Archives in 1975 as an archaeological "deposit,"[36] and in a letter to Roy Miki explains that finding that catalogue was "like a stroke of lightning. I just knew, looking at that thing, that I had the other half of my poem. There it was, all I had to do was work it out."[37] Dennis Cooley cites the two halves referred to in this quotation as *Seed Catalogue* and *The Ledger*, but I think that the terms are more fluid than that. The catalogue itself is perhaps the "other half" of the already-in-process poem. Regardless, Kroetsch clearly saw the two, catalogue and poem, as symbiotic. In fact, Kroetsch writes that one "problem for a people who seldom see images of themselves in literature or art" is that "we fail to recognize the connection between art and life. We separate the two fatally."[38] This fatal separation between art and life is restored to some degree in the text of the poem, but also in its design. The seed catalogue is quoted in "Seed Catalogue" textually and visually—it is insistently present.

In light of such comments, not only on the poem itself, but on the forms of Canadian long-poem *books* in the 1970s, Fritsch's vital role as a collaborator in the construction of the many meanings of *Seed Catalogue* comes into focus. Julia Moss, discussing *The Ledger*, notes that Kroetsch approved of the various changes made to that poem across distinct editions: "This flexibility implies that Kroetsch allows his poem a multiplicity created by others. He resists asserting a definitive edition, even though this means a reduction of his own control over the text."[39] Indeed, as Moss writes, "many people have laboured under the title of author,"[40] an assertion that is equally true of *Seed Catalogue*. There is further evidence of Kroetsch's openness to editorial and publishing intervention and collaboration in one of the poem's most recognizable passages:

> But how —
>
> >Adam and Eve and Pinch-Me
> >went down to the river to swim —
> >Adam and Even got drownded.[41]

Dennis Cooley, in his retrospective narrative of the production of *Seed Catalogue*, credits David Arnason with "drownded": "Somewhere about here Arnason rereads the manuscript. The word is 'drownded,' he says. Kids say 'drownded.' 'You're right,' Kroetsch says, and changes the word on the spot."[42] Kroetsch's approach to writing and publishing demonstrates a pattern of openness to the ideas and contributions of others and encourages a reading of the poem and book informed by its full production history.

In *The Crow Journals* (1980), Kroetsch records his excitement about the upcoming publication of *Seed Catalogue* in an entry from September 22, 1976:

> *Seed Catalogue* will become a book. Thanks to Turnstone Press and those four adventurers: Arnason, Cooley, Enright, John Beaver. They dare to be culture-makers, the givers of new form, in a city that prides itself on having grown old young. When high culture threatens to become fossilized – when it threatens to become mere imitation of distance culture, the prophets come into town. From Gimli. From

Estevan. From Saskatoon. And John Beaver, a scholar from Britain who studies French-Canadian writing. Making it new.[43]

Kroetsch's faith in Turnstone was amply repaid by the eventual design and publication of the book, but was not universally supported when he made the decision. As Dennis Cooley recalls,

> Kroetsch's support for small literary presses leads him to Turnstone. He asks Robert Enright and I one day (Sept 22, 1976) as we are dispersing from the student pub: might we be interested in publishing it? A senior professor in the Department of English registers his scorn. He will eat the manuscript if Turnstone publishes it.[44]

The publication took longer than anticipated. Fritsch believes it was finally completed in the fall of 1977, fully one year after Kroetsch recorded his excitement in his journal. In February 1977, he expressed frustration at how long it was taking: "I wish the rumor about *Seed Catalogue* would find its realization: but no, the book ain't out yet. I'm a believer in the local, and last fall I agreed to have Turnstone Press do a limited edition of the poem. Nothing has happened, but the manuscript is finished, complete. Perhaps it's waiting for spring, as a seed catalogue should."[45] This follows Fritsch's notes: "April 1977 I was working on some pages and proofreading, on the 19th 'took Kroetsch in to printers.'"[46] Despite the delays, however, Kroetsch was ultimately happy. Upon seeing the completed book, Kroetsch was so pleased with Fritsch's design that he gave her his royalty cheque.[47]

I want to be clear that I am not suggesting that the designs of reprints and anthologies are failures on the part of editors, publishers, or designers. There are editorial, financial, and practical reasons that poems are printed in tight quarters on simple white pages. The poems are necessarily reconstituted in relation to one another in a collection like *Completed Field Notes*. *The Ledger*, for example, as outlined by Julia Moss, has its own complex print history, including a transition from a large format page to a smaller page and typographic adjustments, and yet, as Moss writes, "discourse on the interaction of text and context in The Ledger tends to gloss over the differences in variant editions."[48, 49] To attempt to sustain the originality of each of these publications and produce a comprehensive volume of Kroetsch's "continuing" works would have been impossible. However, I do want to hold up Fritsch's original design as an example of fine small-press book design that paired text and book-object in a way that was always irreproducible. Three recent reprintings from Talonbooks are instructive here—Fred Wah's *Scree: The Collected Earlier Poems, 1962–1991* (2015), Daphne Marlatt's *Intertidal: The Collected Earlier Poems 1968–2008* (2017), and Phyllis Webb's *Peacock Blue: Collected Poems* (2014) take pains to reprint distinctive book-objects as faithfully as possible given the restraints of their new material forms.[50] In Wah and Marlatt, the reader is given facsimile reproductions of coloured pages and original typesetting. In Webb, we see an effort to typographically reproduce significant elements of the typesetting of original publications. See the use of space in *Naked Poems* in particular, a poem with meanings that are regularly damaged in anthologies by misrepresentation of the essential spatial and concrete elements of its composition.

This paper is, in part, a plea to go back as far as possible when studying small-press books. The Canadian small-press has a rich history of daring design work that is sometimes successful, sometimes not, but often at least tries to do something with the book that renders the reading experience distinct. Reprints, particularly once a book or poem is anthologized and absorbed into the more "official" verse cultures of Canada, put particular material and economic pressures on a text during design and production. Clearly, it is unfeasible to reprint "Seed Catalogue" in *15 Canadian Poets x3* looking like the first edition; the goal of that anthology is to be taught and read widely, and therefore to offer as much material as possible for as low a cost as possible. The small-press, however, in a range of ways, has always resisted the imperatives of the capitalist market. What was once a small-press book, or a small-press poem, is something different when repackaged to serve non-small-press goals.

The visual information of the first edition of *Seed Catalogue* has faded significantly in the forty years since it was published. In the two copies of the first edition I examined while writing this paper, the catalogue reproductions have faded to the point that only headings from the catalogue pages are legible. The images of seeds and their products have largely been reduced to silhouettes, and the full text of the advertising copy cannot be read. The possible meanings contained in these reproductions are eroding, and many have already been lost. Moreover, one library copy I examined has been so roughly handled during its years in the stacks, and its glue has become so dried and cracked, that the pages are no longer bound and instead sit loosely between the damaged hardcover binding, held together with an elastic. *Seed*

Catalogue has become a fragile and rare edition. It could be digitized as is—and should be—but that would not restore the original experience of reading the first edition at the time of publication. Robert Bringhurst, discussing the difficulties of photographic reproductions of books, notes that the success of such efforts is to be measured by "the degree to which they leave you uncontented with any reproduction and eager to encounter the originals instead."[51] *Seed Catalogue* is precisely such a book and, unfortunately, the original state of its first edition is no longer intact. The poem is inescapable if one studies Canadian literature, but its print history has not been adequately recorded and the material conditions of its first edition have been lost, to the detriment of possible readings.

For the myriad academic studies of *Seed Catalogue*, one rarely finds mention of Eva Fritsch's name, or discussion of the material design and production of the first edition—only Laurie Ricou's review and Dennis Cooley's writings address these issues in any depth. Scholars of the small-press can do more to attend to the principles that animate the material forms of such publishing work. In "Seed Catalogue" and *Seed Catalogue*, we can trace a compelling piece of Canadian small-press publishing, book, and design history, but also the transition of a small-press book and poem from a restricted to a general market. In that transition, the visual signifiers of the book and poem are degraded, rendering it a different and potentially less rich poem to read. The publisher and the book designer, as mediators between reader and poem, are clearly collaborators in the production of a book's meaning. These histories need to be sought out and incorporated into more traditional textual analysis when studying the small-press in Canada, and in the case of *Seed Catalogue* and other books from its era, there is an urgency to attend to these issues now as pages and ink deteriorate. There is a loss of visual context and information that, although it feels appropriate relative to the textual fragments of the poem, is nonetheless another layer, another "archaeological deposit," being lost. If Kroetsch's archival gesture—that is, his excavation and remediation of the seed catalogue discovered in the Glenbow archives—is significant to the poem as existing criticism suggests, then we must acknowledge and wrestle with the archaeological gesture it was met with by Eva Fritsch and Turnstone Press during the production of the first edition of the book.[52]

Works Cited

Brahms, Flemming. 1980. "Interview." *Kunapipi* 2 (2): 117–27.

Bringhurst, Robert. 2008. *The Surface of Meaning: Books and Book Design in Canada*. Burnaby: Canadian Institute for Studies in Publishing.

Campbell, Wanda. 1996. "Strange Plantings: Robert Kroetsch's Seed Catalogue." *Studies in Canadian Literature* 21 (1): 17–36.

Cooley, Dennis. 2016. *The Home Place: Essays on Robert Kroetsch's Poetry*. Edmonton: University of Alberta Press.

———. 2016/2017. "On Robert Kroetsch and Turnstone." *Prairie Fire* 37 (4) (Winter): 86–88.

Davey, Frank. 1970. *Weeds*. Toronto: Coach House Press.

Geddes, Gary. 2001. *15 Canadian Poets x3*. Toronto: Oxford University Press.

Jones, Manina. 1993. *That Art of Difference: 'Documentary-Collage' in English-Canadian Writing*. Toronto: University of Toronto Press.

Kamboureli, Smaro. 1991. *On the Edge of Genre: The Contemporary Canadian Long Poem*. Toronto: University of Toronto Press.

Kroetsch, Robert. 1989. *Completed Field Notes: The Long Poems of Robert Kroetsch*. Toronto: McClelland and Stewart.

———. 2000. *Completed Field Notes: The Long Poems of Robert Kroetsch*. Edmonton: University of Alberta Press.

———. 1980. *The Crow Journals*. Edmonton: NeWest.

———. 1981. *Field Notes: The Collected Poetry of Robert Kroetsch*. Don Mills, ON: General Publishing.

———. 1983. "For Play and Entrance: The Contemporary Canadian Long Poem." *Open Letter* 5 (4) (Spring): 91–110.

———. 1983. "On Being an Alberta Writer." *Open Letter* 5 (4) (Spring): 69–80.

———. 1977. *Seed Catalogue*. Winnipeg: Turnstone Press.

———. 1979. *Seed Catalogue*. Winnipeg: Turnstone Press.

———. 1986. *Seed Catalogue*. Winnipeg: Turnstone Press.

———. 2004. *Seed Catalogue*. Calgary: Red Deer Press.

Marlatt, Daphne. 2017. *Intertidal: The Collected Earlier Poems 1968–2008*. Vancouver: Talonbooks.

Moss, Julia. 1998. "The Particulars of Space: Looking at Robert Kroetsch's The Ledger." *Textual Studies in Canada* 10/11 (Winter): 43–54.

Ondaatje, Michael, ed. 1979. *The Long Poem Anthology*. Toronto: Coach House Press.

Ricou, Laurie. 1978. "Review of Seed Catalogue by Robert Kroetsch." *Arts Manitoba* 1 (3/4): 114–15.

Van Herk, Aritha. 2008. "Ardently Archiving." *Topia: Canadian Journal of Cultural Studies* 20: 155–66.

Wah, Fred. 2000. Introduction to *Completed Field Notes: The Long Poems of Robert Kroetsch*, by Robert Kroetsch, ix–xvi. Edmonton: The University of Alberta Press.

———. 2015. *Scree: The Collected Earlier Poems, 1962–1991*. Vancouver: Talonbooks.

Webb, Phyllis. 2014. *Peacock Blue: The Collected Poems*. Vancouver: Talonbooks.

Notes

1. Van Herk, Aritha, "Ardently Archiving," *Topia: Canadian Journal of Cultural Studies* 20 (2008): 164.
2. The first three editions were published by Turnstone Press (Winnipeg) in 1977, 1979, and 1986 (reprinted in 1997), respectively, and the fourth was published by Red Deer Press (Calgary) in 2004 (with wood engravings by Jim Westergard).
3. Bringhurst, Robert, *The Surface of Meaning: Books and Book Design in Canada* (Burnaby, BC: Canadian Institute for Studies in Publishing, 2008), 12.
4. Ondaatje, Michael, ed., *The Long Poem Anthology* (Toronto: Coach House Press, 1979), 312.
5. Moss, Julia, "The Particulars of Space: Looking at Robert Kroetsch's *The Ledger*," *Textual Studies in Canada* 10/11 (Winter 1998): 46.
6. Jones, Manina, *That Art of Difference: 'Documentary-Collage' in English-Canadian Writing* (Toronto: University of Toronto Press, 1993), 52.
7. Kamboureli, Smaro, *On the Edge of Genre: The Contemporary Canadian Long Poem* (Toronto: University of Toronto Press, 1991), 109.
8. Ondaatje, *Long Poem Anthology*, 312.
9. Kroetsch, *Seed Catalogue*, 35.
10. Bringhurst, *Surface of Meaning*, 12.
11. Fritsch, Eva, email to the author, March 25, 2017.
12. Kroetsch, *Seed Catalogue*, n.p.
13. Ricou, Laurie, Review of *Seed Catalogue* by Robert Kroetsch, *Arts Manitoba* 1 (3/4) (1978): 115.
14. Cooley, Dennis, *The Home Place: Essays on Robert Kroetsch's Poetry* (Edmonton: University of Alberta Press, 2016), 154.

15 Cooley describes part of the production process: "Enright and I head over to the print shop on campus which then was publishing the Turnstone books. We look over their stock, choose a light blue paper we agree is the very thing. Eva Fritsch works on layout, carefully choosing pages from the commercial seed catalogue that resonate with the text of Kroetsch's poem, and then setting them painstakingly by hand. Why not coloured ink while were about it, when we print it? Why not? says Fritsch, and she completes the design sometime over the next several months" (Cooley, "On Robert Kroetsch," 87).

16 Wah, Fred, "Introduction," *Completed Field Notes: The Long Poems of Robert Kroetsch. By Robert Kroetsch* (Edmonton: University of Alberta Press, 2000), xiii.

17 Kroetsch, *Seed Catalogue*, 27.

18 Cooley, "On Robert Kroetsch," 88.

19 The Westergard edition contains only "Seed Catalogue" and is beyond the scope of this paper. It presents a new visual reimagining and re-engagement with the poem through wood engravings.

20 Campbell, Wanda, "Strange Plantings: Robert Kroetsch's *Seed Catalogue*," *Studies in Canadian Literature* 21 (1) (1996): 19.

21 Campbell, "Strange Plantings," 18.

22 Kroetsch, *Seed Catalogue*, 27.

23 Cooley, *The Home Place: Essays on Robert Kroetsch's Poetry*, 145.

24 Brahms, Flemming, "Interview," *Kunapipi* 2 (2) (1980): 121.

25 Kroetsch, *Seed Catalogue*, 11.

26 Kroetsch, *Seed Catalogue*, 35.

27 Kroetsch, *Seed Catalogue*, 19.

28 Kroetsch, *Seed Catalogue*, 41.

29 Kroetsch, *Seed Catalogue*, 43.

30 Kroetsch, *Seed Catalogue*, 43.

31 Kroetsch, Robert, "For Play and Entrance: The Contemporary Canadian ong Poem," *Open Letter* 5 (4) (Spring 1983): 93.

32 Kroetsch, "For Play and Entrance," 93.

33 Kroetsch, "For Play and Entrance," 94.

34 Kroetsch, "For Play and Entrance," 103.

35 Kroetsch, "For Play and Entrance," 104.

36 Kroetsch, "On Being an Alberta Writer," 76.

37 Cooley, *The Home Place: Essays on Robert Kroetsch's Poetry*, 87.

38 Kroetsch, "On Being an Alberta Writer," 73.

39 Moss, "The Particulars of Space," 51.
40 Moss, "The Particulars of Space," 53.
41 Kroetsch, *Seed Catalogue*, 21.
42 Cooley, "On Robert Kroetsch," 87.
43 Kroetsch, *The Crow Journals*, 60.
44 Cooley, "On Robert Kroetsch," 86.
45 Cooley, *The Home Place: Essays on Robert Kroetsch's Poetry*, 153.
46 Fritsch, Eva, email to the author, May 1, 2017.
47 Fritsch, Eva, email to the author, March 25, 2017.
48 Moss, "The Particulars of Space," 43.
49 The first edition is 8.25" wide by 10.25" tall, while the second edition is 6.5" wide by 7.75" tall.
50 Roy Miki has also been published in the series—*Flow: Poems Collected and New* (2018)—but I have yet to examine a copy so cannot speak to it here.
51 Bringhurst, *Surface of Meaning*, 14.
52 Thank you to Dennis Cooley and Eva Fritsch for their kindness and generosity with memories, time, and details; to Phil Hall for discussing this paper with me (before it existed) in Montréal; to Kate Sutherland for her efforts to supply me with a copy of Laurie Ricou's review; to Joseph Cassidy-Skof, Chris Johnson, and Mark Sokolowski for information on different Turnstone editions of *Seed Catalogue*; and to Lindsey Childs, Janine Tschuncky, and *Prairie Fire* for kindly sending me a digital copy of their "Turnstone at 40" issue on short notice.

"letter as basic form right now":
Kroetsch's Epistolary Poetics
JASON WIENS

In a folder containing notes for and drafts of Robert Kroetsch's "Postcards from China" in the Robert Kroetsch fonds at the University of Calgary, one note reads:

> letter as basic form right now—
>
> letters to Smaro
> letters to Ron—containing the whole book, in a way
> letters to…to myself, about China? ("Note," n.p.)

Composed around the time Kroetsch would write and publish "Letters to Salonika" and "Postcards from China" in *Advice to My Friends* (1985), this note reveals his self-consciousness about the epistolary poem as a genre, and as a productive new direction in his poetics. Further investigation in Kroetsch's papers reveals that "Letters to Salonika" are composed almost entirely of excerpts from actual letters Kroetsch wrote to Smaro Kamboureli while she was in Greece in May and June 1981, while "Postcards from China," ostensibly addressed to his daughters, were not derived from actual letters at all. I want to read "Letters to Salonika" and "Postcards from China" in relation to each other, to the archive they both draw from and supplement, and to the tradition of the epistolary poem. The two sequences, and epistolary poetry generally, confound the distinction between private and public discourses, between life and art, and as such are exemplary of the general thrust of Kroetsch's poetics in the 1980s.

"Letters to Salonika" and "Postcards from China" can be read productively as companion pieces. In addition to their appearing in sequence in both *Advice to My Friends* and *Completed Field Notes*, "Letters to Salonika" anticipates and references Kroetsch's pending trip to China, which "Postcards from China" documents. "Letters" ends with a Greek translation of the closing lines to Pound's "The River Merchant's Wife": "Please let me know before hand / And I will come out to meet you / As far as Cho-Fu-Sa." The lines from Pound's poem—itself a letter poem, and at least in part a translation—serves as a transition from the Greek context to the Chinese, and of Kroetsch's transition from Canada to China. "Letters to Salonika" and "Postcards from China" also mirror each other in interesting ways. Beyond their differing histories and circumstances of composition, in the two sequences the epistolary persona's position is inverted. As signified by the prepositional shift from "to" to "from," "Kroetsch" writes from a static position in domestic space in "Letters," and from a dynamic position in foreign space in "Postcards." They are both love-letter sequences of sorts: in "Letters," the love is erotic; in "Postcards," filial. Each epistolary sequence also engages with other established literary genres: "Letters" is clearly in dialogue with the Petrarchan tradition; "Postcards" with ethnography and travel writing. But in typical Kroetschian fashion, the dialogue with the established genres works to either parody the conventions of the genre (in the case of "Letters to Salonika") or deconstruct them (in the case of "Postcards from China").

It would appear that the epistolary form was somewhat topical around the time that Kroetsch noted the letter was "a basic form right now." Jacques Derrida published his sequence of poetic prose love letters that also function as ruminations on correspondence, in *La carte postale* in 1980; the letters themselves were written in 1977. A special issue of *Northwest Review* dedicated to the letter-poem came out in winter 1981, the same year Kroetsch would write the letters that would form the foundation for "Letters to Salonika." Hank Lazer's contribution to that issue addresses a very Kroetschian concern: how to begin. As Lazer puts it:

> The letter-poem immediately provides a great solution to a problem that any poet faces, the problem of address. The very form, the

salutation, helps to shape the poem. Private reference and gossip may follow. And so the poet, after the poem is done, must wonder if the poem speaks to more than one person. (Lazer 236)

In "Letters to Salonika" we see how the address to the particular addressee allows for a ready entrance to the poem, but Kroetsch, rather than turning to the letter poem as a genre that solves the problem of address, discovers a poetic potential in actual letters he has composed. In the same issue of *Northwest Review* Sam Hamill observes that the "poem as letter allows a privacy of speech, and a certain confidentiality of tone that other genres tend to repel. Epistolary poetry may be said to be the first expression of the 'confessional school' since its tendency is to include and/or refer to autobiographical and biographical detail not generally known to the public" (229). The epistolary form thus also permits Kroetsch, always wary about many of the assumptions underwriting the confessional lyric, to allow the autobiographical and the confessional to enter his work while maintaining a necessary aesthetic distancing and postmodern skepticism. As Thornton Wilder puts it, in an essay delivered in 1928 but published in 1979, between "the fictional character of fiction and the all-too-graphic character of biographic work, there are letters" (Wilder 164).

As we know, many of Kroetsch's early poems draw on archival materials, most obviously "The Ledger" and "Seed Catalogue." Beyond the conventional archive, Kroetsch's use of found materials in his poetry is well established; in "Seed Catalogue" alone, we have citations from the titular catalogue, literary criticism, a will, and, of course, letters, such as the letter from "Amie" which helps "conclude" the poem. In "Letters to Salonika," Kroetsch again turns to the archive, though in this case the archival material is his own. The letters incorporated into "Letters to Salonika" are not "found" in the conventional sense, but rather become found materials when Kroetsch decides to repurpose them. As a passage in *Labyrinths of Voice* recalls,

> *I was writing...intensely pained love letters...and one day I realized the signifier / signified thing was happening again, and I couldn't help but notice, Hey, these letters are kind of interesting...there was this awful moment when I started to notice, and I said, I'd better make a carbon copy of this letter.* (Kroetsch 1982, 198; emphasis in original)

Examination of the archived copies of the letters reveal that Kroetsch (presumably) would read through copies of the letters he had sent, selecting text to be included in the poems by marking passages from the letters with a check mark. Much of this text he incorporated into the poem verbatim, but he would occasionally—and revealingly—revise it.

For instance, in the letter of June 3, 1981, Kroetsch has put check marks beside text that he would eventually incorporate into the published poem, with revisions. We see in this example a pattern emerge of inclusions and exclusions. Here is the original letter as it appears in the archive:

June 3 81

Dear Smaro,

- ✓ Today is census day in Canada. I put you down as a citizen living forever right here in Canada. And I put your tax refund—$611.80—into your account.

- ✓ I'm outlining the Greek chapters of the book. Sudden and abrupt changes in the story, as I'm back to writing first drafts. It's obvious now that I'll be finishing the book next summer, not this summer. The Greek chapters have become much longer as a section in the story. Wild, good stuff. I like what's happening. And I now feel less pressure to get the book done. It has got to be a good book, Kamboureli. I don't at this point need what is merely another book: reach, reach.

- ✓ Would you check something for me. Dorf gets a message from the international police service. Interpol, I believe it's called. Would the message be delivered by the local police in Salonika?

- ✓ And—I'm hoping the message would be delivered by then—I'll need an exact description of how they look/dress.

My head is also running over with poetry at the moment. Not having to teach is great. We have to hang in until my sabbatical—then we have to make a great year of it. Both of us writing. And after that I hope to be teaching less. Half-time, possibly. Depending on what you're doing. Writing a lot, I hope. Teaching somewhere? West coast? Edmonton? We'll do the making strange of our lives, don't worry. (I love you.)

(69) (hmmm)

Later, that same morning:

> Smaro, I have commenced such a loathing for the most of mankind that my joking about becoming a hermit is no longer quite a joke. I suffered my drinking companions for an hour and a half yesterday, then fled the Pembina Hotel, a place that used to be a favourite haunt of mine. Dorf, just a few minutes ago, was sitting in a taverna in Saloniki, lamenting that to love is a great fault.
>
> The ultimate catch is, however, that I don't want to be a hermit alone. I want you to be with me. You must find our hermitry, there in Greece. My daughters, your parents and grandmother, possibly your aunt that I haven't yet met, four or five people from the far west of Canada—these will be allowed to visit us, briefly. The rest: us and solitude and books and ouzo and my tongue between your legs.
>
> i   just   barely   endure (and, no, endurance
> is something other than love: love is   love is

Here is the poem of June 3 published in "Letters to Salonika":

> June 3.
>
> Today is census day in Canada. I put you down as a
> citizen living forever right here in Canada.
>
> I'm outlining the Greek chapters of the novel. Sudden
> and abrupt changes in the story, so I'm back to writing
> first drafts. It's obvious that I'll be finishing
> the book next summer, not this summer. And now I feel less
> pressure to get the book finished.
>
> Would you check something for me? Dorf gets a message from
> the international police service. Interpol, I believe it's
> called. Would the message be delivered by the local police
> in Salonika? And—if that's the case—I'll need an exact
> description of how the police look, dress…I can't
> remember… Dorf, just a few minutes ago, was sitting
> in a taverna in Salonika, lamenting that to love is a great
> fault. (Kroetsch 1989a, 145)

We can see that in the revision process Kroetsch has retained the more subtle flirtations (the note about putting her down in the census) and excluded the less subtle ("my tongue between your legs"). References to money—and there are many in the letters—are excluded, as are more mundane academic concerns. Discussion of the writing process of *Alibi* is included, as is the case throughout the poetic sequence, demonstrating the extent to which the process of writing the novel was both a collaborative effort and generative of other creative texts, such as this poetic sequence "We write books to avoid / writing books" reads part of the June 28 entry (166). The exclusion of the discussion of Kroetsch's desire for a hermetic life seems appropriate: the intense desire for extreme privacy, included in the private discourse of the letter, is excluded from the public discourse of the poem.

We see another example of this revisionary process in the entry for June 8, specifically an anecdote about going for lunch with Ken Probert at the new Burger King that had recently opened on Pembina Highway in Winnipeg. In the letter, Kroetsch writes that he had "wanted to ask for a crown, a comic crown, to wear," while in the published version he revises the anecdote so that he "asked for a crown. The young gentleman in charge of crowns was offended" (150). Here Kroetsch twice takes advantage of the medium of writing to revise the humorous anecdote to make it more effective, while the revisions remind us of the Kroetschian instability of narration and decoupling of story from incident. In revisions to a later letter, Kroetsch also manipulates dates, changing the date of the letter of June 10th to the 15th in the poetic version, and changing the number of letters he enthusiastically acknowledges receiving from her from "three THREE *three*" to "five FIVE *five*" (152). Kroetsch's adjustment of the number of letters received here might seem incongruous with the persona's Petrarchan construction of the absent lover as uncaring throughout the sequence, but as a moment in which the persona expresses delight at the reestablishment of the circuit of epistolary communication, more letters received seems appropriate (and perhaps a latent expression of subconscious desire for that contact).

This speaks to perhaps the most striking difference between the letters and the poems: the extent to which Kroetsch rewrites his persona as pained lover in the letters to a kind of parody of the Petrarchan lover in the poems. In a letter of June 17, for example, he writes to Kamboureli, after what had apparently been a difficult phone conversation: "If my letters fail, then I can only ask again what is a letter? I think they have been, my letters, most of them, messages to you, unbearable cries of pain." These sincere and often straightforward expressions of pain and of concern for the status of the relationship become reframed in the poems, likely in part by the shift in genre itself, to a construction of a Petrarchan lover, metaphysically dissecting his pain so as to render it numb. The opening of the June 17 entry, for example, presents a speaker who reframes his "unbearable cries of pain" as an aesthetic question: "Form. I want to talk to you about the relationship of the erotic to form. But I fall silent. I receive a letter from you and it's so old that you are already someone else, the letter is out of joint with the reality that I imagine. A problem in form, a dislocation that is real" (155). The poems, as rewritings of the letters, offer a demonstration of the "relationship of the erotic to form" that Kroetsch references here: the erotic becomes encoded differently in a private, epistolary discourse than in a public, poetic discourse.

Because Kroetsch's papers are housed in Archives and Special Collections in the Taylor Family Digital Library at the University of Calgary, where I teach, I have been able to have students work with archival materials relating to works of Kroetsch we are studying. In the academic year 2016–17, I had students work with materials relating to "Letters to Salonika" in two different courses: the first a third-year course on Canadian literature since 1950, and the second a senior undergraduate seminar on Kroetsch and the archive. In the former course, students were asked to examine copies of the letters Kroetsch sent to Kamboureli alongside the poetic sequence, noting substantive variations (as I am doing here), and posting images of the letters to our online course delivery platform. In the latter course students did much the same exercise, but then digitized selected materials and created archival exhibits in an Omeka site that has been built from this and other courses. Most of this material consists of drafts of poems and novels, but they have digitized other artefacts of interest, including the photograph of Kroetsch's mother ekphrastically rendered in "Sounding the Name," and an attempt to digitize the stone hammer of "Stone Hammer Poem."[1] This sort of genetic critical work on drafts of, say, *The Ledger* or *The Studhorse Man* is fundamentally different from the work on "Letters to Salonika," a difference turning on the ontological distinction between the draft and the letters, and the differences in compositional process between them.

The students who worked on "Letters to Salonika" in the archive course noted that the June 26 entry, which consists solely of "THE POET,

ALONE ON HIS 54TH BIRTHDAY, REFLECTS ON HIS 54TH BIRTHDAY" (164), was followed in the letter Kroetsch sent to Kamboureli by four pages of text—the longest letter among the archived copies. The students decided to digitize this letter and include it in the exhibit, in part because of the stark contrast between the abundance of text Kroetsch produced, and the blankness of the page in the poetic sequence. If in the sequence the blank page conveys a note of sadness, even self-pity, following the capitalized caption at the head of the page, our awareness of the amount of text that has been removed only heightens this pathos. Telltale checkmarks beside sections of the archived letter suggest that at one point Kroetsch was going to include excerpts from this letter, but ultimately decided against it. The letter is not unlike many of the others in the sequence—Kroetsch writes of drinking, of their relationship, his love and frustrations therewith, of academic work, of evenings spent with friends, of his own struggles as an artist—so its exclusion seems to me based not on anything exceptional in the letter itself (and in any case Kroetsch is editing out problematic material throughout the process) but rather, it would seem, to respond to silence with silence. As he puts it in the first page of the letter, "I speak my letters into your silence" (Kroetsch n.p.), but here the silence the poet encounters on the occasion of his fifty-fourth birthday can only be met with an equivalent silence, and, as archival investigations reveal, a silence produced by the erasure of an intimate, confessional discourse.

One significant difference between the letters and the poems concerns the identity of the addressee. Nowhere in "Letters to Salonika" is Smaro Kamboureli's name used; in part this is likely out of respect for her privacy, but also, as Méira Cook points out "[i]n the selfconscious transformation of these letters from private to public artefacts, we may even ask if it were possible to construct the lover at all except in the scopic field of the observing other" (Cook n.p.). Although Ann Munton argues "[t]hese entries encode a specific reader," the particular historical correspondent here becomes transformed in the generic shift from letter to poem to an anonymous cipher, a structural position as addressee which every reader of the poem mobilizes through the act of reading. The transition from letter to poem does indeed mark a movement from a private to a public discourse; however, given the demographics of the audience for Kroetsch's work, indeed the narrowly defined readership for poetry in Canada in general, it is quite likely many if not most readers would be aware of the identity of the addressee. Moreover, the existence of the letters in the archives raises certain ethical questions relating to the work I have students do with this archival material and indeed with my critical examination of the letters here. Reading the poems alongside the letters illuminates the former in productive ways, and yet the letters often relate intimate information relating to the relationship between Kroetsch and Kambboureli. "Letters to Salonika" are quite explicit about matters relating to sex and the body, and the letters are even more so. Kroetsch proceeds in "Letters to Salonika" by reshaping the lover's discourse of the correspondence, and the poetic persona, through a winnowing process, through editorial acts of exclusion. Our recognition that Kroetsch is constructing a persona in the "Letters to Salonika," and indeed, is engaged in self-fashioning in the original letters themselves, does not make the content of the latter any less personal and potentially embarrassing, nor does it absolve me, as teacher and critic, in the classroom or in publication venues such as this, of the imperative to deal responsibly with these materials. Further complicating the matter is that Kamboureli's letters to Kroetsch, while included in the Kroetsch fonds, are restricted. It would be an interesting project indeed to consider the epistolary dialogue between the two, but the restrictions on her letters reinforce the sense one has when reading "Letters to Salonika"—and that the lover laments repeatedly—that the lover is writing into silence, that there is a lack of epistolary reciprocity. The archival injunction, one might say, puts the frustrated researcher in a comparable position to that of the frustrated lover: seeking after a response, only to be met with silence.

In an essay on the epistolary mode in the work of James Schuyler, Daniel Katz cites Vincent Kaufmann's observation that "in terms of traditional divisions between 'life' and 'work,' a writer's correspondence has always occupied an uneasy position, a kind of 'vacant lot,'" as Kaufmann puts it, "hidden between the life and the work; an enigmatic zone connecting what he [the writer] is to what he writes, where life sometimes seeps into the work, and vice versa" (Katz 150). A key difference between letter and poem, according to Katz, would be that "whereas poems, subject to the aesthetic, are fit objects of contemplation, a letter would be seen to have above all a utilitarian function. To blur the distinction letter/poem is precisely to unsettle the category of the aesthetic as that of disinterested contemplation" (150). If the letter is a private discourse, or rather a discourse with a narrowly construed audience, and the poem is a public discourse, albeit one also with a limited audience, how might the distinctions between them be further unsettled when the letters move from the private possession of the writer to the more public possession of the institutional archive, and therefore become potentially accessible by a wider public? And what happens when those archival documents are digitized? The *potential* to be accessed, in the case of both poetry and archives, is of course not the same as the actualization of that potential. Once a writer is aware his materials are destined for a public archive, surely this shapes the production of the drafts, as well as his self-fashioning—and his construction of others. That is to say, just as a writer constructs a persona in the poem with an awareness of a future anonymous audience, so too does the writer who knows his papers are destined for the archive construct a persona in his letters.

Kroetsch himself has publicly commented on the relationship of the author to the persona in "Letters to Salonika." In a 1989 CBC "Morningside" interview with Peter Gzowski (they are discussing the recently released *Completed Field Notes*), Gzowski observes that the "amazing series of love poems," as he terms "Letters to Salonika," takes the form of a "journal," and indeed these "letters" ostensibly addressed to an other come to more closely resemble the even more private and confessional form of the diary, if only because we have access to just one side of the correspondence. Gzowksi interrogates Kroetsch on what parts of the sequence are invented and what are "real," asking Kroetsch if he wrote the poems down "in the moment"; Kroetsch misleadingly claims he did. Kroetsch then comments on the persona in the sequence: "[A]nd then in that poem ["Letters to Salonika"] I play with the notion that the persona might literally be me, which is an outrageous thing in poetry, because poets are always inventing other selves who speak the poem." Kroetsch then speaks of "dislocating" the association of the figurative persona with his literal subjectivity, something most sophisticated readers can readily accept. As Cook puts it, "[t]he narrator of 'Letters to Salonika,' like most of Kroetsch's protagonists, constructs himself in the telling of his story. And like most of these, does not exist until told as story" (Cook n.p.). But it is perhaps more complicated in this case: Kroetsch's story is not the only one he is telling here, after all. Susan Rudy Dorscht is no doubt correct when she observes, "[i]n writing letters, in appropriating selves, we are never the selves we write we are" (Rudy Dorscht 100) and that "[b]oth 'Letters to Salonika' and 'Postcards from China' are…attempts to write the self off" (99), but surely the selves written "off" here bear some relationship to the historical subjects both scripting and scripted. Kroetsch himself seems well aware of this in his own revision process: disparaging comments about colleagues or other writers in the private letters, for example, do not find their way into the poems. As Simona Bertacco observes, "Kroetsch's long poems flirt with the genre of autobiography since there is not only an extraordinary occurrence of the first-person personal pronoun, but also a remarkable coincidence of fictional events and actual facts of the writer's life" (Bertacco 216–17).

"Letters to Salonika" and "Postcards from China" are distinguished by the inverted circumstances of their composition. In the case of "Letters to Salonika," Kroetsch is creating poems through selecting sections of actual letters he wrote—mining his own archive. In "Postcards from China," Kroetsch is retrospectively inventing a scene of writing: although written in the present tense, and following the conventions of the postcard form in relating sights seen, Kroetsch actually wrote the "postcards" from notes he accumulated while there. In a draft of a letter to his daughter Margaret, included in the folder containing drafts of the texts that would comprise "Postcards from China," Kroetsch suggests that the sequence is written as a kind of compensation for paternal failure, for an epistolary silence that he would lament on the part of the absent lover in "Letters to Salonika":

Dear Meg,

This is the letter that I should have written you from China. If I had been the father I like to imagine I might have been. But even then, there in China, I knew that I could not yet write the letter. I write it now as if I had been able, then, to write it then.

Whether this is a draft of a letter or a poem is uncertain, but it seems to me more likely to be the latter, suggesting that at one point Kroetsch considered including it in the sequence itself. In a letter to Gary Geddes he confesses "Somewhere in the (near?) future—I want to, must, confront these 'postcard' notes and try to go for the real thing." The "Postcards" sequence therefore becomes a supplement to Kroetsch's failure to correspond with his daughters from China. They are in fact a retroactive attempt to write letters from China that he was somehow blocked from writing while there. And although we have no reason to consider the truth claims of either "Letters to Salonika" or "Postcards from China" and their biographical relationship to the historical subject "Robert Kroetsch" as having more or less authority based on this, the compositional circumstances of the sequences still differ.

The sequences also differ in terms of how the reader, as third party, is implicated in the correspondence. As Cook suggests of "Letters to Salonika," "since the letters are no longer private devotions, but in the context of the book, public declarations, he implicates the reader in this transaction, inserting him/her as third term in a lover's discourse structured as triangle" (Cook n.p.). Because the letters are more intimate than the postcards in both address and content, and because the writer of the letters comes across as more vulnerable in the letters than in the postcards, the reader is situated more voyeuristically when reading the letters than the postcards. This becomes compounded when we read the poems of "Letters to Salonika" alongside the letters themselves: because the "Letters to Salonika" drew upon actual correspondence, whereas "Postcards from China" evidently did not, the reader is situated as more intrusive within the earlier sequence.

Unlike the "Letters to Salonika," the "Postcards" sequence appears written through a more conventional writing and revising process. The evolution of the July 1 entry, the first in the sequence, for example, reveals that the explicit address to the daughters comes later, while the association of China and water is consistent from the beginning. Here is an excerpt from an earlier draft of the opening of the sequence:

> My first impression of China: water. Crossing the
> coast. Flying, then, over a green land that was
> designed by water.
>
> China, like Canada, is a place of rivers.
>
> | Yellow | St. Lawrence |
> |---------|--------------|
> | Yangzi | Fraser |
> | Pearl | Saskatchewan |
> | | Columbia |
> | | Mackenzie |
> | | Yukon |
>
> We saw all three of those Chinese rivers from
> the air. And then by accident, through the misfortune
> of a monsoon, we saw the Lijiang River. Peach River.

The "original order" of the drafts that would become the opening "July 1" entry of "Postcards from China" suggests a particular linear development.² This first, more "open form" poetic draft, is followed by a draft in prose-poem form of what would become the first "stanza" of the July 1 entry. This is followed by a draft which appears in more conventional epistolary form, with an opening salutation ("Dear Meg"), and then a more conventional letter, with holograph revisions, and which includes reference to other figures in the poem, such as "Mr. Wong," "Mr. Bi," and "Madame Fan," as well as Joseph Conrad. This draft then functions as a kind of outline, or rather a seed that would germinate into the sequence. The third paragraph of this "letter draft" would end up as the opening stanza of the sequence, in slightly revised form:

> Flying over the Chinese coast, off the China Sea and
> towards Shanghai; in the green land far below us, what I
> took to be roads. There cannot be so many roads in China,
> I thought, roads everywhere. And then, a few minutes later,
> I realized that what I took to be roads were canals, ditches,
> waterways. It was a web of water below us, the Chinese land.
> (Kroetsch 1989a, 167)

The drafts reveal, or perhaps suggest, that Kroetsch turned to the conventional letter form in composing the drafts of the poems, and then winnowed these letter drafts down to the prose poem form, partly because, presumably, it is more consistent with the discourse of the postcard.

That discourse is a particularly laconic epistolary form due to spatial and temporal constraints: the limited space of the card itself, and the limited time available to compose while travelling. As Jacques Derrida puts it, the postcard "limits and justifies, from the outside, by means of the borders, the indigence of the discourse, the insignificance of the anecdoque [sic]" (21–22). And yet the entries in "Postcards from China" elaborate a discourse that is hardly indigent, and exceeds the borders of which Derrida writes—Kroetsch does relate anecdotes about his travel, but tends to expound on their significance beyond what one would find in a conventional postcard. Perhaps more importantly, Kroetsch invents encounters that he relates, as in this passage with Buddha, Tu Fu, and Joseph Conrad:

> Unexpectedly, I saw Buddha. But there were three of him,
> three statues, surrounded by eighteen disciples, in a hall
> I entered when I was looking for the place where the great

> poet, Tu Fu, got drunk and wrote poems. Tu Fu, the Tang
> poet, was up on top of the Greater Wild Good Pagoda,
> having a sip of wine with Joseph Conrad.
> (Kroetsch 1989a, 175)

If the postcard is a writing that relates wonders seen and heard in a laconic discourse, Kroetsch plays with that discourse here by inventing such wonders. Moreover, conventional postcards include a pictorial element that is absent here, and which the epistolary discourse might conventionally comment on and supplement. Instead, Kroetsch provides description that aspires to the condition of the pictorial, with the advantage that the temporal medium communicates movement more effectively than the spatial: "And everywhere the hard fact of the peasants' lives. People stooped in the rice paddies. Two fishermen on a raft, fishing with cormorants. Four women digging a ditch. The commune houses, low, blending into the earth" (173–74).

The imagined encounter with Conrad is, as Munton observes, for Kroetsch an encounter with a literary father, but the appearance of Conrad in the text also calls attention to the "Postcards," and to the postcard's relationship to travel writing—a genre Conrad's work both draws upon and contributes to. Certainly "Postcards from China" repeats tropes common to travel writing:

> Here, where the Silk Route began. This morning I got up early and had my tea, and then I went for a walk in the bright morning light to watch people doing their exercises, in the parks. And I saw an old man, walking. In a garden. In a garden that seemed to me to be a maze, a pattern of hedges and paths; one of those gardens designed especially to tease us out of our habitual ways. Like the Forbidden City, in Peking, that unfolds and contradicts and confuses with impossible repetitions.
> (Kroetsch 1989a, 176)

Here the foreign locale becomes a site appropriated to the perspective of the bourgeois Western subject as a space for the transformation of that subject, "to tease us out of our habitual ways." Kroetsch writes throughout the sequence of using chopsticks, and of a certain subtle cultural and even corporeal transformation he underwent: "Today we had lunch in the Canadian embassy. How quickly knives and forks have come to seem affected, strange, not immediate and direct. Chopsticks, Meggie, become the hand, the fingers. They are becoming"

(172). However, by framing the ethnographic discourse not within the public discourse of the travel book, but rather within the private discourse of the postcard, Kroetsch's text could be read as evading the more colonial implications of such discourse. In their address to specific correspondents and intimates of Kroetsch, namely his daughters, "Postcards from China" exceeds the genres of travel writing and ethnography while retaining many of their conventions. Besides the dedication to his daughters, a number of times in the sequence the speaker makes reference to a shared memory or directly addresses one of the daughters by name:

> The National Museum. My ecstasy at seeing the Tang horses. I experienced ecstasy, Meggie. Whatever that is. The Tang Dynasty, 618–907. The horses are singing. What you used to say, Laura, when we rode the carousel, there in the park in Binghamton, New York. Those perfect horses gave me transport. I was, for almost a minute, resident and present and alive in the Tang Dynasty. (174)

The relationship with his daughters provides Kroetsch a frame of reference through which to contemplate his own experience: "Now, a few hours later, in Peking, I think of you, my daughters, there on the other side of the world, as innocent of China today as I was yesterday. We come unaware to these tidal changes in our lives" (168). Rather than writing for an anonymous public a privileged Orientalist discourse, Kroetsch articulates his experiences through a more intimate address that invokes anecdote and memory.

Derrida writes: "What I like about postcards is that, even if in an envelope, they are made to circulate like an open but illegible letter" (12). That is, the epistolary discourse of a postcard already circulates publicly, potentially readable by anyone literate in the language who encounters it, and so the shift from epistle to poem that I discuss above is less a movement from private to public than an amplification of an already public discourse. Moreover, postcards sent periodically over the course of travel are a fragmentary, serial discourse. Derrida, again, is on point here: "I have so much to tell you and it will all have to hold on snapshot postcards—and immediately be divided among them. Letters in small pieces, torn in advance, cut out, recut. So much to tell you, but all and nothing, more than all, less than nothing—to tell you is all, and a post card supports it well" (22). The postcard sequence, then, seems congruent with Kroetsch's own ideas on how poetic fragments accumulate into a provisional narrative. As he puts it in "For Play and Entrance": "We threaten to write stanzas (fragments, pieces, journals, 'takes,' cantos even) that cannot become the poem" (Kroetsch 1989b, 126).

One of the epigraphs to "Letters to Salonika" reads, "Time rewrites every book. We try so to construct a book that time, rewriting, makes it better" (Kroetsch 1989a, 138). Reading these sequences through the archive is one way of allowing time this process of rewriting; investigations into the archives reveal that these epistolary poems were both rewritings of sorts: rewritings of letters sent, and rewritings of letters unwritten. The orientation to the other fundamental to the epistolary genre masks the degree to which, in these poems, Kroetsch is rewriting his life to himself. The act of writing a life necessarily excludes through the act of inclusion. Kroetsch's poetry has always both engaged with the archive and been an archival act itself, but in this period of the early to mid-1980s, from the epistolary poems I have discussed here to the journal poems of *Excerpts from the Real World*, he would turn increasingly to his own life as an act of self-archiving. If "every act of memory is also an act of forgetting" (Taylor 243), these archival investigations reveal at least something of what is forgotten in Kroetsch's poetic re-memberings.

Works Cited

Bertacco, Simona. 2002. *Out of Place: The Writings of Robert Kroetsch*. Bern: Peter Lang.

Cook, Méira. 1995. "Postscript for 'Letters to Salonika.'" *Canadian Poetry* 37: 42–61. http://www.canadianpoetry.ca/cpjrn/vol37/cook.htm.

Derrida, Jacques. 1987. *The Post Card: From Socrates to Freud and Beyond*. Translated by Alan Bass. Chicago: University of Chicago Press.

Gzowski, Peter. 1989. Interview with Robert Kroetsch. University of Calgary Special Collections, Acc 591 / 96.6.71.17a.

Hamill, Sam. 1981. "Epistolary Poetry: The Poem as Letter; the Letter as Poem." *Northwest Review* 19 (1) (January): 228–234.

Katz, Daniel. 2010. "James Schuyler's Epistolary Poetry: Things, Postcards, Ekphrasis." *Journal of Modern Literature* 34 (1) (Fall): 143–161.

Kroetsch, Robert. 1981. Letter to Smaro Kamboureli. 3 June 1981. University of Calgary Special Collections, Acc 591 / 96.6.48.8.

———. Letter to Smaro Kamboureli. 8 June 1981. University of Calgary Special Collections, Acc 591 / 96.6.48.8.

———. Letter to Smaro Kamboureli. 10 June 1981. University of Calgary Special Collections, Acc 591 / 96.6.48.8.

———. Letter to Smaro Kamboureli. 17 June 1981. University of Calgary Special Collections, Acc 591 / 96.6.48.8.

———. Letter to Smaro Kamboureli. 26 June 1981. University of Calgary Special Collections, Acc 591 / 96.6.48.8.

———. Letter to Smaro Kamboureli. 28 June 1981. University of Calgary Special Collections, Acc 591 / 96.6.48.8.

———. Letter to Gary Geddes. 19 November 1982. University of Calgary Special Collections, Acc 591 / 96.6.48.2.

———. Note. Robert Kroetsch fonds, University of Calgary Special Collections, Acc 591 / 96.6.48.2.

———. Typescript draft of "Postcards from China." University of Calgary Special Collections, Acc 591 / 96.6.48.2.

———. 1982. *Labyrinths of Voice*. Edited by Shirley Neuman and Robert Wilson. Edmonton: NeWest Press.

———. 1989a. *Completed Field Notes*. Toronto: McClelland and Stewart.

———. 1989b. *The Lovely Treachery of Words*. Toronto: Oxford University Press.

Lazer, Hank. 1981 "The Letter-Poem." *Northwest Review* 19 (1) (Winter): 235–45.

Munton, Ann. 1992. *Robert Kroetsch and His Works*. Toronto: ECW Press.

Rudy Dorscht, Susan. 1991. *Women, Reading, Kroetsch: Telling the Difference*. Waterloo, ON: Wilfrid Laurier University Press.

Taylor, Jane. 2002. "Holdings: Refiguring the Archive." *Refiguring the Archive*, edited by Carolyn Hamilton et al., 243–282. Springer, Netherland: Kluwer Academic Publishers.

Wilder, Thornton. [1928] 1979. "On Reading the Great Letter Writers." In *American Characteristics and Other Essays*, edited by Donald Gallup, 151–64. New York: Harper and Row.

Notes

1   See omeka.ucalgary.ca/collections/show/5 for materials from the Kroetsch papers, including the letter I discuss at some length here.

2   "Original order" is of course a problematic concept upon which to make presumptions about any "linear development" of a text. Even if the archivist processing the accession was careful to maintain the original order of the documents as they were received, there is no guarantee that Kroetsch kept his papers in careful linear sequence, nor that subsequent researchers were careful to preserve original order themselves. I can make assumptions

about the development of the sequence based upon the closer resemblance of one draft to the "completed" version, but when dealing with any archival documents, and perhaps Kroetsch's in particular, we must guard against any notions of a "linear" genetic sequence to the compositional process.

Kroetsch Abroad: The Travel Poems

DENNIS COOLEY

Though Kroetsch has spoken of the travel poem as originating with Homer, his own travel writing is far from epic. His travellers move tentatively, respectfully, self-mockingly. The characters, who function also as narrators, are not thrown into exile, nor are they refugees, nor are they heroic figures striving toward some large goal. Most of their trips are spill-offs from professional work or, less often, personal and familial journeys. In most cases, they are sponsored by agencies in Canada. Only in the "Delphic" poem does Kroetsch himself chose the route and the destination. Though he doesn't presume on his privilege, he does enjoy as visitor the benefits of being expected and honoured. His visits are brief and guaranteed by an imminent and easy return to home. The awayness creates no special estrangement, though it presents experiences that can disorient as much as please the wayfaring figure.

Only in "Postcards from China" does Kroetsch actually write of home (more precisely, "to" his daughters who are at "home"). Two of the sites he visits (Germany and Greece) are hardly unfamiliar. Only China is genuinely exotic, and there he is bolstered by the company of six fellow writers, all known to him; he is supported by provincial and national agencies in Canada; and welcomed and guided by the Chinese Writers' Association. None of the trips seem particularly daunting, though in a 1979 letter he declared "I'm so ferociously North American that I go to all those Old Countries with mixed feelings."[1]

The travel poems may well have been prompted by an invitation from David Staines: "This paper was first presented at the meeting of The Modern Languages Association in Houston, December 29, 1980 [...]. It was Staines who asked me the question," Kroetsch later said (1989, "For Play and Entrance," *Open Letter*, 110). The response appeared almost immediately as a memorable statement on the Canadian long poem.[2] In rapid fire, as if primed by the Houston talk, Kroetsch wrote an ambitious new series of poems. It arced across the early 1980s—from "Letters to Salonika" (1981), to "Postcards from China" (1982), to "Delphi: Commentary" (1984),[3] and to "The Frankfurt *Hauptbahnhof*" (1984). The four of them, published within three years (1982–1984), appeared together for the first time in 1986 as sections in *Advice to My Friends*.[4]

For years Kroetsch had been intrigued with the long poem, and he had already published several major long poems: "The Ledger" (1975) "Stone Hammer Poem" (1976), "Seed Catalogue" (1977), and "The Sad Phoenician" (1979). In a very real sense the travel poems represent an extension of that first trajectory. And though, if Kroetsch is to be believed, these are not travel poems, the new publications do address the mutualities of travel and writing that had come to intrigue him.

"LETTERS TO SALONIKA"

> *I've read more of Michaux, a fascinating travel journal, Ecuador. A kind of mad poem. Or perhaps it really is a travel journal. I don't know.* (2000a, *Completed Field Notes* 138)

The travel poems open in "Letters to Salonika" with a narrator who does not travel. He is the anti-traveller, the abject wayfarer who, life on hold, lingers at home while the beloved ventures. Restlessly domesticated, he reads, daydreams, cooks, gets his shoes repaired, joins friends for beer and lunch. Feeling destitute, marking time, he measures out the desultory details of his days. It is Penelope who journeys—she's off to Greece. Back home the narrator expands the trope. He decides he has become "a strange Columbus" (131). He understands himself to be abandoned and housebound: "I am, today, my own widow" (134). In a manuscript "letter" dated "June 25" or possibly "June 26" (his birthday), he similarly writes: "I am the hurt wife. The male allowance gone to you, the inwardness to me [...] and me going all the way to China to stop hurting" (591/96.6 46.8).

The slow pace of "Salonika"—its inconsequential information, the awkward phrasings, the acute anxiety, the lassitude, the lamentations—gains weight between May 27 and June 28, 1981, as the narrator almost daily sends distraught "letters" derived from (or giving rise to) material now stored in the archives. Those letters are neatly typed, virtually without error or alteration, suggesting that they are not the "original" letters, but tidied and possibly edited versions of what might have been written in an "actual" correspondence. What Kroetsch has said in *Labyrinths of Voice* points to their existence: "*I was writing... intensely pained love letters...and one day I realized [...] Hey, these letters are kind of interesting...and I said, I'd better make a carbon copy of this letter*" (1982, *Labyrinths*, 198).[5]

The story of a stricken man thickens: "Sometimes I think this going away of yours has hurt me beyond all repair. I am not myself and cannot ever be again" (132).[6] The stay-at-home narrator breaks out in sudden lyric as answer to his state: "What is a letter? Sometimes it is a star that fell. / Sometimes it is a rock, a stone" (145). For several days the events are middling, the speaker frozen in waiting. On June 1, he begins to stir: "The trip begins to look definite" (136). By June 4, he is on his feet: "I went downtown in the rain to look for books on China. [...] Yes, I am to leave here on the 29th of June" (139). By June 15, quickened in anticipation, he supposes, "I do not have enough stories of China to be able to imagine the China that I should be imagining" (144). The future starts to move in on him.

And so it is "Cathay. Li Po and Tu Fu, those contrary poets" to whom he turns (149). An archival letter for "19 June 81," from which these words are taken, says more about the poets' appeal: "Those contrary poets: Li Po and Tu Fu. Li Po the romantic. [...And] Tu Fu. The introspective man, the poet of discipline. Both of them, in me. [...] I was both and daring to live with both" (591/96.6 46.8). The penultimate entry in "Salonika" speaks to the power and to the fit of their work: "I think of the Chinese poems I'm reading these days, so many of them about travel and separation" (157). The last page blends present concerns and literary precedents: "[F]rom you, from Pound, from the Chinese." The final four lines, Shirley Neuman tells us (1984, 184), are written by George Seferis[7] (he of the June 19 entry) in modern Greek as a translation of the poignant ending to Li Po's poem, best known in English through Ezra Pound's "The River Merchant's Wife: A Letter."

The step from one poem to the other is typical of the series, the work on one project already being invaded by thoughts for the next. That pattern holds for all of Kroetsch's writing. A plan, Kroetsch has on more than one occasion said—you need a plan. He had written to Robert Harlow, May 22, 1976: "I suspect we're alike in not envying the young writers who flash onto stage with one book. It's the idea of ouvre [sic] that compels us. The books that are the book. The range, the testing of possibilities, the winning and losing, the risking it again" (27.1.2 3.11).[8] Somewhere between design and accident he writes the trajectory of his work.

And he's on to the China poem.

"Postcards from China"

From the outset of "Postcards from China" the entries are alive, excited. The first thing Kroetsch sees, the irrigation canals, please him to simplicity: "[T]he fingering water, holding the land green; it was like that, I was happy to see that, and I understood"; "we begin to sing because we are happy" (2000b, *Completed Field Notes* 159–60). The entries become playful, even childlike, susceptible to surprise. They unroll in speculation, tumble into comical invention, happy fantasy. The roofs of Peking, Kroetsch writes in almost innocent whimsy, are "so beautiful that I knew, secretly, that if I tried I could fly like a dragon and land on a roof" (162). Joseph Conrad shows up in a droll skid of anachronisms (163). To Kroetsch's delight, an old man walks happily through a maze: "He was following paths, the old man, making turns, pleasing himself with surprise and mystery [...] while I watched him watching" (167). Day after day Kroetsch writes of gladness in serendipity: two men on different occasions show astonishment that when they speak English they make sense (166, 159); the ancient Chinese poet Tu Fu shows up to drink and visit with Joseph Conrad on top of the Grater Wild Goose Pagoda (166).

The intensity increases when Kroetsch finds the Tang horses and is catapulted into "Ecstasy" and "transport" (166), and his mind swings back to his daughters' girlhood and his life with them then. A day or two later he is elated to find the emperor's buried army: "Six thousand figures, horses and men. [...] ghostly figures in the earth. [...T]he handsome men, the proud horses, rising into this scalding heat from the Chinese earth. This breaking into light" (167). Next day he is still haunted: "The soldiers of that first emperor, back there in Xi'an, turned into stone. Forever and never, breaking into light" (168). The trope is rare in Kroetsch and it brings him about as close to revelation as he ever gets.

The events provoke brief moments of personal understanding. A sense of awe emerges in the quiet brio of the traveller's departing words: "I watch through the large windows of this modern train. I watch through the windows. [...] The water buffaloes [...] The thousands of people, in the fields, in the ditches, on the roads [...] Men and animals, wading in the water. Men and women and children, together" (168–69). The enumerations exceed the need for information and spill into the music of a special knowing. Kroetsch conveys the results in a "speaking" voice which lingers in quiet astonishment. The lift and pacing perfectly convey his spellbound watching.

It may seem strange in "Postcards from China" that, though the writers who accompanied Kroetsch mention one another, he rarely brings up their names. Day after day the pages are directed in high excitement and affection to his beloved daughters, Meg and Laura. An early mention of them is almost ceremonial, a deeply touching overture: "I think of you, my daughters, there on the other side of the world" (160). In other moments the father's voice wakens personally to them. It projects and intensifies his wish to bring them into what he is finding: "I know that you would love him too, if you were here" (161). The daughters enter the poem as nouns of address that are appended to an event, as if no further explanation were needed when we speak to those who are close to us. They function as conditionals to happiness, and as sparks to personal memory: "And the voice, Laura; you should have heard him" (163); "What you used to say, Laura" (166). The father writes in ellipses, in wonder of what he finds, confident in knowing he will be heard: "Chopsticks, Meggie, become the hand, the fingers" (164); "I experienced ecstasy, Meggie"; "The cat is delicious, Meggie" (168). Meggie, Laura—the names are foremost in his mind, and it is to them that the poet, renowned for his formidable silences, so familiarly speaks. He phatically speaks connections elsewhere, too, as we see in Adele Wiseman's amusing anecdote about him. Though he cannot speak a word of Japanese, he reassures a panicked Japanese taxi driver: "Robert soothes him with sounds that grow ever more expressively musical, communicating a largeness of goodwill that must inevitably lead to mutual understanding on some higher level than the merely verbal" (1982, *Chinada*, 103).

"Salonika" was written from the outset in an epistolary form. "Postcards from China" was written out of that same impulse, though it quickly muted the intention. The dedication, "To my daughters, / Margaret and Laura," introduces the two chief silent correspondents who appear in the poem and in hints of actual, or contemplated, messages. What remains of Kroetsch's working papers indicates that he had in mind something more than the odd address. He had considered composing the text, or much of it, in the form of letters or postcards, perhaps emulating his own decades of practice when he was travelling. The following snippets, all handwritten, and appearing as single entries on one page, attest to his thoughts for the China poem:

> "to write a Chinese 'letter'"; "to Meg?"; "subject of so many Chinese poems—separation"; "10 letters to Meg from China"; "10 letters to Smaro—Greece"; "> letter to Spanos—"; ">letters to and from Ron"

Another page includes these typed ruminations:

> letter as basic form right now—; letters to smaro; letters to Ron— containing the whole book, in a way; letters to…to myself, about China (591/96.6 48.2)

A handwritten note on the bottom mentions "letters to Joseph Conrad about China." The most conspicuous concern his daughters. Several are directed, but perhaps never sent, to Meg. The words about Meg align "Postcards" with Li Po's powerful depictions of separation and loneliness:

> (time of separation—
>
> > from Meg
> > parallel to Chinese poems (591/96.6 48.2)

One version of a letter to Meg is intimate and excruciatingly tender:

> This is the letter I should have written you from China.
> If I had been the father I like to imagine I might have
> been. But even then, there in China, I knew that I
> xxxxxxx could not yet write the letter. I write it now
> as if I had been able, then, to write it

The most developed letter, dated "July 1," includes these simple, touching words:

> I'm thinking about you tonight, here, in China. I think
> of you, my daughter, on the other side of the world, there
> in Upstate New York, and me here in my room in the Friendship
> Hotel in Peking, and how, of all the people I know, I wish
> it could be you, here, to share this with me. (591/96.6 48.2)[9]

"DELPHI: COMMENTARY"

> *Delphi: Commentary is a devotional poem, in praise of daughters.*
> —Robert Kroetsch, "Statement" 363

In "Postcards from China" Kroetsch had written, "You must have a guide when you go on a journey to a mysterious, unknown place; that's one of the rules of literature, and maybe of life also" (2000b, CFN 160). The "Delphi" poem assumes its own questing shape and its own beneficent guides.[10] It makes every sense for someone, such as Kroetsch, who had long thought of the Mediterranean as a source of inspiration. So strong was the pull that in 1968 Kroetsch had written from England to a friend back home: "Got to Rome for the first time in my life—and it exceeded all my expectations. The Colosseum held me strangely; I couldn't leave it. [...] The idea of the Muse, and of Parnassus, and of poetry seemed so natural there" (27.2.2.29).

The passion for Greece never abated: "Strange, that I so long ago borrowed the sound of Greece. I always heard the biblical stories as something a little bit bizarre, grotesque. [...] But the Greek stories, for all their passion and violence, spoke *exactly* to me" (2000a, CFN 146).

Kroetsch was prepared for the journey and well aware of the mediations that would govern it. The anticipation makes for clever use of textual precedents. As the poet moves through the ordinary days of a visitor, he strikes up a lively conversation with an ancient and invisible Greek, Pausanias. That long-dead visitor appears in a translation by Sir James Frazer in the form of a book that Kroetsch in (apparent) prospect consults and in retrospect quotes. With that ancient and printed advisor, and with his two vital daughters whose voices will lead him in their affection and their laughter, the poet sets out. On the way he plays ingeniously with the antecedents given to him. He alters them, adds to them, sets them against one another, amends them, puts them up against his own and others' words. The texts of ancient Greece sit illuminatingly alongside the language of contemporary tourists.

The bravado of a list bears signs of the strategy. The column of items embodies the very essence of epic, we might suppose—a roll-call of honoured and classical names. Kroetsch cites the names to be found on the Delphic trophy as he has found them in Frazer's work: twenty-seven of them, plus four more. "How are these discrepancies to be explained?" Frazer wonders. To the right of the page in a long thin column Kroetsch supplies in their entirety the roll of the recognized people, arrayed in a proper and respectful way—all thirty-one. Except, Kroetsch's list includes thirty-two. Hidden quietly within the others is (as twenty-third): "Canadians." The intercession generates a sly adjustment. When the visitors are positioned equitably among the grand names of classical antiquity, the enumeration wobbles (2000c, CFN 171).

The early parts of "Delphi" revel in irony and humour, and they parody the quest upon which Kroetsch and his daughters are embarked. We find in the comic text what readers of Kroetsch may have come to expect.

In notes and drafts Kroetsch had graphically sketched out possible layouts for the poem. On empty pages he drew empty blocks at one place or another on a page and added arrows to indicate probable repositionings of them. The parts in counterpoint apparently would bounce off and alter one other. In one instance a tour guide's chatty and worldly speaking waits its chance on the page. It sits immediately and dramatically below the more troubled, personal, and inward words of the poet. Strategic locations of passages also involve Pausanias, who appears on the bottom of the page, almost margin-to-margin):

> I have also heard say
> that the water of the Selemnus is a cure for love in man
> and woman for they wash in the river and forget their
> love.

Above the passage and half way across the page we watch the narrator's words collide with his aid's in comic and poignant effect:

> What did he eat, along the
> way? What drinks did he
> stop for? Did he meet [as Kroetsch did] old
> ladies who spoke to strangers
> of husbands dead in the wars?

> What was the road like,
> without buses? Were the
> washrooms clean? Did fathers
> travel with their daughters,
> and weep in the night for
> love?
> (2000c, CFN 174)

Despite its undercutting, the poem is realized within known conventions. For one thing, a guide, as Kroetsch has mentioned. He supposes he will need help, even though his guide is not always to be trusted, if he is to be prepared to hear the voice at Delphi. Kroetsch shakes out colourful and often jarring collisions between what Pausanias, a long-ago tourist to the site, and what he, himself, happens upon. The old Greek tourist, we read, identifies the priestess at Delphi as a woman over fifty years old and dressed as a virgin. In stinging adjacency, Kroetsch notes among the tourists on his bus "three braggart women, baggy-faced, rich-bitch…and one of them painted to look like a child, all of them jangling their gold in our ears" and showing contempt for the place to which they are going (175). Their sacrilege jars against the silent respect shown by the daughter and others in the poem, such as the elegant Japanese lady who "brought along her smile" (171), and the Australian woman who spoke quietly of her lost husbands (175). Their unassuming passages could well have been lifted, and perhaps were raised, with little alteration from a journal.

Another passage comically splices the unspoken words of the poet (wry, informing, contemplative) with the loud and public words of a tour leader (practiced, hurried, offhand, comical). The guide's expressions comically threaten to overrun the tourists. The poet keeps his words to himself, though Kroetsch has chosen to slide his thoughts parenthetically into the guide's breakneck shtick. The square parentheses that mark the poet's words effectively set them aside in quiet protest, or stunned silence:

> Marathon. That
> place over there [that we've just passed, that you almost
> saw] is Marathon. The messenger, when the Persians were
> defeated, ran all the way to Athens. They had no Key Tour
> buses then [laughter]. He ran those twenty-two miles [the
> precious words, locked on his tongue]. His message spoken
> [the victory spoken, the city saved] he fell down dead. (173)

Kroetsch, no epic hero, persists in entertaining jokes on himself. His daughters tease him, take confident pleasure in disabusing him of his fantasies, as in their jocular debate about the presumed reality of an unpublished "eggplant" poem.[11] The collective voices, precisely rendered in Kroetsch's lineation, and assured in their reception, are perfect:

> You mean, it doesn't
> exist, Laura said. Now
> wait a minute, I said.
> ...
> Yes, Laura said. Yes, Meggie said. We have references to
> the lost Greek poem, I presume, Laura said [...] True, I said.
> True enough. (182)

The friend "Joe," who wrote so enthusiastically about *Advice to My Friends*, testifies admiringly in that same letter to Kroetsch's skill in conveying the girls' talk: "[M]y recollection of their expressions as I remembered them seemed to fit into the moments that are the poems. And then back even farther, I remember you as a father to them back in '69 and '70 etc. and how I now see your fathering quite clear in these poems" (775/04.25 5.3b). Infused with colloquial verve, "Delphi" rollicks along as the two young women guide their writer-father to the age-old origin. Through scene after scene Kroetsch revels in impish anecdotes at his own expense. Amused at his own forays into poetry, many of them unpretendingly prosaic, he seeks exoneration in textual precedents:

> Frazer: Even in his best days / he [Apollo] did not always rise / to verse, and in Plutarch's / time the god appears to have / given up the attempt in despair / and to have generally confined / himself to plain, if not lucid, / prose. (2000c, 179)

Small lurches in the narrative are liable to a crafty (re)telling:

> (we were climbing toward
> his temple; we stopped to
> stare at the Treasury of
> the Athenians; we stopped
> to catch our breath) (178)

The daughters' voices continue in fond scepticism to weave among the father's fabrications. The tones and rhythms are utterly convincing. In the following passage the first sentence unfolds and amplifies in an apparently assured way; the next sentences shorten and stiffen in resistance:

> I want to be an *olive* tree, I explained, not just any old
> tree; one of those ancient olive trees, with holes clean
> through the trunk, where you can see out the other side.
> To what? Meg said. To other olive trees, I explained (172)

Yet, the poem is "serious." It mulls over messages, raises questions, needingly seeks. It talks of "precious words, locked" on the tongue, lost and abandoned poems, riddles, labyrinths, letters, clues, acts of divination, words folded on themselves, puzzles, poses, apt and surprising rhymes, interpretations, gods and myths of the underworld, prophecies. These are the complex and dazzling signs by which the Canadian writer travels: "[A]nd, going to Delphi, going to Delphi, I had expected to ask a question." The phrase—"going to Delphi"—appears five times on one page (172). We hear in those recursions signs of something. What? Hope? Determination? Are these rhythms of anxiety? "Delphi" gathers on this uncertainty toward its end. As the journey takes on age-old shape, it migrates toward ancient and sacerdotal rhythms: "It is always that way, the poem, the abandoned poem, in / which the hero seeking the answer to the impossible question, seeking the impossible / question, takes to the road" (176). The compelling rhythms cross the text in grammatical parallels: "One day, one night, before Pausanias, before Socrates, before Apollo (?)" (180). The patient and persistent patterns press past the line endings, spill into daily, even profane, events:

> It is always that way:
> Swing with the road's high
> curve, upward, past the
> bauxite mines (spilling the
> mountain ochre and orange). (176)

A quiet resolve has led the poet up the road, but when the Kroetsches reach the temple he feels tired, befuddled. He is depleted by the heat and scoured by the dust. Kroetsch has instructed himself at this point to "use specific detail." Remembering perhaps injunctions to make the stone stony, the world palpable, he tells himself to make us "feel the heat" (591/96.6 43.3), a lesion to our inattention. He seems to have succeeded within a simple syntax and memorable details of a world rubbing against skin, the dry and gritty air, the striking spare colours of the place:

> The wind was a dry wind,
> There might have been
> no sea at all, far below,
> where the Pleistos River
> winds its way through the
> silver-green of olive
> groves, out to blue
> water. The dust was a
> tight and grainy dust. (2000c, 181)

Worn and exhausted, disoriented in the wind and the dust, eyes closed (the better to hear?), he lingers behind as his daughters leave him to his listening and his asking. He brilliantly constructs the scene in which he is led, not though the eye, that old organ of distance, but through the nearness of touch and smell and sound and, still more rare and powerful, a visceral kinaesthesia:

> I heard only the wind.
> I was tired from the climbing, dusty, trying there to follow
> after my young daughters....
>
> The blown dust had closed my eyes. The cicadas were loud
> in the pines. The pines smelled of their own sweating.
> What I heard was a smaller sound, in the wind itself,
> under the pulsing rhythm of the cicadas. (183)

The poem lives a long way from tourist writing of the kind that W. J. T. Mitchell describes. There's a good chance, Mitchell tells us, that a leisured tourist, taking in the sights, seeking pleasurable ease, will see the world as landscape in a version of "the Ideal, the Heroic, the Pastoral, the Beautiful, the Sublime, and the Picturesque" (1994, 14). According to Mitchell the ocular bias turns a place into "a marketable commodity [...] in 'packaged tours,' an object to be purchased, consumed, and even brought home in the form of souvenirs such as postcards and photo albums" (15).[12] It distances and nullifies the local realities, certainly those that pinch and scour and spark the body. The tourist flirts with "scopophilia, voyeurism, and the desire to see without being seen." Enthralled, he remains "safe in another place—outside the frame, behind the binoculars, the camera, or the eyeball, in the dark refuge of the skull" (16). The tourist's gaze readily turns place into scene and acts with imperial power, as Frank Davey, with devastating irony, shows in his long travel poem *The Abbotsford Guide to India*. The Delphi venturer, vulnerable, unhurried, opens his body to the event and navigates by all his senses.

Kroetsch's text leads us skillfully through the bodily apprehensions toward the arrival. The poet, noted as uncertain, unguarded, has in heightened sensation become susceptible to change. In what happens, or seems to happen, at Delphi—Kroetsch is very careful to leave the actuality in doubt—the roles of solicitor and speaker collapse. The visitor does ask a question, and he is received with one. When the traveller catches up to the waiting daughters and they ask what it is that their father has asked, Kroetsch sounds confounded in explaining: "I was surprised when I offered my explanation. I didn't have a chance, I said. My father asked the question first" (2000c, 185). Another turn: the father, not the priestess, speaks. We arrive at a moment of crisis surprisingly close to visionary experience—unexpected because the author in postmodern bent has forever sought the palpable world and railed against transcendence. What's needed, he once said with robust irreverence, is "effing the ineffable" (1976, "voice/in prose" 35).

> "This poem is a thanks poem for my father who, from the underworld, called me again to my task and my joy."
> (1991, "Statement" 336)

The reversal takes a still odder turn when Kroetsch tells his wary daughters what his father has actually said: "What are you doing here? / my father said. / Did I teach you nothing?" (2000c, 186). Why his father? Why this speech? Why here? The weight of the message is one that Kroetsch continues to feel when he repeats it in closing (187). We could place the event within a biographical reading—the exhausted and guilt-stricken son faces his memories of a father disappointed that his son had abandoned the family farm. Do we hear exasperation? The father's questions, a bit unnervingly perhaps, do not anticipate answers. His voice is challenging, judgmental. Shirley Neuman's reading of

"Delphi," which patiently works out the father/son connections, draws attention to the poet's words on "the dangerous road to Delphi, Oedipus, King of Thebes: // The Cleft Way," where Oedipus killed his father. She emphasizes that in Kroetsch's poem "the encounter with the father is displaced from the crossroads to the temple of Apollo at Delphi (omphalos) and imagery of granary floor, harvest and grain dust effects the leap from the Alberta farm of the father to Apollonian temple" (188). In one of many twists in the poem, the refused father farmer speaks from the dead at an ancient site of harvest.

But there *was* a voice, apparently. Something or somebody spoke: "I had missed the moment; the voice spoke and I was not quite ready for my own hearing" (183). Kroetsch affirms his testimony by stressing in the line endings the agents "it" and "I": "The voice reminded / me that *it* / had spoken. *I* / had heard it" (184). The avowal is not unexpected. Kroetsch prepared us when earlier he spoke of Croesus who "heard, but did not understand" a prophecy (181). Past stories and present events cross into one another. In an almost cinematic scene, Kroetsch fills in the related circumstances:

> After the hard questions we ask the question, What? What
> did you say? And the wind blowing. And how the wind
> came up, and the dust, I don't know. The wind was blowing.
> The feet of the tourists powdered the dust. What was it I
> said I said? I said to Laura. (179)

The chaining ("I said, I said, I said") borders on enigma and riddle and confirms the poet's simple admission, "I don't know." Readers can hardly be surprised because Kroetsch has supposed "we spend our lives finding clues, fragments, shards, leading or misleading details, chipped tablets written over in a forgotten language" (1989, "For Play and Entrance," 117–34). Here, the family, picking their way through the site at Delphi, speak in slightly perturbed stichomythia. The poem stutters. "What? What did you say?...What was it I said..." "What?" "What?" "What?" Words fail us, we say, and we turn that inadequacy into a knotty eloquence. The eddy pulls the tourists into a shared confusion. The drastically abrupt sentences refuse the judicious measuring to be had in a grammar of proportion and explanation. The iterations (the wind, the wind, the dust, the wind, the dust; as, earlier, the rhyming of "hero" and "eros") present an immediacy—an elemental condition we might say—that finds similitude in the haptic apprehension of wind and dust. The passage goads: there is no end to "what?"; no answer to "how"; only: "I don't know." Words whirl in their weather of the journey and the narrative halts to summon itself.

Or, supposing. Supposing the daughters, so supportive and so admiring of their father, can't quite bring themselves to credit his report? That is what he supposes in the beautifully cadenced report of their impudence and their happy authoring of a family romance. In willing abnegation he becomes a creation of their speech:

> Only my two daughters, smiling in their sceptical delight;
> their father had heard the oracle speak. They were so
> pleased with me, already I was a story to tell their friends.
> ...Do you know what? they would begin, they were
> already beginning, to their smiling, amused, delighted
> friends. Do you know what happened... (2000c, 187)

Their reservations find more studied equivalencies across the text: "As to the story that" (181); Pausanias raises doubt about divination (175); the poet wonders: "How does one pose" (179). But what the speaker feels for his daughters and what they feel for him abides. Later, the Delphi poem in hand, Meg responded enthusiastically to it:

> Dad,
>   I read the Delphi poem for the 2nd
>   time tonight.
>   I love it!!
>   and you too!
>   Sleep well,
>   Meg (591/96.6 43.51)

Kroetsch, modest listener, persists quietly in his belief: "I had heard / the speaking in the wind" (2000c, 187). The statement culminates a series of small acceptances: "It is always that way," "It is always that way" (176), "That's the way it is" (180), "this is what it is / to love daughters" (184). It is the way of all things. We are carried by bits of wisdom, not so much accepted in resignation, but willingly received and knowingly repeated. It is the way of the ambitious poem too—one that speaks of misreading and losing language to tricks of the eye and failures of the ear. In "poetical statements [...] made under the influence of frenzy and the inspiration of the god" (184) we are asked to suppose that the narrator has heard the oracle. Accompanied by his guides, he has journeyed to Delphi to get the word. He goes "back" to where it all began, where everything comes from. But what can he find? The story jams and unsettles the understanding. The homecoming delivers Kroetsch to what he folksily calls the "belly // button // of the world" (179), and it takes him to a personal and familial home.

What Kroetsch later said about the status of his father during the Delphi trip takes us in startling directions:

> It was again one of those things—I didn't hear him say it but I suddenly realized he had said it to me and I hadn't heard it. And it was right on. [...] that the place you know is that patch of rural Alberta. What the hell are you doing in a sacred place in Greece? And yet my being there was precisely what made me hear it, realize that. (Gunnars 60)[13]

In that understanding the traveller faces not remonstrance for presumption (how dare he?), but reprimand for turning away from his first and real home.

In the end, we are left wondering whether to accept the words as anything more than accident or illusion. The oracle speaks in a perplexing voice from an undefinable world. The poem hesitates between disquiet and assent. Perhaps that is the nature of the poet's words. We have George Steiner's understanding of the enigmatic messages that classical oracles were prone to deliver:

> Gods and chosen mortals can be virtuosos of mendacity, contrivers of elaborate untruths for the sake of the very craft (a key, slippery term) and intellectual energy involved. [...] A very ancient conception of the vitality of 'mis-statement' and 'mis-understanding' [...] seems implicit in the notorious style of Greek oracles. ([1975] 1998, *After Babel* 219)

Kroetsch's texts, unable to commit themselves wholeheartedly to what seems extraordinarily to have happened, leave us never the less with an unease about what exactly did happen—at that fissure in the Greek rocks, at the archaeological sites in China, in the plane over it, and in the train ride through China; and, as we shall soon see, at a noisy train station in Germany. At the cracks and rifts in what we say and do we come into another speech. It is at the jerks and wrenchings in the narrative, Kroetsch surmises, that the poetry escapes, like vapour: "The long poem is the crack in the glaze that goes by the name of literature.

The long poem tells us that underneath the glaze is the exquisite clay that we call writing. Birds, walking along the edges of rivers, taught us to write" (1991, "Statement" 363). The feet and hands press into the soft matter as once in ancient cuneiform they left their traces. The crazed markings, rough and nearly covered by refined surfaces, then, speak the poetry of our deepest and least assured lives.

At the same time Kroetsch's poems retain, and celebrate, a wonderful sense of dailyness. He rubs our brief bodies against our days. He brings us to the verge of revelation. The poems leave us with a sense that what most dramatically occurs in his narratives is tantalizing and electrifying. The words come to him and leave their inexplicable and waking residue. They show that the intense scenes of discovery are authored by fortuity, or, in relinquishing authority, by the poet's measures of wit and folly.

Place is where when you go there things happen. To you. You are caught by surprise. But then—

"The Frankfurt *Hauptbahnhof*"

In "For Play and Entrance" Kroetsch invokes as exemplary "the field notes kept by the archaeologist, by the finding man, the finding man who is essentially lost" (1989, *Treachery* 129). This is what he said in that defining talk on December 29, 1980, almost as if in prophecy. He went on to create in rapid succession the remarkable set of travel poems—from "Letters to Salonika" to "Postcards from China" to "Delphi: Commentary" and to "The Frankfurt *Hauptbahnhof*." Immediately on the heels of them he visited "*das alte* country" (2000d, CFN 189) and launched into "The Frankfurt *Hauptbahnhof*."

From January 8 to January 22, 1983, Kroetsch undertook an ambitious academic and literary trip, which took him to a dozen sessions to Berlin, Trier, Siegen, Vienna, Graz, and Strasbourg.[14] What most immediately he took away in his writing can be seen in "The Frankfurt *Hauptbahnhof*," whose primary event turned on a disoriented encounter with a perfect stranger.

Kroetsch's experiences on the trip quickly led to metalingual entries that gathered in the margins of the developing text and invaded it. According to Kroetsch, "it all began for me with the marginal notes in *The Rime of the Ancient Mariner*, when I realized that marginality was central to the poem" (591.96.6 40.9). The impetus gained momentum when on "Sept 24 82," only days before Kroetsch left for Europe, bpNichol wrote asking for a statement on notation: he "would particularly like to include something from you partic in term of course the shifts that go on in FIELD NOTES" (591/96.6 44.9).[15] The effect on the poem was almost immediate. The "whirlwinds of crows, up there above us, under the wind-ripped clouds" (591/96.6 44.9), with which, in Vienna, Kroetsch is spellbound (591/96.6 44.9), become "a notation inscribed /.../ on a flighty sky" (2000d, CFN 192). The trope attaches to the New World, too, migrating to Kroetsch's favoured bird, the blackbirds moving "here to there, forth and back, charging the sky electric with intent" (2000d, CFN 197),[16] in their turning and returning resembling perhaps the verses and reverses followed in Greek ploughing of the land and in Greek poetry where it bends back into the next line. A turning away and back, in vice versa. He continued to thicken and amplify the language.[17]

The score of the scraggly crows' flight, it turns out, is more than poetic conceit. It draws us to the story of the unknown stranger in the Frankfurt train station: it "was the crows' / notations that / told me / how to meet // the gone stranger" (2000d, CFN 193). The birds' calligraphy offers pre-diction, a sort of knowing before naming, apparently. A sign of where the poet is or might be going. An omen in their moment. The poet traces the swift and shifting trajectories of an ink which is so immediately erased. Their whirling and wind-ripped flight we might read as emblem of the poet's rhythms, the traveller's erratic journey and agitated mind when, seeking the train, he is thrown into panic and into the path of the inscrutable stranger. The disarming encounter culminates what Kroetsch thinks of as acts of reading and writing.

The poem consists of eleven parts, though only part 2 (Kroetsch's first arrival at the station, on his way to Trier), part 5 (Kroetsch's ruminations on the mysterious guide), and part 10 (Kroetsch's visit to the station on his way to the airport for a flight home), centrally deal with the stranger, who sets off the drama. The poet went looking, half-heartedly, for an ancestor, and he found a stranger. What we make of that anonymous figure or, more importantly, what Kroetsch makes of him, is intriguing.

The narrative begins in a comical grouse, a good-natured bitching: "me, swinging / at the old / suckerball again" (2000d, CFN 189). The breezy self-direction would seem to promise few insights, though what is left of a previous passage has stripped the sort of detail that might have foreshadowed that outcome. The plane from Berlin arrived, Kroetsch noted in his crabbed handwriting, to a day that was "dark, cloudy, drizzling rain" (591/96.6 44.90).

Kroetsch liked to write about the traveller who gets lost, but his figures usually had some idea, vague or small, of what they were looking for. If you aren't watching for something, he surmised, you might not see anything. The poet, fumbling to read a strange place and an unfamiliar language, carries his anticipations like a suitcase, "even into the unknown." He seldom is looking for anything in particular, certainly no transfiguring or shattering illumination. Expectations for Kroetsch, however, serve as inevitable and enabling parts of the journey (disabling too).[18] For Kroetsch they often produce comical misadventure and deflating surprise:

> I expected to see the birthplace of one of my ancestors.
> We go into the unknown, even into the unknown, with
> expectations. I expected to find a *Kirche* where my
> *Urgrossmutter* went to pray. I found a plaque marking
> the birthplace of Karl Marx. I found a Roman spa that
> dated back to Constantine the (280?–337) Great.
> (2000d 191)

The sought is nowhere to be found. Foreknowledge gets him nowhere. In his groping and self-mocking, the character is not very sanguine about actually happening upon any understanding. "I hate tourist poems where they actually think they understand the place," he has said. "At best I'm getting a glimpse into that complex of things that is my own poem" (Gunnars 60). He now, in the "Frankfurt" poem, engages in a travel poem in which he refuses to be a tourist. Yet the lost (poet) is found and himself finds himself. Or a version of himself.

The text disorients us and puts us, like the narrator, into a crisis of understanding. "The Frankfurt *Hauptbahnhof*" threads its way through evasions, contradictions, ellipses, paradoxes. The text tumbles down the page in double columns, boxes of text, clumps of words. It opts for anagrams, slangy quips, sudden departures, apparent irrelevancies, gnomic little pieces. As much as the text helps us with notation, it dislocates us too, and we join the searching man who is himself lost.

The grandmother herself, ostensible object of the journey, may be gone beyond discovery—there is "not a trace of the old girl" (195) Kroetsch announces with a folksy nonchalance—but all is not lost, for the lost man, it turns out, is found. Confounded about making his way, Kroetsch wobbles in the loud and cavernous Frankfurt train station. His staccato style of that report scores his anxiety—abrupt sentence fragments (some without subjects, some lacking verbs), declined capitals, insistent repetitions, persistent wishes broken in endless negations, broken and incomplete expressions, curt and spastic rhythms. He is caught in a commotion much as earlier in the "Delphi" poem he had stood in the midst of wind and dust, waiting. In the "Frankfurt" poem he is brought into virtual paralysis at a place that escapes his knowing:

> couldn't find the train. couldn't. twenty-five parallel
> and anonymous tracks. in the iron cave that is the main
> station. had to catch a train to Koblenz, transfer there
> and proceed to Trier. the train, couldn't find the train;
> couldn't. two minutes to departure time, and the clock
> running, galloping conundrum of the ricocheting sun. had
> to catch the train to Koblenz:
> (2000d, CFN 190)

The truncated sentences and heavy punctuation brilliantly convey the speaker's jerky starts and stops. And then these two small lines, by themselves:

> the/ train
> the train/

The unusual appearance of the virgule—notation on the spot—scores the patterns of his distress. First the intonation of arrival. Yes, that's what I'm looking for: "the/ train." Ja, ja, ja. *The* train apparently, the sought train—*that* train. Where is it? And then, a small burst of, panic, is it?: "the train/" Oh, the *train*! It's here, somewhere, leaving leaving, my god where is it? The lines skitter. Against an urgency to move, to get going, *now*, the halts and spasms register a near immobility. The layout conveys a confused urgency within the hubbub that is the Frankfurt station, and that is in the traveller's head: "couldn't find the: couldn't. one minute. paralyzed / whistlecall. and the clang-shutting of doors; on this / track, here, on that track, there, trains, to trains. / no minutes" (190). This is the time for a transfiguring moment, surely. The vulnerable man, frozen in the echoing clatter and the shotgun splatter of punctuation, stands in need of help. A fusion of nominals and verbals ("whistlecall" and "clang-shutting") powerfully undoes the comfort of usual categories. Time for the voice from the cave.

Bizarrely, into those minutes of sweaty confusion a rescuer appears. Kroetsch disperses the report of that deliverance across the larger text, reinforcing details and withholding information as he goes along. First, a man, telling him he is "getting / onto the wrong train" and "pointing me right" (190). More than a bit unexpected—for him and for us—this guide arrives out of nowhere. How could it be that he knows the rail system, knows the sought route, knows what Kroetsch needs to know, and is willing to intercede? Who is he? A few pages later Kroetsch returns to the figure when in a more settled punctuation and syntax he explains what has happened. He adds and curiously glosses information about the man:

> Like me, he was pushing a cart with his luggage on it. he was wearing a green corduroy jacket, like mine. he was slightly younger than I, but only slightly, a matter of a year or two. he was shorter, but only a little. his beard was more carefully trimmed than mine, the frames of his glasses were of a light-coloured plastic, the sort I should be wearing instead of metal. (193)

How could this be—all those matchings in manner and occasion, in dress, in age and grooming, even to the very glasses the two of them were wearing, or he ought to have been wearing? Consider Kroetsch in a later text also informed by a visit to Frankfurt: "You must practice, she told me, and this in no uncertain terms, to confound the possibility of encountering your own double" (2001, *The Hornbooks of Rita K* 47).

The verb moves in its own contradictions from clear repudiation, to deep bafflement. To confront: to disprove, refute, rebut. To be thrown into distress, confusion, fluster. To mistake one thing for another, to muddle, mix up, confuse. To be thrown into distraction, bewilderment, perplexity. The meeting in the Frankfurt station rouses its own confounding. What are we to make of all those mirrorings?

Might we consider Kroetsch's own collusion in finding the doppelgänger and extracting the resemblances? A determination to realize the outcome? We have some reason for supposing that is the case. At the symposium on Kroetsch held at the University of Ottawa in 2017, Smaro Kamboureli reported that Kroetsch, having heard of Eli Mandel's encounter with his doppelganger (in Mandel's *Out of Place*), had been eager to find a double of his own. And we ask: How prepared is he to find the familiar in the strange, even in the very moments of its happening? He certainly lingers over the possibilities. The two men's ages, we hear, are the same. But no, not quite. Kroetsch has begun the passage with some confidence, forthrightly announcing the similarities: "Like me, he was," and he wore a "jacket, like mine." But he then adjusts the claims in small equivocations: he was "slightly" younger than me, a mere wink of a difference, however. The diminishing of the gap is heard more distinctly in his next demurral—"a matter of a year or two." The comparison in height receives similar treatment, the distance being only a "little" and presumably therefore of no real consequence. True, the stranger clipped his beard a bit close, but it was a beard, wasn't it, a real beard, much like the speaker's own?

The greatest divergence occurs in what he has to say about glasses. Both men wear glasses, yes, but they look quite different. Does Kroetsch's regret in saying he "should" be wearing glasses like his anonymous rescuer reveal a resolve to efface the discrepancies and find his match? Is the reach for the double at this moment acknowledged? It would seem so, and that in writing these words Kroetsch knows that it is. His attempt to dissolve the disparity provides options so inadequate that he himself, even in the moment, would smilingly have been less than convinced, or convincing. A Kroetsch we have long known emerges, confident that we too will see through the feeble move, amused with him at the obvious audacity. The reading provides us with an affable trickster who laughs at his transparent ruses when he poses as an innocent who is easily but not wholly taken in.

The "double" reappears once more, near the end of the text, when a reassured Kroetsch returns to the station on his way back to Canada. In this passage, though Kroetsch himself is hatless, and the double had been wearing a hat, Kroetsch on the spot decides that "only a day before our encounter I had in fact, while shopping in Berlin, attempted to buy a hat for myself" (198). The attempt to take a tenuous coincidence as deeply meaningful recapitulates the pattern of almost willful delusion. Even so, he cannot fully commit himself to the irrational and the inexplicable.

Few readers would predict what next emerges, however. Kroetsch has carefully gathered the parallels bit by bit. Only at the very end, climactically, does he say that the voice of the stranger, though it was "foreign," sounded "familiar." Upon his return to the Frankfurt station with a new capacity to read the timetables, he professes that "I recognized only then, there"—the adverbial stresses drawing out the immediacy of the drama and the tension in awaiting the forthcoming realization. The stranger's voice, more than "familiar," more than "recognizable," the narrator decides, still delaying the revelation and upping the suspense in the rhythms of a man nudging toward a big truth, "had been exactly my own" (198). The adverb outrageously revokes all equivocation. (Kroetsch, you might be interested in knowing, came back from that trip—shades of the Ancient Mariner, wild-eyed and electrified emissary from a world of mystery— so taken with what had happened that he repeated the story with real verve to his friends in Winnipeg.)

An open hearing resides at the heart of Kroetsch's travel poems. He listens to the strange man in the Frankfurt train station, listens to the oracle at Delphi, listens to Pausanias. He listens to the Australian woman talk trustingly about her life. Listens to the offensive tourists, the garrulous bus driver. Listens to his daughters. Listens to the cicadas. Listens to the wind—no, to "a smaller sound, in the wind itself." Listens as the person we know as Kroetsch listened to the rest of us. Kroetsch shows no inclination—no more in his life than in his writing—to talk at the world or to overpower it with his speech. In a passage that could apply to Kroetsch, Corradi Fiumara has noted that active listening, as opposed to assertive speaking, "faces all difficulties unarmed and lets unfold what must happen" (1990, *The Other Side of Language* 61). Understanding (what Fiumara calls "A genuinely philosophical activity") "begins at the point in which we are exposed to being disconcerted and disorientated by the unthought-of, and unthinkable, nature of the answer" (126).[19]

Though the transforming scene in "Postcards from China" perhaps provides a mild exception to the figure, he immerses himself, bodily, in the worlds he visits (as in "Delphi" he stood in the wind and the grit and the sun). He builds his poems out of a scattering of "voices," but the pieces are more than an agglomeration of poetic and prosaic language.[20] He lets the world reach him in felt proximities—the smell of sweating pines, the sun hot on the neck, the noise of cicadas, the clang and clatter of a huge train station. He includes the words of actual speaking subjects. The dialogue—and in these poems it **is** a dialogue—guides him through the unfamiliar spaces. What did you say, they ask, he and his daughters, what did you say?

But this listening supposes something more. This voice, the one in the Frankfurt *Hauptbahnhof*, was "exactly" Kroetsch's own? The claim of identity brings us up short. Then there **was** more to the brief meeting in the train station, though the insistence is somewhat lessened in the epilogue, when the speaker abruptly allows, "I never / wear a hat"

(2000d, 199). The words moderately revoke the extravagant earlier claim. Now: we two in the train station, we who were both (potential or actual) hat-wearers, we who were the same, are not quite the same because I am not a hat-wearer, not really. The denial seems sharpened in the adverb "never." Not: I wasn't wearing a hat; and not even: I don't wear a hat; but: I never—surely "NEV-*er*"—wear a hat. The poet never comes clean about these things. His notes on the Oracle scene in "Delphi" say as much: "(write it so the reader must guess at what it means)" (591/96.6 43.3).

The negation is strengthened, and we remain in uncertainty, perhaps in the state that Todorov has found central to the "fantastic." The reality is left somewhat comically in doubt. What kind of double was this, really? Did he actually know what it was Kroetsch needed to know? How could he know? How is it that in his banal costume and mild courtesy he could be bearer of provident wisdom? The text never resolves the doubt and we are left hovering between credulity and disbelief. True, the intercessor does seem "real." Kroetsch describes him in some detail—his dress and grooming primarily. Yet we never read his face and he remains for many reasons unfixed and undefinable. When an "inexplicable phenomenon occurs," Todorov supposes,

> the reader finds himself obliged to choose between two solutions: either to reduce this phenomenon to known causes, to the natural order, describing the unwonted events as imaginary, or else to admit the existence of the supernatural, thereby to effect a modification in all the representations which form his image of the world. The fantastic lasts as long as this uncertainty lasts; once the reader opts for one solution or the other, he is in the realm of the uncanny or of the marvelous. (1977, "The Ghosts of Henry James" 179)

Whatever the stranger represents, he serves as enigma to a slightly comical Kroetschean traveller, who feels his way haltingly into an inexplicable discovery.

Place is where, unpredictably, you find things and things find you. "We come unaware to these tidal changes in our lives," Kroetsch had written upon arriving "in China without a language" (159). For Kroetsch's traveller there are no send-offs and no welcomings home, no ceremonies of coming or going. The journey is never clearly laid out or directed, nor is it sustained or radically transforming. The breakthroughs, even if they take unexpected and sometimes painful directions, even as they rupture an otherwise quotidian narrative, are sought and welcomed, however obliquely. At the moments of intensified doubt and discovery the language quickens; the lines shift in rhythms of stress and elation. The hinge events are borne in an undercurrent of poignancy and a humour edging into self-mockery—into perhaps what in "Delphi" the traveller has spoken of as "that comic poem / with a fool for its hero" (183). The scenes are accepted and, later, in understated tones, celebrated. They remain unresolved and the experiences of which they speak are still mysterious.

Place is where you find yourself. You find yourself in trouble. You find yourself surprised out of your boots.

By then Kroetsch had already begun work on the mother poems.

Works Cited

Primary

Kroetsch, Robert. 1976. "voice/in prose: effing the ineffable." *freelance* 8 (2): 35–36.

———. 1981. "For Play and Entrance: The Contemporary Canadian Long Poem." *Dandelion* 8 (1): 61–65.

———. 1982. *Labyrinths of Voice*. Edited by Shirley Neuman and Robert Wilson. Edmonton: NeWest Press.

———. 1983a. "For Play and Entrance: The Contemporary Canadian Long Poem." "Robert Kroetsch: Essays." *Open Letter* 5 (4): 91–110.

———. 1989. "For Play and Entrance: The Contemporary Canadian Long Poem." In *The Lovely Treachery of Words: Essays Selected and New*, 117–34. Toronto: Oxford University Press.

———. 1982. "Postcards from China." In Geddes, *Chinada*, 21–31.

———. 1983b. "Letters to Salonika." *Letters to Salonika*. Toronto: Grand Union Press.

———. 1984a. "Delphi: Commentary." Robert Kroetsch: Reflections. *Open Letter* 5 (8–9): 22–40.

———. 1984b. "The Frankfurt *Hauptbahnhof*." *Open Letter* 5 (7): 83–93.

———. 1984c. "Delphi: Commentary." *Open Letter* 5 (8–9): 22–40.

———. 1991. "Statement." In *The New Long Poem Anthology*, edited by Sharon Thesen, 336. Toronto: Coach House.

———. 2000a. "Letters to Salonika." In *Completed Field Notes: The Long Poems of Robert Kroetsch*, 130–58. Edmonton: University of Alberta Press.

———. 2000b. "Postcards from China." In *Completed Field Notes: The Long Poems of Robert Kroetsch*, 159–69. Edmonton: University of Alberta Press.

———. 2000c. "Delphi: Commentary." In *Completed Field Notes: The Long Poems of Robert Kroetsch*, 170–88. Edmonton: University of Alberta Press.

———. 2000d. "The Frankfurt *Hauptbahnhof*." In *Completed Field Notes: The Long Poems of Robert Kroetsch*, 189–201. Edmonton: University of of Alberta Press.

———. 2001. *The Hornbooks of Rita K*. Edmonton: University of Alberta Press.

Secondary

Cook, Méira. 1995. "Postscripts for 'Letters to Salonika.'" *Canadian Poetry* 37: 42–61.

Cooley, Dennis. 2016. *The Home Place: Essays on Robert Kroetsch's Poetry*. Edmonton: University of Alberta Press.

Davey, Frank. 1986. *The Abbotsford Guide to India*. Victoria: Press Porcépic.

Dragland, Stan. 1995. "Potatoes and the Moths of Just History." *Essays on Canadian Writing* 55: 98–114.

Fiumara, Temma Corradi. 1990. *The Other Side of Language: A Philosophy of Listening*. Translated by Charles Lambert. London: Routledge.

Geddes, Gary. 1982. "Chinadiary." In *Chinada: Memoirs of the Gang of Seven*, edited by Gary Geddes, 9–20. Dunvegan, ON: Quadrant.

Gunnars, Kristjana. 1987–1988. "'Meditation on a Snowy Morning:' A Conversation with Robert Kroetsch." *Prairie Fire* 8 (4): 54–67.

Mandel, Eli. 1981. *Life Sentence: Poems and Journals: 1976–1980*. Victoria: Press Porcépic.

Miki, Roy. 1989. "Self on Self: Robert Kroetsch Interviewed." *Line* 14: 108–42.

Mitchell, W. J. T. 1994. "Imperial Landscape." In *Landscape and Power*, edited by W. J. T. Mitchell, 5–34. Chicago: University of Chicago Press.

Neuman, Shirley. 1984. "Figuring the Reader, Figuring the Self in *Field Notes*: Double or Noting." "Reflections." *Open Letter* 5 (8–9): 176–194.

Steiner, George. [1975] 1998. *After Babel: Aspects of Language and Translation*. Oxford: Oxford University Press.

Todorov, Tzvetan. 1977. "The Ghosts of Henry James." In *The Poetics of Prose*, translated by Richard Howard, 179–189. Ithaca: Cornell.

Wiseman, Adele. 1982. "How to Get to China: Core Samples from a Continuous Journey." In Geddes, *Chinada*, 98 -137.

Notes

1. Courtesy of Dick Harrison. A few years earlier, on "12 Sept 68," Kroetsch had likewise told Rudy Wiebe that "The experience in/of England was good. It freed me of a need I had; some damned fool desire simply to live there for a while. If I ever go back I'll go as an oldfashioned tourist" (334/84.1 6.32).

2. *Dandelion* 8.1 (1981): 61–65. The paper was republished in 1983 in a special issue of *Open Letter* and in 1989 in Kroetsch's collection of essays, *The Lovely Treachery of Words*.

3. The poem was first published as: "Delphi: Commentary." Robert Kroetsch: Reflections, *Open Letter* 5.8–9 (1984): 22–40.

4. "Joe," an old friend from Kroetsch's days in upstate New York, wrote to him on "2 February 1986," immediately and enthusiastically thanking him for the new title: "I read ADVICE TO MY FRIENDS today—a splendid book, rich in complexity, strong in tenderness. [. . .] For me, the collection really comes alive with 'Letters to Salonika' and I can't quite believe my response to 'Postcards from' and 'Delphi'" (775/04.25 5.3b).

5. The *Labyrinths* interviews took place from "April to November 1981" (*Labyrinths* 209) and so would have actively accompanied the writing of "Salonika" from May 7 to June 28, 1981. The projects show several signs of interaction, including among the Salonika papers indications of Kroetsch's near despair about how *Labyrinths* was shaping up.

6. Against the angst of those frequent entries, there are moments of conflicted happiness. The entry for May 31, say, describes a violent thunderstorm that pounds exhilaratingly at the apartment window (*Completed Field Notes* 135).

7. About the time that Kroetsch would have been writing "Salonika" he told me how greatly he esteemed Seferis' writing and how powerful he found Chinese poetry.

8. In that spirit Kroetsch praises Robert Harlow: "The new project will extend Harlow's oeuvre—and he is one of the few writers presently writing who are aware of creating just that—a total and lifetime work" (27.1.1 3.11).

9. These words in one page of the "China" folder show that Kroetsch thought about using "The Divorced Father" as a "title for the book (III)":

    –sequence dealing with my
    dreams / nightmarish about
    Meg and Laura (591/96.6 43.6)

The lines are followed by a refrain, "in the eyes of my daughters," to which is attached the beginnings of a poem that strongly resembles Kroetsch's "The Poet's Mother." The archives also contain seven sketchy one-page letters addressed "Dear Meg" and dated July 3, July 4, July 5, July 6, July 7, July 8, and July 9 (591/ 966 48.2).

10 Kroetsch had considered several other titles for the collection: "DELPHI," "DELPHI: A VISIT," "DELPHI: DIVINATIONS," "DELPHI: INTERPRETATIONS" (591/96.6 43.3).

11 There is at least one eggplant poem in print—the poignant and almost absurdly comical one that appears in the "May 30" entry found in "Letters to Salonika."

12 Kroetsch's own infamous blizzards of postcards, hundreds and hundreds of them assembled with an ice-cream cone in hand, and a stamp in the other, which were posted freely into the world, never depicted scenic beauty, or if they did, they put the scenes into a comical or ironical or personal reception. The postings were overwhelmingly phatic and sought contact with friends, colleagues, and family.

13 Stan Dragland reads the father as severely crippling and as replicating the actual father's constraints:

> If the voice is taken seriously, Kroetsch's work everywhere questions the authority of Fathers, but here the father is no abstract superego; he has a familiar voice that has rebuking power after all these years—it reduces a middle-aged man to a kid. The fulfilment of the quest is a failure (1995, "Potatoes and the Moths of Just History" 110).

Yet, something in the poem suggests otherwise: "It was his awkward stating / (his farmer's patient / voice)" (Kroetsch, 186). In drafts for the poem the father is clearly sympathetic: "I heard the meaning of the wind that [meant? wants? (writing unclear)] its way / through my father." On another page in which the father asks his question Kroetsch has added these words: "[E]cstatic moment: he realizes what it was like in Greek times; after the sounds and smells of the animals sacrifice; the prophetess speaking—." Another abandoned passage speaks in realist detail drawn from the poet's vital childhood on the farm:

> It was the wind I had heard. I knew it was a voice from the earth. It was the wind, that prairie wind, and my head full of ripening wheat and the hot sun of August, the men in the yard, repairing binders, driving the bronze rivets flat on the canvas slats, and always the wind. (591/96.6 43.3)

14 As I tried to show in *The Home Place*, the signs of Kroetsch's unbounded outwardness are plentiful:

The flurry of trips was typical of Kroetsch's professional life. A journal entry dated "April 17, 1976," from the time when Kroetsch was writer-in-residence in Lethbridge, notes: "This year, so far: 46 airplane flights" (The "Crow" Journals 51). That's 46 flights in about 110 days! Other numbers are just as dumbfounding. In 1986, ten years later, an astonished Roy Miki remarks on Kroetsch's "incredible restlessness" ("Self on Self" 140): "[Y]ou're on the move more than any single Canadian writer I've ever talked to." Kroetsch, who has just identified himself as "a kind of vagabond in my life," responds: "Oh, there was a time [that same year, 1976, possibly] when I was on, I think, 75 flights in one year" ("Self on Self" 111) (2016, *The Home Place* 9).

15 Kroetsch replied on "Sept 24 82" to say "well, okay, i'll tackle it—something on the shifts that go on in Field Notes" (591/96.6 44.9). On "Dec 22, 1982" Kroetsch, immersed in the topography of his work, wrote to Frank Davey at *Open Letter* with directions on arranging his manuscript: "Here is a new section of Field Notes—'Delphi: Commentary.' each page of the ms is intended as a page in the published version" (591/96.6 43.5). A few days later, on Jan 2, 1983, he again wrote to explain in detail: "My reorganization (notation?) of the right-hand column in the middle allows for some silence following horses ran: on the left; it works better in relation to the next page, in its visual patterning and anticipation; and the stanza of lines consisting each of two words echoes page 15, with its stanza of three-word lines" (591/96.6 43.5).

16 On that same day, in Vienna, January 15, Kroetsch's thoughts characteristically had begun to reach ahead to the next long poem, which would become "Sounding the Name." When his Viennese guide took him to the Kunsthistorisches Museum he picked up three postcards:

"The painter's mother"
"The painter's mother, Detail"
"Rembrandt's mother"

The folder containing the postcards includes a picture of a young woman, standing beside a chair and before a window. On the back of the picture are these words: "HILDA WELLER (KROETSCH) age 16 or 17" This has to be the picture that Kroetsch speaks of in "Birthday: June 26, 1983" (*Completed Field Notes*, 201). The file also contains a note written in Kroetsch's hand: "[S]ee commentary on 'Whistler's Mother*" (591/96.6 47.15)

17 In *Completed Field Notes*, Kroetsch drops a number of passages that had talked about margins (on Nicole Brossard, Derrida, Culler), or sat in the margins—in Latinate diction (196), in puzzling ruminations (197), and in epigrammatic definitions (189). Shirley Neumann has in "Figuring the Reader" patiently worked out the permutations of notation in the poem.

18 When Kroetsch was about to begin *Alberta*, his first travel book, he wrote in gratitude for the help his publisher had provided: "The travel book is beginning to take shape, thanks to Jim Bacque's giving me a peek at Edward McCourt's manuscript. [...] I was somewhat puzzled as to where to begin. Now, when I start to travel about the countryside, I'll know what I'm looking for" (27.1.5).

19 Fiumara identifies "modes of thinking" that we might apply to the listener who moves through Kroetsch's travel poems, "Delphi: Commentary" most of all: "'mild,' 'moderate,' 'modest,' 'available,' 'vulnerable,' 'welcoming,' 'patient,' 'contained,' 'tolerant,' 'conciliating,' 'receptive,' 'pitiful' [...] 'humble' [...] 'poor' [...] 'disciplined' [...], 'vital' (1990, *The Other Side of Language* 69).

20 Fred Wah followed a similar strategy: "I had worked at the utanikki, the poetic journal. [...] I loved that tension between prose and poetry; hence the prose poem. So the prose poem became a compromise for me." www.theglobeandmail.com/arts/books-and-media/fred-wah-a-portrait-in-his-own-words-and-a-few-others/article6628165.

"like when the sun, similarly": Fragmented Fragments in Robert Kroetsch's Chapbook Poetry

Nicole Markotić

1. "as if flight itself was merely"
(*Revisions of Letters Already Sent*)

In a letter to a fellow poet Mário de Sá-Carneiro in March 1916, Fernando Pessoa writes: "I'm having one of those days *in which I never had a future.*"[1] He's speaking of a sorrow that, for him, on this day, is "bottomless," even as he understands the absurdity of such a statement. A month later de Sá-Carneiro killed himself in Paris, another poet whose depression led to a deficient future.

I begin this literary gloom because I often read a touch of analogous melancholy in Robert Kroetsch's poetry, explicitly showing up in *The Sad Phoenician*, but permeating many of his long poems. I'm not suggesting that readers speculate about the poet's frame of mind through a poem's content, but rather that there is a characteristic quixotic melancholia informing much of Kroetsch's poetics. Dennis Cooley notes that "[a]n understated melancholy will eddy through almost everything Kroetsch ever wrote,"[2] Jeffery Donaldson that *The Snowbird Poems* encompass "melancholic nostalgia and beach-ball whimsy,"[3] and Beverly Rasporich that underlying Kroetsch's work is a mournful, romantic, sexual ego, observing that even his fiction is "littered with corpses and bones."[4] But for many critics, the melancholic has been overshadowed by the experimental and the madcap in Kroetsch's writing.

Much has been written about Kroetsch's postmodern fragmentation. Eli Mandel, for example, argues that Kroetsch's *Seed Catalogue* arises "out of terror, out of the losses, out of the shards and fragments of lives, their letters, documents, memories, speech, stories, big stories and little stories, invocations and epilogues, first and last words, loves and deaths, emptiness, all that the prairie wasn't, could not be, its absences, emptiness and fulfillment, the plenitude of being."[5] And Nathan Dueck, writing about "Sketches of a Lemon," says that, "Kroetsch entices readers with fragments vis-à-vis Georges Braque"[6] the painter, a contemporary of Pessoa and de Sá-Carneiro.

Kroetsch's interest in Fernando Pessoa reached across many years and writers. In her review of *Too Bad: Sketches Toward a Self-Portrait*, Judith Fitzgerald calls Pessoa "Kroetsch's "go-to guy.""[7] For good reason! Pessoa's projection of layered alter egos unwrites the conventions of autobiography, as does Kroetsch. In *The Book of Disquiet*, Pessoa's semi-heteronym,[8] Bernardo Soares writes, "I only get up from my chair by making a monstrous effort, but I have the impression that I'm carrying the chair with me, and that it has grown heavier, because it is the chair of subjectivity."[9] Like Kroetsch after him, Pessoa/Soares, feels the weight not only of identity but of the burden of perpetuating a continual and consistent self. "It is Kroetsch, after all," writes Lee Spinks, "who has consistently argued that the post-colonial crisis of identity is engendered by the tyranny of the requirement to produce images of self within the constraints of a colonising discourse."[10] Spinks writes of "Canadian identity," here, his words attesting to the scripted relationship Kroetsch invokes between history and self. In Kroetsch's poem "Pessoa and His Heteronyms" in *Too Bad*, the persona and his daughters sit under a statue of Pessoa in Lisbon; they regard the poet cast in bronze, an immovable weight, and invite him to join them for coffee. "Pessoa didn't so much as crack a smile. / It was one of his many voices that spoke. / From the empty chair I was sitting on."[11] The persona, here, seems to occupy the chair no more than the dead poet he and his daughters address, who is and is not Pessoa; the persona does and does not occupy his chair. Kroetsch and Pessoa: they do and do not present themselves as individuated selves.

2. "It's always already too late to turn back" (*Writer's Block*)

In his poetry made up of sequential fragments, Kroetsch leans into both a disjunctive and narrative impetus. Kroetsch's (mostly uncollected) chapbook poetry consists of numerous small-press publications, in particular the quest narratives *The New World And Finding It* (1999) and *The Lost Narrative of David Thompson & Ten Simple Questions for David Thompson* (2009), the pithy verses itemizing potential ruptures, unfilled gaps[12] in *Writer's Block* (2011), and fragmentary palimpsests in *Revisions of Letters Already Sent* (1993). In *Revisions*, the persona attempts to edit letters previously sent (and presumably already read). For example, he asks a fictional reader to delete the statement that "catastrophe is a shade of blue" and to insert the phrase "the butterfly by the water tank."[13] The entire chapbook consists of fragmented and out-of-context phrases. But these lines do not pretend to be *drafts* of still unfinished letters; rather, they are original lines written after the original letter has already been sent (and supposedly received). These are lines that the persona gifts to the world, though perhaps not to the letter's original recipient. Each page begins with the subtitle "please delete, where indicated" or "please insert, where indicated," but the poem does not offer further typographical (or even fanciful) "indications." The Barthesian writerly reader implicitly knows where the lines belong (wherever they please), just as the Kroetsch reader knows that his lines belong inside unbelonging, "not the usual usual, no, but not the unusual either"[14] is one suggested "insert"; and one suggested deletion promises that "allegories of ice cream announce that angels eat."[15] In these limited edition chapbooks, Kroetsch investigates a challenging poetics that envelopes "the demands fragment makes on us for shaping, for telling, for imagining."[16]

3. "What if I say I love you, and thereby end the poem?" (*Revisions*)

In his "Course in Melancholy," which he led in the fall 2011 at the University of Windsor, poet Alan Davies said that the seventeenth-century English scholar and author of *The Anatomy of Melancholy*, Robert Burton, "both suffered from melancholy, and flourished creatively in the midst of it."[17] Publishing in 1621, Burton designates melancholy as both a passion (of the heart) and a peculiar "anguish of the mind."[18]

For Burton, the cause could be artistic endeavour (writing), as was the treatment (writing); for a poet suffering from melancholy, then, to write operates simultaneously as toxin and remedy. For Burton, melancholy is deeply connected to romantic love as well as to art, explaining why the force of the imagination contributes so greatly to its cause.[19] Pessoa might readily agree. In his letter to Sá-Carneiro, he goes on to strikingly describe periods of overwhelming sadness as "days of the soul."[20] For Pessoa/Soares, "days of the soul" encompass sadness and despair and pain, and are "full of the here and now."[21] Such days send the artist spiralling through anguish, but also prompt innovation's sincere ambition. I cannot help but honour and admire the many "days of the soul" that reverberate from reading Kroetsch's poetry: directing readers toward the inexpressible, grounding us in the here and the now. Inside many of his fragment poems, inside those bits and pieces and splinters, readers may discover elaborate worlds: blistering and desperate and electric and exquisite.

The New World and Finding It conveys the settler story of North America. Indeed, the persona includes advice such as "If sailing, steer towards the setting sun"[22] and the pointed observation that "The New World has, as you might not / have noticed, strings attached."[23] This "New World," the persona avows, "is the color of blood."[24] The title gestures toward the instability of the discovery narrative within colonial exploration (and subsequent exploitation upon "finding" a continent already inhabited): first comes the idea of a "New World," and then follows an adventure aimed at the fertile ideal.

The persona in this chapbook shows up as interested in seduction as much as in exploration: the two intertwine repeatedly. Yet, even as he mentions that explorers must "Consider the consequences / of a first kiss,"[25] he adds that "The New World is its own alibi. It was never there,"[26] conflating the need to cloak an exploitative narrative with the need to achieve imaginary identity, even an identity with—and maybe especially for—place. Given that where we're heading does not exist in the present (maybe never will), the aim to get there becomes tinged with sorrow: "Try crossing the street with your eyes shut to get to what / you read in the morning newspaper is absolutely / A New World."[27] This new world is difficult to pin down, a world hiding inside the declared self, a drastic version of what we think we know, a beckoning by the alien and the familiar, a trust in the partial story: "The poem as big as a continent."[28]

4. "How does one prepare for disorder? (Do not repeat the question)" (*The New World and Finding It*)

But sadness is not necessarily sad, any more than debris need be trash. "What if the scraps *are* the story?"[29] Kroetsch asks. He wishes, he says, to "read the gaps, the silences, the long story behind the snapshot that captures a split second of time and fixes it in a small and unmoving frame."[30] Kroetsch's writings show a wariness with regards to displays of authorial dominance and clout, and so disrupt and disturb genre expectations as a way to subvert the story (such as by writing an "autobiography of a wedding dress" in *The Puppeteer*, or by dispersing the concept of a "life story" when one persona finds he can "hack into his life"[31] in *Too Bad*).

According to Cooley, Kroetsch "warns against notions that one's very own personal and unique voice speaks in a text. He endorses polyvocality and recommends a mix of discourses, not to mention awareness that in writing one is always in a position of derivation and refraction."[32] The short poem "Self-Expression," in *Writer's Block*, parodies the possibility of its title: "The poet meant to show off / his new underwear. / He forgot he wasn't wearing any."[33] Aside from the obvious punchline humour, the poem's scenario also challenges the certainty of a unified subject. The poet who "shows off" hasn't the same sense of his body as the individual who decided to get dressed without underwear. There is a temporal gap in memory between dressing and undressing, just as there are many generative gaps between the imagined and the real. To adapt Adorno, art mediates the imaginary through fragments. For Kroetsch, poetry and disjunctive narrative occupy the same literary frame; the investment in progress (social and literary) now correlates to hesitation and indeterminacy, wherein, one "should, if not in doubt, turn back."[34]

Brian McHale says that what to poetry readers may come across as "authentic autobiography, spoken in the poet's own persona," is surely "a fallacy, an optical illusion."[35] Kroetsch's own words play with, perpetuate, and underline such optical illusions. In the long poem "Spending the Morning on the Beach," in *Seed Catalogue*, the persona announces: "I can no longer keep a journal. My life erases everything I write."[36] Debra Dudek posits that after that line, "the poet's persona no longer exists in the first person";[37] from that point in the series, "the poet becomes *he*."[38] That "third-person *he*," says Dudek, "apprehends the poem or poetry as an object of his thought from which he is separated.

He exists in an independent clause performing an action that is not the act of writing poetry."[39] For Kroetsch, that dynamic separation helps generate the writing act. Writing against projected implications infuse Kroetsch's essays and also generate poems that acclaim the fragment. As I noted above, *Revisions of Letters Already Sent* revels in the partial, the edited out, the incomplete. The poems include ambiguous lines— such as "crowned with a radish crown, the first," "stenography, among other," and "the noon's slice of cucumber, the ancient"[40]—that unambiguously cut into an unknown, yet decisively prior text.

Speaking about the long poem, Kroetsch writes: "The story as fragment *becomes* the long poem: the story becomes its own narrative; i.e., our interest is in, not story, but the *act* of telling the story."[41] Such a declaration is not far from Adorno's examination of aesthetics when he writes: "The fragment is that part of the totality of the work that opposes totality."[42] For Kroetsch, the *process* comprises the artistic moment. "Completing" a world settles the dynamic fragments too categorically, too successfully. For Kroetsch and Adorno, the world is comprised of splinters and slivers, not an immaculate and solid whole. "Compulsory unification serves only to fragment,"[43] says Adorno, whereas multiplicity grounds art's "truth-content"; Kroetsch, metaphorically nodding, adds that the falling apart of the Canadian story is what holds it together.[44] Stability is a dream, a reverie that, crashing, anticipates the "days of the soul." The "limits of language are such," writes Kroetsch, "that all should be written down."[45] Ultimately, the ending delays us: "The way is old and lined with corpses."[46]

5. "The blunder allows us into the world" (*New World*)

Kroetsch's fragment is an oblique act of narrative poetics. When asked about the function of narrative in his poetry, Kroetsch replied that the reason he likes the anecdote is because we "think by story."[47] Ultimately, "we're fragmented human beings and the fragment speaks to what we are."[48] Kroetsch here flirts with the possibility that fragments can make a grander world, but that only the fragment can engage a reader's interest. Anything larger is by default less productive for writer and reader. How then to fit entire worlds into each word?

Ironically, Kroetsch's fragment-tilting poems tend to fall into the category of "long poem." As Dennis Cooley remarks, for Kroetsch, objects serve as "a pretext for a long poem": "A stone hammer. A ledger. A seed catalogue."[49] But in *The Sad Phoenician*, Cooley argues, the poet taps not a found object *per se*, but the "compendium of words available in the public domain—invented by no one apparently, and belonging to no one."⁵⁰ Ultimately, says Cooley, *The Sad Phoenician* is a joyful assortment of "puzzling references, contradictions, nagging repetitions" and "what may or may not be non sequiturs."⁵¹ And when Spinks insists that for Kroetsch "the idea of identity is inextricably linked to the function of language as a model of representation and communication,"⁵² he expands his argument to include an understanding of "the freedom and the terror" of the enduringly linguistic relationship between the self and world."⁵³ Those pesky "and/but" reprises that open every line, or line every opening: How can the poet ever *complete* himself when there's so much more language to consider? Or as Pessoa declares: "Without syntax, there is no lasting emotion."⁵⁴

The letter I quote at this essay's opening—from Pessoa to de Sá-Carneiro—forms the epigraph to a book ostensibly written by one of Pessoa's alter egos, Bernardo Soares. In a splendid resemblance to the narrative arc in *The Hornbooks of Rita K*, Pessoa's uncompleted manuscript was literally found written on disordered scraps of paper in a trunk after his death. In *The Hornbooks of Rita K*, the archivist, "Raymond," organizes scraps into a somewhat cohesive book-length manuscript. But "Rita's hornbooks," Dawne McCance argues, "subvert the perspectivist illusion of a detached and confinable subject; autobiography as trait [...] enacts the possibility, the necessity, of going outside of oneself."⁵⁵ Again and again in Kroetsch's poetry, the persona "goes outside" the constructed aura of the forlorn self. According to McCance, the self is "caught in a double bind, where to write is, already, to differ from oneself."⁵⁶ Pessoa/Soares writing about art and love (and melancholia) beckon to Kroetsch, infusing his ideas about literary estrangement and the fragmentary nature of writing any taxonomy of "self."

6. "What does your map map?"
(TEN SIMPLE QUESTIONS FOR DAVID THOMPSON)

Ryan Fitzpatrick makes the claim that "Kroetsch's stabilizing spatial production works alongside a postmodern practice that values the destabilizing tactics of fragmentation and discontinuity."⁵⁷ So, the very repetitions that provide structure also give clues to the subverting of structure itself.

In his "scraps" of books, those chapbook poems that accentuate the fragment, Kroetsch turns to an emphatic theme of his work, the idea of discovering thing or place (the New World, David Thompson's travels, corrections to missives). "Life impairs the expression of life. If I were to live a great love, I would never be able to describe it,"[58] writes Pessoa/ Soares, in a small essay, "Aesthetics of Artifice." I read these words and hear echoes of Kroetsch's parallel summons to his lover/companion in *The New World and Finding It*. "The New World," the persona claims, "is over there. It is always over there. You cannot avoid finding it. Nor can it be found."[59] Not being able to do the thing that you're doing, might be the quintessential definition of Kroetschian writing.

Frequently, in formal talks and in casual conversation, I have heard Kroetsch paraphrase Gertrude Stein: "If you can do a thing, why bother?" That question invigorates his writing,[60] and appears as a defining paradox throughout his poetry and much of his fiction. In preparing for the journey of discovering the "New World," Kroetsch's persona offers tongue-in-cheek advice: "You must read opening paragraphs only." You must "[r]emember to carry a toothbrush," and you must "[t]hrow away all current maps and read the palm of your / lover's left hand."[61] Art guides the multiplicity of the heart to the world; art ushers in further worlds.

7. "yes, but I meant" (*REVISIONS*)

In the push and pull of fabulated meanderings, Kroetsch both rejoices in and undercuts the authority of the conqueror. In *The New World and Finding It* and *The Lost Narrative of David Thompson & Ten Simple Questions for David Thompson*, each persona's preoccupations become high concepts the poet must unearth and expose, in order to interrogate the not-yet-discovered as somehow pristine cultural capital. *The New World and Finding It* plays on the narrative of colonialization (in what way is the world new? to whom?), yet also delights in persona and reader claiming love as fresh or innovative or in any way untried. Adorno remarks that "[t]he new is the longing for the new, not the new itself."[62] Kroetsch captures that impossibility when his persona advises: "Take with you, on a journey, since you feel you must, seeds. Sterile / seeds, preferably. Let the garden grow you, not you the garden."[63] In these lines, he gives advice and makes admonishments—"take with you" since "you feel you must"; the colonizer brings the old world with him, even as he forages into the new. Go, wander into this unfamiliar place, and immediately plant something to make it familiar to you. A contradiction that has demarcated history; a folly that has invented the present tense.

But will the person who insists on bringing seeds from another soil be able to heed the advice to *not* plant a garden, but to let the garden grow him? Or does Kroetsch wryly point out that the concept of garden itself might be an old-world concept? "Proceed knowing nothing," the persona recommends and, one stanza later "[p]roceed as planned."[64] One cannot, of course, do both. To fully explore the poem, one must, of course, manage both. Deceitful contradictions and dazzling ambiguities lie at the heart of Kroetsch's poetry. Inside the heart sprout sentence morsels. And inside those morsel sequences flourishes an achingly gorgeous melancholy.

8. "you say you could not live in the landscape and yet you" (*REVISIONS*)

The Lost Narrative of David Thompson takes on the vast topic of explorers and the so-called untouched lands they surveyed. In this chapbook, purportedly "edited" by Robert Kroetsch, the bits and pieces of narrative come to the reader via Charlotte Small, the Indigenous woman who married explorer David Thompson. Charlotte wears a necklace of porcupine quills, but David Thompson doesn't notice, even as he inscribes every detail of his explorations onto paper. "The West is tangled," the male persona tells readers, "A sheet of paper is neat,"[65] presumably at its most tidy when still blank, pristine, awaiting the certainty of ink. According to Charlotte, while David embraces tomorrow, she rinses the heart of a caribou, and in doing so, prompts readers to recognize her vibrant role in the explorations: she is the guide with knowledge of the flora and fauna, she is the one who "could smell water," she is the narrative core of David's story, even as he, with his "courage and arithmetic" measures the "wisdom of coffins."[66] The two characters love in the direction of heartache, and David Thompson persists in writing that direction onto his maps.

In Kroetsch's companion chapbook, ostensibly addressed to the explorer by an unnamed, obdurate persona, *Ten Simple Questions for David Thompson* invokes the historical figure at the same time that it speaks to his poetic resonance. The text constructs Thompson as a literary anecdote, remarking that contemporary provincial officials, in naming the David Thompson Highway, "think you were a road."[67] With a metonymical remark like that, Kroetsch plunges readers into what Camelia Elias calls "oracular reading."[68] The answer is not the answer, but the question bestows a particular attention onto the word as world.

Elias wants to read the literary fragment not only as a perception of partiality, but as a "force," denoting a state both real and imagined, through which, Kroetsch might add, "poetry and potatoes certainly may appear in the same / sentence."[69] The fragment, says Elias, through "definitions of incompleteness," imply ruin and residue,[70] rather than a long (though perhaps jagged around the edges) poem. But fragments don't just offer pieces of a narrative whole, the pieces propose information that does not require more story: a grocery list, or an inventory of absences in the prairies, or the repetition of why one should not bite into a freshly squeezed lemon. As Cooley reminds readers, that list of absences in *Seed Catalogue* "unlists itself."[71]

Thus the fragment operates in Kroetsch as a positive force. The fragment, in his poetry, suggests the incomplete and the unfinished at the same time as it insists on resistance and resilience. The fragment threatens hegemonic power structures, cultivating incredulity toward unquestioned authority. Though the colonizer narrative prevails, as do those meta-narratives that secure us all inside fixed and knowable mythos, the fragment cracks open cracks. An alibi that flows and eludes, that splinters and dis-locates. As Adorno notes, "Hegel was the first to realize that the end of art is implicit in its concept."[72] The new creatively bursts forth from the prior, and in the process ruptures itself. And the residue of those ruptures do not offer a unifying whole (despite the persistence of such seductive narratives), but promise further euphoric rupturing.

9. "Home is a tent peg. / Home is a man crying in his sleep." (*The Lost Narrative of Mrs. David Thompson*)

The last lines in the *Revisions* chapbook (I won't say, "the ending") kick off with a simile:

> like when the sun, similarly, sinks, or when the last bird leans
> out of the red horizon, or when night fastens, tongue stiff,
> to choke cherry blossom[73]

"[L]ike when the sun, similarly," might read as unnecessary recurrence, but without the "original" already-sent letter, how can the reader possibly know whether the "similarly" emphasizes the "like" or points to another similarity with suns and whatever comparison the writer has hitherto made? The long line in the long poem pushes farther and farther away from the left-justified margin. Not to get away, and not to blossom into reiterative completeness. But for the pleasure of the leaving and coming home and leaving, for the breathlessness of that melancholic turn.

> The tern, migrating. The seed gone to flower. Metaphor is
> For longing only. Migrating. The turn.[74]

Works Cited

Adorno, Theodore. 1997. *Aesthetic Theory*. Edited by Gretel Adorno and Rolf Tiedemann. Translated by Robert Hullot-Kentor. London: Bloomsbury.

Burton, Robert. 1938. *The Anatomy of Melancholy*. Edited by Floyd Dell and Paul Jordan-Smith. New York: Tudor.

Cooley, Dennis. 2016. *The Home Place: Essays on Robert Kroetsch's Poetry*. Edmonton: University of Alberta Press.

Davies, Alan. 2011. "A Course in Melancholy." Seminar discussion, University of Windsor, September 19, 2011.

Donaldson, Jeffery. 2006. "Prairie Poetry Reviews." *The University of Toronto Quarterly* 75 (1) (Winter): 39–48.

Dudek, Debra. 2008. "'Prairie as Flat as the Sea': Realizing Robert Kroetsch's 'Spending the Morning on the Beach.'" *West of Eden: Essays on Canadian Prairie Literature*, edited by Sue Sorensen, 260–71. Winnipeg: CMU Press.

Dueck, Nathan. 2017. "Drafts of Kroetsch's 'Sketches of a Lemon'." *Robert Kroetsch: Essays on His Works*, edited by Nicole Markotić, 166–69. Toronto: Guernica.

Elias, Camelia. 2004. *The Fragment: Towards a History and Poetics of a Performative Genre*. Berlin: Peter Lang Publishers.

Fitzgerald, Judith. 2010."Review: Too Bad." *The Globe and Mail*. May 7, 2010. Accessed August 2, 2017. https://beta.theglobeandmail.com/arts/books-and-media/review-too-bad-sketches-toward-a-self-portrait-by-robert-kroetsch/article4318387/?ref=http://www.theglobeandmail.com&.

Fitzpatrick, Ryan. 2017. "'Does the City Give Us the Poems? Or Do the Poems Give Us the City?': Robert Kroetsch's Spatial Assemblages." In *Robert Kroetsch: Essays on His Works*, edited by Nicole Markotić, 57–76. Toronto: Guernica.

Kroetsch, Robert. 1995. "D-Day and After: Remember a Scrapbook I Cannot Find." In *A Likely Story*, 127–147. Red Deer, AB: Red Deer College Press.

———. 2001. *The Hornbooks of Rita K.* Edmonton: University of Alberta Press.

———. 2017. "How Do You Interview a Poet? A Conversation with Robert Kroetsch." Interview by University of Windsor graduate students. In *Robert Kroetsch: Essays on His Works*, edited by Nicole Markotić, 205–22. Toronto: Guernica.

———. 1982. *Labyrinths of Voice: Conversations with Robert Kroetsch.* Edmonton: NeWest Press.

———. 2009. *The Lost Narrative of Mrs. David Thompson*, edited by Robert Kroetsch. Windsor, ON: Wrinkle Press.

———. 1989. *The Lovely Treachery of Words: Essays Selected and New.* Oxford: Oxford University Press.

———. 1999. *The New World and Finding It.* Salt Spring Island, BC: (m)Öthêr Tøñgué Preš.

———. 1993. *Revisions of Letters Already Sent.* Calgary: disOrientation chapbooks.

———. 1986. "Spending the Morning on the Beach." In *Seed Catalogue*, 29–43. Winnipeg: Turnstone Press.

———. 1979. "Statements by the Poets: Seed Catalogue." In *The Long Poem Anthology*, edited by Michael Ondaatje, 311. Toronto: Coach House Press.

———. 2009. *Ten Simple Questions for David Thompson.* Windsor, ON: Wrinkle Press.

———. 2010. *Too Bad.* Edmonton: University of Alberta Press.

———. 2011. *Writer's Block.* Vernon, BC: Greenboathouse Press.

Lee, Spinks. 1993. "Towards a Poetic Economy of the Self: Robert Kroetsch's The Sad Phoenician." *British Journal of Canadian Studies* 8 (2): 219–29.

McHale, Brian. 2004. *The Obligation toward the Difficult Whole: Postmodernist Long Poems.* Tuscaloosa: University of Alabama Press.

McCance, Dawne. 1998. "On the Art of Building in Ten Hornbooks." *The New Quarterly* 18 (1) (Spring): 161–73.

Pessoa, Fernando. 1998. *The Book of Disquiet: Composed by Bernardo Soares, Assistant Bookkeeper in the City of Lisbon.* Translated by Alfred Mac Adam Boston: Exact Change.

———. 2001. *The Book of Disquiet.* Edited and translated by Richard Zenith. London: Penguin.

Rasporich, Beverly J. 2015. "Studly Men and Postmodern Possibilities: Robert Kroetsch and Leonard Cohen." *Made-in-Canada Humour: Literary, Folk, and Popular Culture*, 144–49. Amsterdam: John Benjamins Publishing.

Notes

1. Fernando Pessoa. 1998. *The Book of Disquiet: Composed by Bernardo Soares, Assistant Bookkeeper in the City of Lisbon*, trans. Alfred Mac Adam (Boston: Exact Change), xxv.
2. Dennis Cooley. 2016. *The Home Place: Essays on Robert Kroetsch's Poetry* (Edmonton: University of Alberta Press), 186.
3. Jeffery Donaldson. "Prairie Poetry Reviews." *The University of Toronto Quarterly.* 75, no. 1 (Winter 2006): 45.
4. Beverly J. Rasporich. 2015. "Studly men and postmodern possibilities: Robert Kroetsch and Leonard Cohen." *Made-in-Canada Humour: literary, folk, and popular culture* (Amsterdam: John Benjamins Publishing), 148.
5. Cooley, 118.
6. Nathan Dueck. 2017. "Drafts of Kroetsch's 'Sketches of a Lemon'." *Robert Kroetsch: Essays on His Works.* Ed. Nicole Markotić (Toronto: Guernica), 167–68.
7. Judith Fitzgerald. "Review: Too Bad." *The Globe and Mail.* 7 May. 2010. Accessed August 2, 2017. https://beta.theglobeandmail.com/arts/books-and-media/review-too-bad-sketches-toward-a-self-portrait-by-robert-kroetsch/article4318387/?ref=http://www.theglobeandmail.com&
8. Pessoa crafted over 70 heteronyms. Of Soares he wrote, "He's a semi-heteronym because his personality, although not my own, doesn't differ from my own but is a mere mutilation of it." Letter to Adolfo Casais Monteiro, 13 Jan. 1935, in *The Book of Disquiet*, trans. Richard Zenith (London: Penguin), 474.
9. Pessoa, 81.
10. Lee Spinks. 1993. "Towards a Poetic Economy of the Self: Robert Kroetsch's The Sad Phoenician." *British Journal of Canadian Studies*, 8, no. 2: 219.
11. Robert Kroetsch. 2010. *Too Bad* (Edmonton: University of Alberta Press), 65.
12. That dreaded phenomenon that Kroetsch, in *The Lovely Treachery of Words*, calls the "speechless clarity of a blank page" (x).
13. Robert Kroetsch. 1993. *Revisions of Letters Already Sent.* (Calgary: disOrientation chapbooks), n.p.
14. Kroetsch, n.p.
15. Kroetsch, n.p.
16. Robert Kroetsch. *Labyrinths of Voice: Conversations with Robert Kroetsch.* 1982 (Edmonton: NeWest Press), 167.
17. Alan Davies. Seminar discussion. September 19, 2011.

18 Robert Burton. 1938. *The Anatomy of Melancholy*. Eds. Floyd Dell and Paul Jordan-Smith (New York: Tudor), 149.

19 Burton, 220. I mention the Davies seminar and the connection Burton makes between writing and melancholy in my critical book, *Disability in Film and Literature*. 2016 (McFarland & Co.), 19–20.

20 Pessoa, xxv.

21 Pessoa, xxvi.

22 Robert Kroetsch. *The New World and Finding It*. (Salt Spring Island, BC: (m)Öthêr Tøñgué Presš, 1999), n.p.

23 Kroetsch, n.p.

24 Kroetsch, n.p.

25 Kroetsch, n.p.

26 Kroetsch, n.p.

27 Kroetsch, n.p.

28 Robert Kroetsch. 1979. "Statements by the Poets: Seed Catalogue." *The Long Poem Anthology*, edited by Michael Ondaatje (Toronto: Coach House), 311.

29 Robert Kroetsch. 1995. "D-Day and After: Remember a Scrapbook I Cannot Find." *A Likely Story* (Red Deer, AB: Red Deer College Press), 136; my emphasis.

30 Robert Kroetsch, 136.

31 *Too Bad*, 78.

32 Cooley, 39.

33 Robert Kroetsch. 2011. *Writer's Block*. (Vernon, BC: Greenboathouse Press), n.p.

34 *The New World*, n.p.

35 Brian McHale. 2004. *The Obligation toward the Difficult Whole: Postmodernist Long Poems* (Tuscaloosa: University of Alabama Press), 149. The example McHale uses is John Ashbery's poem "The Skaters."

36 Robert Kroetsch. 1986. "Spending the Morning on the Beach." *Seed Catalogue* (Winnipeg: Turnstone Press), 31.

37 Debra Dudek. 2008. "'Prairie as Flat as the Sea': Realizing Robert Kroetsch's 'Spending the Morning on the Beach'." *West of Eden: Essays on Canadian Prairie Literature*. Ed. Sue Sorensen (Winnipeg: CMU Press), 268.

38 Dudek, 268.

39 Dudek, 269.

40 *Revisions of Letters*, n.p.

41 *The Lovely Treachery of Words*, 120.

42 Theodore Adorno. 1997. *Aesthetic Theory*, eds. Gretel Adorno and Rolf Tiedemann, trans. Robert Hullot-Kentor (London: Bloomsbury,) 61.
43 Adorno, xii.
44 *The Lovely Treachery of Words*, 21–22.
45 *The Lovely Treachery of Words*, 120.
46 *Writer's Block*, n.p.
47 Robert Kroetsch. 2017. "How Do You Interview a Poet? A Conversation with Robert Kroetsch" interview by University of Windsor graduate students. *Robert Kroetsch: Essays on His Works*. Ed. Nicole Markotić, (Toronto: Guernica), 207.
48 Kroetsch, 206–7.
49 Cooley, 201.
50 Cooley, 201.
51 Cooley, 213.
52 Spinks, 220.
53 Spinks, 221.
54 Pessoa, 8.
55 Dawne McCance. "On the Art of Building in Ten Hornbooks." *The New Quarterly*, vol 18, no. 1 (Spring 1998): 164.
56 McCance, 168.
57 Ryan Fitzpatrick. 2017. "'Does the city give us the poems? Or do the poems give us the city?': Robert Kroetsch's Spatial Assemblages." *Robert Kroetsch: Essays on His Works*. Ed. Nicole Markotić (Toronto: Guernica, 61).
58 Pessoa, 148.
59 *The New World*, n.p.
60 As questions often did; in his essay on the scrapbook as literary form, Kroetsch writes, "I am much more interested in the questions we ask ourselves, than in the answers we hide behind" ("D-Day and After…" 131).
61 *The New World*, n.p.
62 Adorno, 44.
63 *The New World*, n.p.
64 *The New World*, n.p.
65 Robert Kroetsch. 2009. *The Lost Narrative of Mrs. David Thompson* (Edited by Robert Kroetsch) (Windsor: Wrinkle Press), n.p.
66 Robert Kroetsch. 2009.
67 Robert Kroetsch. 2009. *Ten Simple Questions for David Thompson* (Windsor: Wrinkle Press), n.p.

68 Camelia Elias. 2004. *The Fragment: Towards a History and Poetics of a Performative Genre* (Berlin: Peter Lang Publishers). Elias defines "oracular reading" as "opening a book and asking a question" (243).
69 *Revisions of Letters*, n.p.
70 Elias, 2.
71 Cooley, 94. Cooley remarks later in the book: "There is an awful lot of [lists] in Kroetsch, ampersands without end" (279).
72 Adorno, 44.
73 *Revisions of Letters*, n.p.
74 *Revisions of Letters*, n.p.

Sketches of a Layman
Laurie Ricou

> *Maybe I'm just a transmitter.*
> —Robert Kroetsch, "On Tour"

> *Risk it, dear reader.*
> — Robert Kroetsch, "Risking It"

> *before you reach conclusions, consider this:*
> *he was mostly unaware most of the time,*
> — Robert Kroetsch, "About Poetic Hope"

1.

We danced, Bob and I, in a slightly stumbling *pas de deux*, at the University College of the Cariboo.[1] We titled our dialogue "Making a Grass of Yourself: Small Cities Up Close" (Kroetsch 2003). We were trying, you see, to get down close to the ground, to feel its textures and plant cover. A few days later, Bob sent me a photocopy of his suite of Kamloops poems titled "This Part of the Country." And scrawled on the first page, in pencil, this message:

> Laurie, just to say, it was great, shamelessly stealing your ideas in public. (Ricou fonds, box 4, folder 5)

Such seemingly casual, cryptic gifting is typical of Kroetsch—the informality of pencil, erasable and faint; the spur of the moment gesture posing as speech; the crafty incidental ("just to say"); alertness to a fleeting truth (*just…*); the stop-and-go syntax (three commas in a short sentence); the hint of risqué exposure. It's great that Bob always lets generosity displace his own achievement and stature. He was writer-in-residence at UCC that term, the artist, the star of the show. Not I. But he deferred. Allegiance to the *small* city, with a self-burlesquing session title. The stuff of a lay poetic.

> *How can one argue that a layman*
> *is truly a layman,*
> *if the question can be argued?*
>
> So much for that.[2]

2.

Here and there I have written about Kroetsch and landscape, and Kroetsch and syntax, and Kroetsch's demotic poetics. Now, from the vantage point of forty-seven years of friendship, forty-seven years of conviviality and delightful orneriness, I just want to speak a tribute: I am going to talk about how Kroetsch has influenced students. Which is to say, of course, that somehow I want to talk about how he is still influencing me.

> RK from Winnipeg, 23 September 1982
>
> the spirit of the students
> is high
> and teaching
> this year
> is a gigantic pleasure
> (Ricou fonds, box 4 folder 3)

Our legacy. His students.

3.

Judi Walker, in a paper for a course titled Prairie Regionalism, proposed that Kroetsch's boisterous zest for the absurd challenges any sense of a sacred landscape. Then she challenges his challenge: "But, alas, too late Kroetsch has already gone after the other big pie. He has dared to rewrite and prairicize (if that's a word) mythology."

Judi, student in high spirits, a dear reader, risked it. Slightly sketchy. Joyfully bemused. Mixing metaphors. Making a verb from a noun. Judi wrote thirty pages when ten were called for.

4.

> Sketches, I reminded myself
> not of a cleric
> nor of a professional
> nor of a Dr Ph D
> nor of a teacher
> nor, for that matter,
> of a writer.

The year Judi prairicized was the year my children first met Bob. He was writer-in-residence at the University of Lethbridge in spring 1976, and a frequent visitor in our home. At a very young age these students—my kids—seem to have been impressed. They trusted this writer because he had no pretensions as a Writer. No clerical role, no obligation to maintain or honour the sacred. The laywriter. Apparently with no formal training. Lay-man from Greek *laikos*, from *laos*, "people." Belongs to the people.

Bob read at the University of British Columbia November 17, 1978, just after I began teaching at UBC. He stayed in our home. My daughter, age six, was trying to write a story. In his letter thanking us for the hospitality, he also made sure to salute his very young student: "Lian[e]'s story," he enthused, "was her first masterpiece" (Ricou fonds box 4 folder 3). So, a few years later, age thirteen or so, when asked to present on a poem for her English class, she is comfortably prompt to make an odd choice—she would discuss Robert Kroetsch's "Sketches of a Lemon" (Kroetsch 2000, 76–80).

5.

> A lemon is almost round
> he'd say
> then
> A lemon is not round.
>
> I don't get it
> I said
>
> Now we're getting somewhere
> he said

Why "Sketches of a Lemon"? Well, as I've said, personal contact encourages risking it. While the poem's indulging a private comfort against self-questioning affirms our need for literature—as for food, the tang of lemon. In my world, the poem bridges a nurturing and enduring friendship—Bob to "Laurie & Treva" to Smaro—and the hopes for futures "glistening with dew" (Kroetsch 2000, 77): father to daughter to granddaughter. Years later, in June 2012, my eldest granddaughter, age six, had written her first story: "un fois," she wrote, "il y a un mouton qui s'appelle moumou."

So, if "Sketches" is not as community voiced as *Seed Catalogue*, nor as politically astute as *Badlands*, it is the very model of a long poem. Which is to say a tartly brief longueur.

6.

So, Dennis and David and Wolfgang and Aritha, I'd say "Sketches of a Lemon" might be Kroetsch's defining astringent poem. It pays homage to plums and to red wheelbarrows, and to blackbirds—and to a dozen ways of *looking at*. It refers explicitly to Francis Ponge: akin to Ponge's blackberry, Bob's fruit is plumped with a drop of ink (Ponge). And it keeps calling out to Smaro, who at the time was raising questions about the essential properties of the long poem.[3] The poem keeps calling out to the poet and critic at home—for help, or support, or simply a response.

"Sketches," as Kroetsch's title modestly signals, is a simple poem about simple things. Which is not to say it's not thoughtful, or intelligent, or intellectually stimulating. It's all of that. But its spare lines and taste for monosyllabic or two-syllable vocabulary tease with promises of directness and accessibility. He asks us to read, in a poem, an unpoetic phrase, an open gesture of non-conclusion: *so much for that*—the poet's poetics of frustrated resignation puts the reader's puzzlement at the heart of reading.

Bob and I used to have a running joke. Every time I spoke at a conference he attended, or had him visit a class, or introduced him as a speaker, I would boast of being his most enthusiastic admirer—and then go on to lament that I didn't understand anything he wrote. And Bob would respond with enthusiasm for all such *not-understanding*. It was the key, he'd imply. By evading understanding he invites (speculative) interpretation, alerts us. Tell it slant, he might have said. Before you reach conclusions, he'd warn. I am mostly unaware most of the time, he'd confess. *Almost* round. [But] *not* round. *Some* lemons. A [single and singular] lemon. All true. All contradictory. Embrace each line, each proposition, in the joy of believing, while simultaneously—imparting the brio—sensing an inherent transience.

7.

That my daughter Liane would choose this poem as a class project—with minimal coaching from her father—rather than Wordsworth's "Daffodils," or "Dover Beach," says something about Kroetsch's influence. "Sketches of a Lemon," however philosophically subtle, or cagily deceptive, inscribes the immediate and available. It has a bit of "Alligator Pie" in it, but without the exotic animal. It muses about a fruit at hand. Lemon repeats in a dozen different contexts: looking for one in the refrigerator; cooking; a cure for colds; biting into one. The routines of daily life. So the play—one could go on—invites extension, demands repetition. I think Liane, in her response, wrote a parody. And the opaque Bigness of capital P Poetry, demanding reverence in classroom and Library, is nicely punctured. Lay: a short narrative poem, especially one to be sung. So much for that.

Bob's poem feels like "kid's stuff"; the "phrasing seems clumsy or naïve," and we, child and adult, sense that "a child could do that" (Chamberlin 2004, 119–20).[4] Let the lemon surprise you he said, or should have.

Now you are recognizing that I don't want to talk much about *whom* he influenced, but about how he influenced. About the process.

Laurie Ricou

8.

Sketches of a lemon to—in his last published book—sketches toward a self-portrait. Not to mention field notes, a kinship genre, also en plein air. Stephen Leacock wrote them, and Emily Carr. Hugh Hood on Leacock (re. his own *Around the Mountain*):

> He's thinking of that water-colour or pencil portfolio that an *amateur* artist might have collected—*perhaps a woman artist*—in the 80s. The characteristics of these are an *agreeable tenuousness*, an endearing tentative quality . . . the lines are done deliberately with haste and with a hit-or-miss accuracy because accuracy is not what is aimed at. Evocation is what is aimed at. (New 1987, 99; my emphases)[5]

So you write about what you know by writing about what you've lived immediately. Maybe not *that you know*, but an illusion about what you persuade yourself you've made contact with. Then you toss it about, floating and burying its sounds and senses until the delta of language changes you (and it) every which way.

Kroetsch's "Letter from China" is addressed to his daughters:

> I think of you, my daughters, there on the other side of the
>   world, as
> innocent of China today as I was yesterday. We come unaware to
>   these tidal
> changes in our lives. (Kroetsch 2000, 160)

And these remarks are in some measure addressed to my daughter. Listen, I would say, to his amazement at the everyday, often intensified, reinforced—and surely complicated—by repetition:

> I saw an old man, walking. In a garden. In a garden that to me seemed to be a maze, a pattern of hedges and paths; one of those gardens designed especially to tease us out of our habitual ways....Himself stopping, now and then; he watched those about him, doing tai chi, while I watched him watching.

Then, immediately, the hesitancy, the utterly commonplace expression, twisted here and there with a quiet bit of trickery and questioning (and surprise):

> I was lost and trying to find a post office. I wanted to mail
> 	you a card I
> had written. In a Chinese post office there's a little brush
> 	and a glue
> pot, so you can seal your letter. (Kroetsch 2000, 167)

You can feel him teaching by not teaching, every syllable.

Here lies the preciousness of friendship and the intensity of memory. Bob the generous teacher, unaware, teaching by declining to teach. I'm stealing your ideas he would say, with delight. That tribute to Liane's "first masterpiece" is both high praise and a challenge to her to work on the second and the twenty-fifth.

Liane was the student closest to home, Kroetsch her surprise tutor. For her, maybe Bob was just a transmitter. Her readiness to tease out the unordinary in the everyday figures in Bob's influence on my postsecondary students, and on me, and through them again on me. Bob wrote his life all his life long in a way that invited his reader to come back with her own stories.

9.

> Anna is mediator
> mediator tells story
> transmitter
> peacemaker

We university types are taught often by the rituals of "scholarship" and peer review and promotion committees not to plagiarize, and always to assimilate and interpret. Here I am shamelessly stealing my students' ideas—without much editing or taming into a thesis.

> [T]he Japanese Morning Glory is a variety of the plant so named because its cultivation and use in décor was hugely popular in nineteenth century Japan. At the very time that Hiroshige was making his woodblock prints of the Tokaido, the Morning Glory was growing in fashion. Here in Kroetsch's poem, the two are brought together again and given further depth through their relationship to The Double Hook. All three, in turn, expand one's reading of The Seed Catalogue. It is a poem about travel, and the stages (or stations) in that travel, always returning to "the home place." Kroetsch's poem can be seen as

> an ode to his mother, each section a reflection on their relationship within their community. As one travels through the poem, one takes the trip back home with the poet. (Peradenic)

I want to respect such comments by letting my student's words stand on their own. I invite you to listen to how they respond and what they guess at. Bob was an influence by being so openly, willingly influenced. Hiroshige to lemons to the Frankfurt Hauptbahnhof. So that he influences you to welcome your own influences. No professional training or designation needed. Sing a lay. Sing like a layman.

> Why, if Anna Dawe is the central character, is so much time spent on her father's expedition?...The important thing is her reactions to and comments on that trip....These parts are, in a sense, her field notes, and chart her progress towards self-realization and a more healthy mental attitude. Thus the main location in the novel is inside her head. She is the mediator of the story, as she says on page 3, in both senses of the word: as the medium through which the story is told, and, in the end, as a kind of peacemaker. (Campbell)

Guesswork. Yet unmade. Tentative. The terms in the vocabulary or architecture of sketchiness create a condition of surprise. In Hugh Hood's phrase, contemplating a sketch the "imagination could wander" (New 1987, 99). The unfinished invigorates. Makes a reader engage where none was before. As Jonah Lehrer wrote in 2012, questioning the protocols of brainstorming: "The obvious answer [stops] being [the] only answer. Even when alternative views are clearly wrong, being exposed to them still expands our creative potential. In a way, the power of dissent is the power of surprise" (Lehrer 2012, 24).

> Kroetsch often wishes to express "noises" for which there are no signs. These [neologisms] and other aspects of Kroetsch's lexicon seem, somehow, to resist their wordness—to try and escape from the hieroglyphics, etymologies, and definitions. (Fero 1991, 18)

> Mine
> This field, this land, this people.
> Repeated over and over until we almost believe
> It's true.

> I'm very suspicious of the word 'truth.' I think those who speak
> of truth often have an agenda. (Ley 2005)

> Bring me the radish seeds,
> my mother whispered.

The radish, like a bulging, pungent, red heart, a basic symbol of life heartens and stimulates....She tends the garden, she nurtures and cultivates the seeds, roots out the latent possibilities, the potentiality of her primary seed, her son....When amid the laughter of the farmhand, he falls off a horse standing still—a horse rooted—without a fuss, but in a somewhat protective manner, she asks for the radish seeds. Thus, the poet's mother, "in / her quiet way of pretend- / ing not to see" [Kroetsch 1995, 114] softens her son's fall....The former voice speaks in the bloom of spring, whereas the latter voice whispers beyond the grave, echoes in memory. By muting his mother's presence, the poet highlights her absence; as a result, her absence becomes her presence. (Szabo)

> The absence of radishes
> The absence of mother
> her absence
> is her presence

Lehm is the German word for loam, clay, mud. The ground in which to insert seed and set roots. A man of the lehm.

10.

I hold on to my students' readings of Kroetsch. And, in turn, when they are given a classroom of their own, they send me the readings their students are trying.[6] Here are two:

> Through...punctuation and chronology, the reader is reminded that the poem is simply Kroetsch's "guesswork," inspired by an ancient rock....The reader must provide his or her own guess as to the function of the stone and the fate of the hand...."[G]uesswork." Despite the

numerical ordering of the sections, the reader soon realizes that any section can precede another [cf. "Sketches of a Lemon"]....[T]he juxtapositions in the poem respond to the juxtapositions which are so much a part of history. Just as no single part of the poem can stand alone, so history, too, must be interlinked with various other events and circumstances.

The maul has been around for millions of years. Thus, to attempt to fix it to a certain point in history would be naïve [note!]. The poem allows us to imagine what functions the stone may have served [will serve?]: however, ultimately this is all guesswork, recognizing as Kroetsch suggests "the primacy of the forthcoming, and *yet* unmade discovery."

11.

> and beer
> with you and Bob
> discussing everything
> in the world
> I did love that

In summer 2011, I was teaching in Trier, staying with Wolfgang Klooss. Bob had emailed: "You are probably, right now,...in that ancient European place, Trier. One of my great-grandmothers was born there. Anna Mormann, b. 1849, married Michael Weller in the USA. Trier and its wine and its beautiful students and those wonderful colleagues who delight in our small giving from the (battered) New World to the Old." The day Bob was killed we received a flurry of emails from many quarters. Several of those came from former students. On June 23, Alanna Fero wrote, perhaps with a touch of whimsy, "I hope you feel there were no words unspoken/written...." The next day Caroline McGechaen, writing from Toronto, remembered "when he came to our class to speak about his writing. He was very engaging." My one-time University of Lethbridge colleague Jeremiah (Jay) Allen wrote at length on June 26 from the Crow's Nest Pass recalling his last encounter with Bob at a poetry reading: "He came to dinner at our house, where he spent most of the evening with Wallis [Jay's wife, a fabric artist], learning about sewing, because a character in the book he was then writing was a seamstress." Now Jay was a good friend when we taught together in Lethbridge, but as will happen, we had neither met nor corresponded since 1980 or 1981. But thirty years later Bob's death prompts Jay's tribute to the term Bob spent with us all as writer-in-residence: "In some ways it may have been the best single semester I had as a professor.... It also seemed to me to represent the very best of liberal arts: me, an economist, always having coffee and beer with you and Bob, discussing everything in the world. I did love that." So, last September we met after those three decades and shared a beer. Bob would love that.

I never heard from any former students when Layton died or Livesay—or even, to choose a more likely figure, when Purdy died. But Bob's influence influenced us differently. Jay wakes us up to our best semester. On June 23 Diana Lake (a student from 1981) wrote from Edmonton with the subject line in lower case "felt the need to connect." Lay. Slang. an instance of sexual intercourse. I remember, she writes, "how you always called him 'Bob Crotch' and I thought you might be feeling sad at his passing." Diana touches on the leman in him. Leman (l-e-m-a-n) ME from lief + man, beloved, willing man. Noun. Archaic. Beloved, sweetheart, mistress. In a sketch we feel a need to connect.

12.

> I had a very strong desire
> To kiss a layman.

In Bob's penultimate email to me, dated 25 April 2011, he surely is transmitting, defining—extravagantly, enigmatically—his own aspirations: "What you have undertaken," he wrote, "as a series of essays on a series of poems/texts is a gift to our culture, from you, a discovery, by you, for us an archaeology of the senses, a language dreaming itself."[7]

> Judi Walker: The writings of Robert Kroetsch are lusty, they're zany, they're spunky, they're wild, they're manic and they're lively. They are also prairie "unmyths" of Odysseys after death. Life and death come together, dance a jig, trade places and become the same thing.

> criticize
> eulogize
> prairicize
> friendship is a risk
> so we risk it
> inventing ourselves again

.

Works Cited

Campbell, Mary. 1976. "Seminar Presentation on Robert Kroetsch's *Badlands*." Unpublished course assignment for English 4001, March 25, 1976. University of Lethbridge.

Chamberlin, J. Edward. 2004. *If This is Your Land, Where Are Your Stories? Finding Common Ground*. Toronto: Vintage Canada/Random House.

Cooley, Dennis. 2016. *The Home Place: Essays on Robert Kroetsch's Poetry*. Edmonton: University of Alberta Press.

———. 1987. "The Vernacular Muse in Prairie Poetry." In *The Vernacular Muse*, 167–222. Winnipeg: Turnstone.

Fero, Alanna. 1991. "Robert Kroetsch Alphabet Book: Sketches of a Thesis." Master's thesis, University of British Columbia.

Kroetsch, Robert. 1995. *A Likely Story: The Writing Life*. Red Deer, AB: Red Deer College Press.

———. 2000. *Completed Field Notes: The Long Poems of Robert Kroetsch*. Edmonton: University of Alberta Press.

———. 2010. *Too Bad: Sketches Toward a Self-Portrait*. Edmonton: University of Alberta Press.

Kroetsch, Robert, and Laurie Ricou. 2003. "Making a Grass of Yourself: Small Cities Up Close." Video Recording. Kamloops, BC: UCC Media Services, Thompson Rivers University Library.

Lehrer, Jonah. 2012. "Groupthink: The Brainstorming Myth." *The New Yorker*, January 30, 2012. Accessed January 19, 2017. http://www.newyorker.com/magazine/2012/01/30/groupthink.

Ley, Susanna. "My Canadian Literature Workbook: The ABCs to Loving Our Words. 'H' Is for Hammer." Unpublished course assignment for English 222/005, November 29, 2005. University of British Columbia.

New, W. H. 1987. *Dreams of Speech and Violence: The Art of the Short Story in Canada and New Zealand*. Toronto: University of Toronto Press.

Peradenic, Amy. 2002. "Annotation #1: *Seed Catalogue*." Unpublished course assignment for English 470B/002, September 26, 2002. University of British Columbia.

Ponge, Francis. 1942. "Blackberries" [Translation of "Les Mures"]. Accessed April 20, 2017. www.babelmatrix.org/works/fr/Ponge,_Francis-1899/Les_Mûres/en/36502-.

Ricou, Laurence (Laurie). Fonds. University of British Columbia Archives.

Szabo, Lisa. 2002. "Cultural Requirements: Robert Kroetsch's *Seed Catalogue*." Unpublished course assignment for English 470B/002, October 17, 2002. University of British Columbia.

Walker, Judith. "Dead or Alive: A Look at Death and Life in the Hit and Myth Writings of Robert Kroetsch." Unpublished course assignment for English 4001, April 9, 1976. University of Lethbridge.

Notes

1. The University College of the Cariboo became Thompson Rivers University in 2005.
2. Fragments of poems not attributed are my parodies or found poems.
3. See Kamboureli, Smaro. 1991. *On the Edge of Genre: The Contemporary Canadian Long Poem*. Toronto: University of Toronto Press.
4. Chamberlin is discussing his ten-year-old daughter's choice of poem to learn in school.
5. W. H. New sketches the characteristics of the form: "[S]hort…stresse[s] the sensorily perceptible…record[s] observable data…a sense of immediacy…the writer is…*present as an observer*" (New 1987, 21–22).
6. These samples of student essays were compiled by Alanna Fero as a teaching aid for English 100/02R. Vancouver, BC. Langara College. Received by the author January 26, 1990. The handout bears the title "Example Essays: *Stone Hammer Poem*." The essay titles are "Parallel Guesswork" and "Flashes of Insight." The authors are not identified.
7. Kroetsch is responding here to a draft of my essay "Binder Twine," later published in *Canadian Literature* 218 (Autumn 2013): 30–44.

Travelling with Kroetsch: Motion, Commotion, Emotion

WOLFGANG KLOOSS

It is the summer of 1998: Kroetsch and Klooss are flying across the River Mosel in a small single-engine airplane.* The world below looks beautiful, the river meandering through meadows and steep hills. And then vineyards. As far as the eye can see—wine.

They had previously driven along the river. Had visited numerous small villages on the banks of the Mosel. But now the world looks different—larger and smaller at the same time. Altitude and velocity open them to new vistas.

Suddenly, a tiny church, carved into the edge of a very steep sandstone cliff, a few nautical miles south of the small town of Saarburg, where, as the name would suggest, a castle presides above the city. Church, town, and castle do not need to be written into existence. They are demonstrably there.

Kroetsch mumbles, his eyes fixed on the seemingly uniform, yet shifting landscape that means region and place. "Look at that, look at that." Later he tells Klooss that he would like to come back, get closer to what he has seen from above. Klooss informs him that there is much more to see. "Is that right?" he enthuses.

---

* The subtitle refers to a short poem Robert Kroetsch wrote for Wolfgang Klooss in 2008. See Metz, Müller, and Schowalter, 3. The author thanks Dennis Cooley and Laurie Ricou for suggestions and editorial advice.

Their meandering is the begining of a journey into the past—a past that resonates in the present, links the remnants of a Celtic sanctuary with a medieval hermitage, a monumental tomb of Bohemian King John the Blind by the Prussian architect Karl Friedrich Schinkel with—as Dennis Cooley has written in a poem—

> [...] graves
> filled with dead soldiers
> many
> 18,19
> Nov 1944
> killed in the last days
>
> *Oct 18, 1944. The call up for the Volkssturm begins in Germany with all able-bodied men from 16 to 60 to be conscripted.*
>
> on a stark cliff above the world going on below
> near a sheer rock
> wall into which men of god had
> burrowed and dug as if for gold
> strange miners lived their lives inside out
> wore like ceintures the rock they had and had not
> spooned out
>
> *they went from strength to strength*
> *their lives were lovely & they died*

(Cooley 2013, 105–06)

Haunting, haunting.

Kroetsch, the poet of graveyards, who writes "in search for the dead" (Kroetsch 1989e, 13), is deeply moved. Here, high above the river, there is no ledger; only endless rows of stones, marked *Unbekannter*—"unknown"—waiting to be turned into story. Cooley asks himself:

> why do we write of the dead to the dead
> *ofthedeadofthedeadofthedead*

> the dead not dead then & we can speak
> to them (must) speak
> for they call & call
> call on us call to us to them (2013, 99)

What do they tell us? How can we fill the haunting silence? It is a journey that connects the Canadian plains with Germany's Rhineland Palatinate.

When Kroetsch first came back to the home country of his German family, he travelled to Trier where he

> expected to see the birthplace of one of [his] ancestors. [He] got into the unknown, even into the unknown, with expectations. [He] expected to find a Kirche where [Anna Mormann, born 1849, his *Urgrossmutter*] went to pray. [He] found a plaque marking the birthplace of Karl Marx. [He] found a Roman spa that dated back to Constantine the (280–337) Great. (Kroetsch 1989d, 200)

Now, in the summer of 1998 the winner of the Governor General's Award for Fiction almost three decades earlier is teaching Canadian literature at Universität Trier, taking his students across the Atlantic to explore with him the prairies of Margaret Laurence, Martha Ostenso, Sinclair Ross, and Frederick Philip Grove, whose German roots were uncovered only decades after he had obscured them in the Canadian west. Among the students are also seniors—real seniors.

Kroetsch presents Hazard Lepage as an agent who glues together fragments of Canadian landscape, history, and people and releases them in a bewildering narrative. In Germany Kroetsch speaks of that story with a mixed group of English majors, non-professional readers of Canadian literature, and retired academics. Given the respectful patience Kroetsch shows for his foreign audience, and his thoughtful and skillful explorations of the assigned readings, students and retirees are quickly drawn into story, become soon acquainted with Hagar Shipley's suppressed emotions, the loneliness of Mark Jordan and Linda Archer, the hardships Mrs. Bentley and Abe Spalding have to endure in a pioneering prairie environment, or the restless wanderings of his own studhorse man across the Canadian plains. All these stories, however alien to the class, echo with the hardships some of the seniors had to cope with in a shaken Germany during the aftermath of the Second World War. And it was in the skies of Cologne, where

Kroetsch's cousin Kenneth MacDonald "was shot down [in 1943] while bombing / the city that was his maternal great grandmother's birthplace. He was the navigator. He guided himself / to that fatal occasion" (Kroetsch 1977, 43). Ironically, MacDonald's return to Germany is a journey into death, to the final destination. Again, prairie Canada and Kroetsch's ancestral home country merge.

Kroetsch's own *"book of final entry / in which a record is kept"* (1989e, 13) reaches deeper into the past. It tells about the long journey his family undertook to get to the New World where Gottlieb Haag's "fortune lay before him." / (*Das ist doch nicht möglich!*) (1989e, 16). What "Old Gottlieb [...] verging on 80 years of age" (1989e, 16), and his relatives found when he reached Ontario and his descendants Alberta in 1905—the year the province was created—is disclosed in a long poem where the stories of Kroetsch's ancestors and their lives in the New World ascend from the graves and collide in a ledger shaped by horizontal and vertical entries. The reader meets James Darling; Nicholas Neubecker; Father Holzer; the Clement family; Joe Hauck, who "got his arm caught in the [mill's] water-wheel [, ...] / screamed [, b]ut no one heard him" (1989e, 20); grandfather Henry; great-grandmother Theresa Tschirhart, "born in Alsace, she spoke / German with a French accent, / English with a German accent, [...] / Married three Bavarians. / Buried three Bavarians. it balances" (1989e, 24); and Aunt Mary, who gave Kroetsch the family ledger. As in so many of his writings, these shifts among local references, anecdotal entries, and plain bookkeeping follow a pattern that mingles geography with history and narrative, to surpass the boundaries of topographical space.

Travel opens up language itself. Accidentally picked-up German words, or contextually motivated phrases such as *Das ist doch nicht möglich!* signal Kroetsch's movement between related, yet diverse linguistic worlds. The language suggests an oral form of transmission, standing in line with the discovery of the obvious: "*Nicht hinauslehnen / Do not lean out*" (1989d, 201). And when Rudy Wiebe showed him Rainer Maria Rilke's word *Lebensgliedes* from the first of "*Sieben Gedichte*" (1915) he inserts it in *Seed Catalogue* (1977, 33) without changing the clause from the genitive to the nominative, which in this context would have been grammatically correct.[1] Quoting Cooley: "It is clear from the archives that what German we find in the long poem has been sought rather than produced with the ease of a native speaker" (Cooley 2016, 309, n. 2).[2] Linguistic borrowings become gifts. At the same time, it shows faith in the non-verbal to overcome the limitations of the dictionary, to—as Kroetsch says—"talk from poetry to prose, from prose into silence" (1989d, 206). How else could the linguistic barriers between an ancient woman with no command of English and her travel companion, the distinguished Canadian writer Robert Kroetsch, be broken down—both of them sharing a train compartment from the city of Graz in Austria's southeast, where Arnold Schwarzenegger was at home, to Switzerland (206). How do words, how does language travel, how do foreign tongues speak to one another?

Movement, travelling, dislocation, disorientation, confusion, and commotion, but also discovery, recognition, and emotion quicken at the core of many of Kroetsch works. When he is lost at Frankfurt Hauptbahnhof, looking for the train to Koblenz, where he would need to find another train to Trier, he encounters a stranger who recognizes his confusion, his inability "to read the schedules and find the track [his] train was on" (207). The man is a little younger, with a beard similar to Kroetsch's. He wears a "green curdoroy jacket, like [Kroetsch's]" (202). The stranger guides the Canadian traveller to the right platform. When Kroetsch is at Frankfurt Hauptbahnhof again, "waiting to take a train out to the airport" (207), he finds it remarkably easy to read the schedules. Kroetsch was saved by his doppelgänger, recognized the self in the other, the other in the self. However far the journey takes the traveller, it ends in self-discovery and it ends at home.

In the summer of 1998, Klooss and Kroetsch were driving along Hunsrück Höhenstraße, where Johannes Bückler (c. 1778–1803), nicknamed Schinderhannes, an apprenticed skinner, was up to mischief in the late eighteenth century; a German outlaw who turned to robbery and break-ins in the Hunsrück region on the west bank of the Rhine, which was then under French occupation. Repeatedly arrested by the Gendarmerie, Bückler again and again escaped his imprisonment, unbuckled the locks as easily as Houdini, and soon became a public hero, before he was sentenced to death and executed by guillotine in Mainz. When they stop at Schinderhannes Turm in the small town of Simmern, Kroetsch is reminded of Bückler's Canadian brother in spirit and action, the Eastern European immigrant John Krafchenko (1881–1914). One hundred years after Schinderhannes, Krafchenko, better known as "Bloody Jack," struck terror on both sides of the US-Canadian border as well as in Europe. Like his "German twin" he repeatedly escaped the police and committed further crimes, until he was finally executed by hangman Arthur Ellis at the provincial jail on Vaughan Street in Winnipeg.[3]

The legend of Schinderhannes has survived in numerous folk tales, in poetry and film—among them Hundshäuter: Aus den versammelten Schriften des Schinderhannes (1996) by Manfred Moßmann. Before Moßmann made himself a name as a poet with a penchant for local colour and the vernacular he was one of Kroetsch's students at Trier. He wrote his thesis on the poems of Louis Riel (1844–1885)—the rebel, archfiend, and lunatic; the hero and founding father of Manitoba—whose "magnificent dream of a Métis nation died at the end of a rope in 1885" (Kroetsch 1968, 15).

In a similar vein the story of the Canadian outlaw Krafchenko has survived in writing and folklore. He comes to life again in Dennis Cooley's *Bloody Jack*, where the Winnipeg poet with a sense for the oral, for "literary parody and poetic extravaganza" (Müller 149), inserts a fake interview with a criminal psychologist, asking the latter: "What if I told you some people think he was a hero?" Dr. Normal L. Braun replies: "I can hear where you are coming from. One might see it that way, sure. However, in my professional opinion the stories about Krafchenko as some kind of charismatic Robin Hood figure are just that—desperate for heroes. They always are" (Cooley 1984, 189). Both Schinderhannes and Bloody Jack evidently were such fascinating, charming figures that they quickly gained legendary status. They were criminal vagrants, striking terror; they were both admired and feared.

Driving along Hunsrück Höhenstraße to Simmern connects the prairies and Rhineland Palatinate once more, evokes the encounter of sites and people, includes the collision of myths and stories that are rooted in region and place, reflecting Kroetsch's vivid interest in local narrative. Distance and proximity collapse. Years before, looking at some seminal Canadian texts, Kroetsch had claimed that

> Canadians are supremely at home when they travel. The departure and initiation and return of travel literature is basic to the narative mode; the urban figures in Canadian literature, when we actually encounter them (in Davies, in Thomas, in Atwood, in Mordecai Richler) are, typically, travelling. (Kroetsch, 1989a, 67)

With this in mind, it cannot come as a surprise that travelling figures prominently in Kroetsch's "domestic" works—even if these do not specifically address urban issues—particularly in the journey book *Alberta* (1968), as well as in his prairie fictions. They signal a continuing search and yearning for the past, often for Kroetsch figured in the home place.

In Alberta Kroetsch describes his experiences during the voyage home to his native province and place of birth. The literary manifestation of homecoming informs nearly all his other writings. The relevant material is carefully researched by a narrator (Kroetsch himself) who becomes immersed in the story, presents comprehensive information about family members, includes eye-witness accounts, and speaks in a lively tongue which bears incalculable traces of the vernacular. Somebody who discovers Europe fairly late in life and who seems to have been little inspired by its cultural sites, who, as he confessed later, turned even angrily on Europe,[4] travels back to the homestead in Heisler, Alberta. "I took a good look at the statues and wanted to go home and drown out some gophers" (quoted in van Herk 1986, xvi). Here is a man whose extended travels have made him homesick, have urged in him a longing for belonging. "Repeatedly and increasingly Kroetsch longs for the world he has left" (Cooley 2016, 14). In a letter to Miriam Waddington, dated January 17, 1972, Kroetsch confirms his attachment to the prairies: "Europe, it now seems to me, is no place to go to work. Rather—to revel. To cut loose, break out, exhaust yourself, rest, begin again to dream. The old dream westward" ("Letter to Miriam Waddington, Jan. 17, 1972"). Alberta enthusiastically reports homecomings to the beer parlour and the tall tale which becomes such a distinctive narrative device in Kroetsch: the "great sub-text of prairie literature is [the] oral tradition" (Kroetsch 1983, 75).

Kroetsch's text is so deeply rooted in the "home place" that it offers an endless sequence of details and reads like a succession of tall tales. It is a compilation of stories telling the stories of his native province and its people—narratives bordering as much on the quotidian and trivial as on the dramatic.

> [...] if you get to a small town when there is no public celebration in progress, I recommend two beers in the local beer parlour. It is customary that you order two glasses per person, on the sane theory that you can't fly on one wing so why make the waiter walk across the floor twice? Thus, for thirty cents per person, you become members of the community; and the prairie beer parlour is as much the community centre as is any pub in Christendom. Here the real news is passed along—the news about those absent, that is—business deals are once again very nearly transacted, friendships are made and daily renewed, the weather is forecast [...]. (1968, 12)

The urban English coffee house where the news was exchanged and which replaced the pub in the late seventeenth century is replaced by the pub in the rural world of the prairies, where gossip becomes a source of information and bullshit a cause for celebration.

Aritha van Herk, close reader of Kroetsch, describes how deeply rooted he is in Alberta. "[It] is his magical kingdom, the centre of his imagination. A world he never left. [...] Alberta required not a travelling away but a return to his childhood home. He had been away for years, a westerner wandering" (van Herk 1986, xv–xvi).

And wandering or rather horsing around the prairies is again at the core of the following work. *The Studhorse Man* (1969) tells a meandering quest story, which Kroetsch began to work on during his "exile" in Cuckfield, England, in 1968. His research for the travel book finds its way into the prize-winning novel. It is a writing of home thoughts from abroad. If there is a text that thematizes motion, commotion, emotion, yearning, anxiety, rejection, evasiveness as well as escape, it is *The Studhorse Man*, Kroetsch's second installment in his out-west triptych.[5]

At the centre of the narrative meanders Hazard Lepage, a protean character who dashes nervously around the Canadian plains during the Second World War, "caught on the wheel of an odyssey that is beyond his control" (van Herk 1986, ixx). Kroetsch's dedication to Klooss's personal copy simply says: "For Wolfgang—journeys, places. Bob Kroetsch. 29 May 92."

Again Kroetsch draws on the tall tale, "not to replace a high literacy, but to supplement it and energize it" (Cooley 2016, 124). Demeter Proudfoot's account of Hazard's journey in search of a mare for his stallion Poseidon bears a larger-than-life quality. It is told by an insane narrator in a bathtub who interferes irrepressibly with the narration and even enters the plot himself, until he identifies himself as Hazard's biographer. Demeter not only keeps meticulous records, which he arranges and manipulates in such a way that they serve his story, he also takes all kinds of liberties in interpreting the protagonist's farings and doings, and finally appropriates them for himself. During the course of the narrative his "identity gradually merges with that of his subject" (Beran 191). In the end he becomes Hazard's doppelgänger. Narrative conventions blur, structures rupture, systems break down. The classical odyssey is turned into a mock quest, Homer's heroic character is displaced by a Kroetschean trickster figure.

With respect to its content, the novel can be read as a travel narrative with an anti-hero who "travel[s] for a living" (Kroetsch 1969,

25) and who, while traversing the Albertan landscape, stumbles into a series of absurd and wicked occurrences. On his ludicrous voyage through the phantastic world surrounding the fictional town of Notikewin, Kroetsch's version of Margaret Laurence's Manawaka, Hazard encounters farmsteads, the notorious beer parlour, a freight train, a milk wagon, a museum, and even a home for incurables, where the protagonist is recruited to a perpetual card game.

Here is one of the few references in Kroetsch's writings where gambling comes into play—though twenty-five years after the release of the novel, in May 1994, Kroetsch himself works the slot machines. As in the home for the incurables, he "hears the clinking of coins" (1969, 46), gets addicted to the sound of money. This happened in the small Alsacian town of Niederbronn-les-Bains, where he together with a group of prairie writers—among them David Arnason, Di Brand, Dennis Cooley, and Doug Reimer from Winnipeg—visited the local casino. In his diary, Cooley recalls that it is Klooss who is up for rescue, "seizing the money before it's lost" (Cooley 1994, n.p.).

Driven by commotion, constantly in motion, Hazard gets entangled in emotional traps and is conquered by women without ever being able to act out his own desires. He specializes in escape and flight, seeks to shake off the (female) domesticity he both longs for and fears.[6] Caught up in his own paradox, he rushes on, only to be finally trampled to death by his precious stallion in the midst of a cold prairie sea.[7] In the words of Cooley, "Kroetsch's rider approaches, always approaches, but he never arrives, for arrival would be fatal to his peripatetic ways" (2016, 176).

At the same time, and perhaps even foremost, *The Studhorse Man* is an exploratory voyage into narrative possibility. After Leonard Cohen's *Beautiful Losers* (1966), which abandons conventions for postmodern modes of narrative,[8] *The Studhorse Man* confirms the shift towards the postmodern in Canadian fiction.[9] It commences Kroetsch's own adventurous journey into "the act of telling the story" (Newman and Wilson, 174), whereby the narrative voice becomes the author's prime concern. This affects the act of reading as well.

The Studhorse Man takes the reader on a tour through a labyrinth of uncertainties and unreliabilities, forcing us to question the trustworthiness of the narration. As Aritha van Herk argues: "The reader is denied any straightforward answer, and the hero (an anagram of whore), is reduced to story, so that 'the only possible heroic act becomes the telling of the story' (LV, 179)" (van Herk 1986, xx). The story is offered by a writer, who like his protagonist and his mad narrator, has himself turned trickster—"the trickster Kroetsch behind the trickster Demeter behind the trickster Hazard" (Beran 187). In the travel book *Alberta*, as well as in the novel *The Studhorse Man*, Kroetsch opens the prairies to his readers as a world of wonders, playing with the formula of an originally orally transmitted epic story whose audience expected to hear about distant lands, strangers, the new and miraculous. Ulysses has arrived in the Canadian west.

As Jonathan P. Sell points out, the traveller-writer in general needs

> to configure the readers' hermeneutic expectations to ensure that his resources would be brought to bear on the interpretation of his representations so that their conceptual probability would be maximized and the making of successful, consensually true meaning guaranteed. In other words, the traveller-writer ha[s] to fix some interpretative parameters for his representations by giving them a recognisable and congruent generic identity. (Sell 2006, 57)[10]

The reader is instructed by both real-world material and elements that belong to the spheres of wonder, both of which come to bear, once a consensual truth is achieved. What Sell claims here for early modern travel accounts applies equally to contemporary Canadian voyage narratives, such as *Alberta* and *The Studhorse Man*.

While Hazard Lepage gets caught up in a horizontal journey across the Canadian plains, in *Badlands* (1975), another "lunatic and yet somehow very moving odyssey" (Laurence) into the Albertan homeland, Kroetsch even takes the reader underground, with a protagonist "[who] was at a loss to explain his own compulsion to recover the past, his maniacal obsession: "Dinosaur—" [...] "We are looking for the bones of the dead. We must find them" (1975, 8), William Dawe declares. How much deeper can one travel into the past than to arrive where dinosaurs sleep? "You are going to the place of the dead?" the girl asked. [...] "Yes" (1975, 8). In the following, Kroetsch constructs a Foucauldian prairie world, offers an archeological reading of history and writing, signals an understanding of region and place which lies also at the core of *The Stone Hammer Poems* (1976). Van Herk writes:

> [...] the prologue poem of Field Notes [...] is about an object that allows the poet/persona to recover history. The stone hammer, which began as a stone, became first, weapon, lost, then an obstruction, then an artefact, lost, returned to stone in a rockpile, found again, became

a talisman for the poet's past, his father and grandfather. The stone/
poem embodies the eternity of prairie. (1986, xi)

William Dawe needs a tool to move beneath a surface where, in a coal mine, he meets a character who is already hidden, who refuses to ever return to the surface, who has chosen to become another invisible man. His journey down the Red Deer River and through the Alberta Badlands takes Dawe not only to the Tail Creek Settlement and the Queen's Hotel in Gleichen, and then past Big Valley Creek and Ghostpine Creek to Drumheller, it also provides a "voyage back into Albertan (pre-)history" (Kuester 1994, 400), all the way into the Mesozoic age. Excavation is genuine to any kind of archeological research. It exposes the scientist like a time traveller to overcast sites and findings, attributes a past to a landscape whose history is supposedly absent, or as Kroetsch argues: "Archaeology allows the fragmentary nature of the story, against the coerced unity of traditional history" (Kroetsch, 1989g, 7).[11] Hence his preference for myth, story, and the tall tale. "Kroetsch subtly suggests [that] the real historian is the novelist [...] who knows that history, like life, must be fleshed out—and in—with marrow and red meat" (Davidson, n.p.). Hazard's horizontal journey has become Dawe's vertical voyage.

Again the travel book *Alberta* and the novel are closely interlinked,[12] just as *Badlands* renews the quest for the dead which had earlier informed "The Ledger." It is a novel filled with graveyards, "riddled with coffins and burials" (Cooley 2016, 179). This notwithstanding, Kroetsch's text strikes a highly comic note as well. Occasionally it even plays on the scatological and it is interspersed with absurd episodes, such as the one in which a skunk has pissed on Claude McBride, "the one among all those travellers who dream[s] insistently of home," who does not care for "his name on a crate of bones [...], but want[s] his children and his wife" (Kroetsch 1975, 42). Now, stripped of his clothes, totally naked, he can be located miles away by the unbearable stink.

Dawe's river passage bears resemblance to the journey of Joseph Conrad's Marlow into *The Heart of Darkness* (1899), which "was like travelling back to the earliest beginnings of the world [...]" (Conrad 61). Towards the end of his increasingly frightening voyage Marlow is confronted with horrifying forebodings of an atavistic world: human skulls posted on wooden sticks.[13] Dawe's destination, on the other hand, *are* the "bonebeds" (Kroetsch 1975, 61). In overbearing vanity he dives deep into (regional) history to unhide the hidden layers of the past. It is a "return to man's own prehistoric source/past" (van Herk

1986, xxii). Yet, after Dawe has reached Drumheller, thinking "this is the last town we have to look at before we get there" (Kroetsch 1975, 64), there are no fossils.

The story of the Badlands expedition is not exactly mediated by Dawe; it is reconstructed from fictional documents. The searcher's field notes enable Dawe's daughter, Anna, to discover her father more than fifty years after he had started his river voyage in the summer of 1916. She wants to "excavate" the man behind the written words, so that she can tell his story and that of his companions who had "no place for women" (1975, 9) in their world. To do so, she has travelled all the way from Ontario to Alberta. As a result, *Badlands* becomes a traversing of gender borders, a passage from male adventure to female narrative, as Willam Dawe's story, based on unreliable notes, becomes swallowed within Anna's story. She has to decipher the text, disclose the truth behind it. She has to fill the written evidence with meaning. Out of his fascination for intertextual practices, Kroetsch marshalls text to interfere with pretexts. In doing so he interrogates supposed evidence, rephrases texts, and parodies speeches as the texts move among one another. Mandel observes:

> One can see Hazard, in *The Studhorse Man*, as the irrational sexual man on a quest for mares, the active sexual body whose life is being "rationalized" by the mind of the static narrator in his bathtub, or conversely see Demeter as the crazed romantic artist looking for a subject for his mad art, and Hazard as merely a series of file cards. One can think of other interpretations, but the rhetoric of the story mocks decision. Similarly, William Dawe is the obsessed quester for bones and Anna Dawe the recorder and keeper of field-notes in Badlands, but Anna also is, initially, a romantic quester for her past, and her father simply the sum of those notes plus a few presercved dinosaur skeletons. Characters exist within each other's fictions in classic Borgesian confusion about who is writing and who is being written. (Mandel 1978, 39)

Like Hazard Lepage, William Dawe dies at the end of his unfulfilled quest. He is not really prepared for this particular voyage and commits suicide by drowning. On his search for the dead he discovers the underworld and descends to Hades—another final destination. In this way, *Badlands* connects western Canada with Greek mythology once more, links the prairies with Europe again.

Finally, returning from Kroetsch's fictional voyages through western Canada to Europe, another journey deserves mentioning. It is again the summer of 1998. Kroetsch and Klooss are travelling to Poland—assisted by the Outreach Programme of the Canadian government, which allowed them to visit the Canadian studies group at Warsaw, the Polish Pen Club, and the English Department of Torun University. Kroetsch reads from his works, discusses with a member of the Pen Club the state of the art, and more specifically the situation of the Canadian writer, and gives advice to students.

Seventeen years later, Anna Branach-Kallas, from Torun, Poland, receives the Pierre Savard Award at the annual meeting of the International Council for Canadian Studies in Peterborough, Ontario—given for a book by a non-Canadian written in French or English. Kroetsch has left his traces.

Upon their return to Trier, Kroetsch was thirsty and hungry. Van Herk remembers: "He wanted a glass of wine. He hoped that an olive or two would materialize. He would have settled for a heel of stale bread" (van Herk 2013, 87). However, at the end of the journey, there was only a lemon. And the lemon was in Klooss's fridge. And the fridge was opened by Kroetsch. He was dumbfounded and he was hungry.

> Men from the Canadian prairies experience profound hunger, hunger of the Battle River strain. He wanted roast chicken. He imagined a lemon meringue pie.
>
> He began, without intending offense, to recite his famous lemon poem, that brilliant *Dinggedicht* contradicting the indigeneity of lemons. (87)
>
> A lemon is almost round.
> Some lemons are almost round.
> A lemon is not round.
>
> So much for that.
>
> How can one argue that a lemon
> Is truly a lemon,
> if the question can be argued?
>
> So much for that. (Kroetsch 1989c, 85)[14]

And so much for travelling with Kroetsch in the summer of 1998—and at other times.

Works Cited

Banting, Pamela. [1995] 1997. *Body Inc*. Winnipeg: Turnstone Press.

Beran, Carol L. 1994. "The Studhorse Man: Translating the Boundaries of Text." *Great Plains Quarterly* 14 (Summer): 185–94.

Bertacco, Simona. 2002. *Out of Place: The Writings of Robert Kroetsch*. Pieterlen, Switzerland: Peter Lang AG.

Breuer, Horst. 1999. "Atavismus bei Joseph Conrad, Bram Stoker und Eugene O'Neill." *Anglia* 117: 368–394.

Conrad, Joseph. [1899] 2012. *Heart of Darkness*. Harmondsworth, UK: Penguin Classics.

Cooley, Dennis. 1984. *Bloody Jack*. Winnipeg: Turnstone Press.

———. 2013. *the stones*. Winnipeg: Turnstone Press.

———. 2016. *The Home Place: Essays on Robert Kroetsch's Poetry*. Edmonton: University of Alberta Press.

———. 1994. Diary. Unpublished manuscript.

Davidson, Arnold E. 1980. "History, Myth, and Time in Robert Kroetsch's Badlands." *Studies in Canadian Literature/Études en littérature canadien*. Accessed October 26, 2016. https://journals.lib.unb.ca/index.php/SCL/article/view/7939.

Engler, Bernd, and Kurt Müller, eds. 1994. *Historiographic Metafiction in Modern American and Canadian Literature*. Paderborn, Germany: Ferdinand Schöningh.

Foucault, Michel. 1972. *The Archeology of Knowledge and the Discourse on Language*. Translated by A. M. Sheridan Smith. New York: Pantheon Books.

Klooss, Wolfgang. 2011. "Flora, Fauna, Monstrous Creatures: Wondrous Discoveries and Scientific Discourse in Early Modern English Travel Writing." Conference presentation, London, England, March 2011.

———. "From Colonial 'Madness' to Postcolonial 'Ex-Centricity': A Story about Stories of Identity Construction in Canadian Historiographic (Meta-) Fiction," In Engler and Müller, 53–79.

———. 2007. "'Through the Eyes of Colonialism': Joseph Conrad's Heart of Darkness and Its Metaphors." In *Conrad in Germany*, edited by Walter Göbel, Hans Ulrich Seeber, and Martin Windisch, 123–52. New York: Columbia University Press.

———. 2009. "Robert Kroetsch, The Studhorse Man." In *Kindlers Neues Literaturlexikon*, edited by Heinz-Ludwig Arnold, 3rd ed., vol. 9: 437. Stuttgart, Germany: Verlag J. B. Metzler.

Kroetsch, Robert. 1968. *Alberta*. Toronto: Macmillan.

———. 1972."Letter to Miriam Waddington, Jan. 17, 1972." MsC.334/84.1 6.20, the Robert Kroetsch Archives at the University of Calgary.

———. 1973. *Gone Indian*. Toronto: new press.

———. 1975. *Badlands*. Toronto: new press.

———. 1977. *Seed Catalogue*. Winnipeg: Turnstone Press.

———. 1983. "On Being and Alberta Writer." In *Robert Kroetsch: Essays*, edited by Frank Davey and bpNicol. Special issue of *Open Letter* 5 (4): 68–80.

———. 1989a. "Beyond Nationalism: A Prologue," In *The Lovely Treachery of Words*, 64–72. Toronto: Oxford University Press.

———. 1989b. *Completed Field Notes: The Long Poems of Robert Kroetsch*. Toronto: McClelland and Stewart.

———. 1989c. "Sketches of a Lemon." In *Completed Field Notes*, 83–87.

———. 1989d. "The Frankfurt *Hauptbahnhof*." In *Completed Field Notes*, 198–208.

———. 1989e. "The Ledger." In *Completed Field Notes*, 11–31.

———. 1989f. *The Lovely Treachery of Words. Essays Selected and New*. Toronto, New York, Oxford: Oxford University Press.

———. 1989g. "The Moment of the Discovery of America Continues." In *The Lovely Treachery of Words*, 1–20.

———. 1969. *The Studhorse Man*. New York: Simon and Schuster.

———. [1966] 2000. *The Words of My Roaring*. Edmonton: University of Alberta Press.

———. 2013. "Motion, Commotion, Emotion." In Metz, Müller, and Schowalter 3.

Kuester, Martin. "Tales Told in the Bathtub: Robert Kroetsch's Historiographic Metafiction." In Engler and Müller, 400–410.

Laurence, Margaret. Cover Text for *Badlands*.

Mandel, Ann. 1978. "Uninventing Structures: Cultural Criticism and the Novels of Robert Kroetsch." *Open Letter* 3 (8): 52–71; reprinted in Markotić, 27–56.

Markotić, Nicole, ed. 2017. *Robert Kroetsch: Essays on His Works*. Toronto, Buffalo, Lancaster: Guernica Editions.

Metz, Annekatrin, Markus M. Müller, and Lutz Schowalter, eds. 2013. *F(e)asting Fitness? Cultural Images, Social Practices, and Histories of Food and Health*. Trier, Germany: WVT Wissenschaftlicher Verlag Trier.

Miki, Roy. 1989. "Self on Self: Robert Kroetsch Interviewed." *Line* 14: 108–42.

Mood, John J. L. 1975. *Rilke on Love and Other Difficulties: Translations and Considerations*. New York, London: W. W. Norton.

Morley, Patricia. 1972. *The Immoral Moralists: Hugh MacLennan and Leonard Cohen*. Vancouver: Clarke, Irwin.

Müller, Markus M. 2004. Review of *Bloody Jack*, by Dennis Cooley. *British Journal of Canadian Studies* 17 (1): 149–150.

Newman, Shirley, and Robert Wilson, eds. 1982. *Labyrinths of Voice: Conversations with Robert Kroetsch*. Edmonton: NeWest.

Ondaatje, Michael. 1970. *Leonard Cohen*. Toronto: McClelland and Stewart.

Rilke, Rainer Maria. 1996. "Sieben Gedichte." In *Werke. Kommentierte Ausgabe in vier Bänden* 2, 138–139. Frankfurt/Main, Leipzig: Insel.

Scobie, Stephen, ed. 2000. *Intricate Preparation: Writing Leonard Cohen*. Toronto: ECW Press.

Sell, Jonathan P. A. 2006. *Rhetoric and Wonder in English Travel Writing, 1560–1613*. Aldershot, UK: Ashgate.

Van Herk, Aritha. 2013. "Kochen und Braten und Schmoren." In *F(e)asting Fitness*, 87–95. Trier, Germany: WVT Wissenschaftlicher Verlag Trier.

———.1986. "Biocritical Essay." *The Robert Kroetsch Papers: First Accession*, edited by Jean F. Tener and Apollonia Steele, ix–xxxix. Calgary: University of Calgary Press. Accessed October 24, 2016. http://www.ucalgary.ca/lib-old/SpecColl/kroetschbioc.htm.

Zellig, Martin. 1998. "The Story of 'Bloody Jack' Krafchenko." *Manitoba History* 35 (Spring/Summer). Accessed October 22, 2016. http://www.mhs.mb.ca/docs/mb_history/35/krafchenko.shtml.

Zichy, Franzis. 2010. *Disenchanted Modernity in Robert Kroetsch's 'The Studhorse Man': Biology and Culture; Sex and Gender; Eugenics and Contraception; Writing and Reading*. New York, Washington: Peter Lang.

Notes

1 Rilke's poem reads as follows: "Auf einmal faßt die Rosenpflückerin / die volle Knospe seines Lebensgliedes, / und an dem Schreck des Unterschiedes / schwinden die linden Gärten in ihr hin" (Rilke, 138). English translation: "The rose-gatherer grasps suddenly / the full bud of his vitality, / and, at fright at the difference, the gentle garden within her shrinks" (Mood, 42).

2 See also Banting, 75–142.

3 Cf. Zellig.

4 Cf. Cooley, *The Home Place: Essays on Robert Kroetsch's Poetry*, 91. Cooley quotes here from Roy Miki, "Self on Self," 121.

5 The trilogy also includes *The Words of My Roaring* (1966) and *Gone Indian* (1973).

6   See Zichy, 12.
7   See also Klooss, "Robert Kroetsch, *The Studhorse Man*."
8   See for full-length studies on Cohen for example Morley, Ondaatje, and Scobie.
9   Cf. Klooss, Out-West, "From Colonial 'Madness' to Postcolonial 'Ex-Centricity,'" esp. 54–56, 70–73.
10 See also Klooss, "Flora, Fauna," 1–3.
11 See also Foucault, esp. 129; Bertacco, 61–62.
12 Cf. van Herk, "Biocritical Essay," xxii–iii.
13 See in this context Breuer.
14 See also "A 'Flight' of Lemons," in Markotić, 163–203.

Driving toward Digression
ARITHA VAN HERK

We would drive. We were driving. We drove.
Robert Kroetsch would insist (often the first sentence out of his mouth after "Hello"): "Let's go for a drive."

So, more often than not, when we met, we went for a drive.

Those drives took on their own momentum and haphazard (already the irony of his characters and their motivations intrudes, Hazard Lepage from *The Studhorse Man* larger than life) destination. We drove around the Battle River country, the shoulders of those hills tracing a remarkable valley, a deep glacial cleft, and my childhood's dream landscape. I grew up a few miles—"Can't you learn metric, Dorf?" (Kroetsch 1983, 19)—south of the Battle River and Kroetsch grew up a few miles north of the Battle; our geography was mirrored despite its different time template. We drove between Edmonton and Calgary, that inimitable stretch of two-laned dispatch, now renamed after Queen Elizabeth. Going south was substantially different from travelling north, the landscape reversed itself, as if upside-down. We drove to Banff, that furtive entrance to the Rockies as cryptic as the rocks. We once drove from Winnipeg to Gimli. Stan Dragland was riding shotgun, and I discovered that he was born and raised in Calgary but had shaken its dust from his feet. We travelled in a van, a rocking, over-crowded van driven by Wolfgang Klooss, down every *autobahn* in Germany, speeding as is required on German freeways, and screeching to a halt only at a *STAU* (traffic jam), in between stopping at obscure places to give readings in celebration of Canadian literature. David Arnason would take off his shoes, and we drove with the windows down to alleviate the stench. The wind brought tears to our eyes.

But we were driving, that meditative limbo between one place and another, the suspension of place inside place, out of place and within the vessel of the car trip, which was sometimes a journey with a destination, sometimes a pure excursion; sometimes an expedition, with planning and an outcome; sometimes merely a jaunt down the street for ice cream; sometimes a pilgrimage, as when we went up to Heisler to take photographs for an article on Kroetsch that I wrote for *Alberta Views* (van Herk 2010), and stopped at a U-pick for saskatoons. Lynette Loeppky and I picked while Kroetsch napped in the barn, and joked with the customers coming to pick up their berries. "I ate your saskatoons," he announced to each one, and the humorously sardonic mouth under his white hair initiated the excursion of their inevitable conversations with him. People confessed unusual particulars to him; he had a way of communicating with strangers that was both endemically Canadian and uniquely his own.

He once tried to teach Rudy Wiebe how to make connection with strangers, service people, and especially waitresses, whom he charmed every time he sat down at a table. We were in a train station café in Berlin, waiting to catch a train to Trier, and Rudy said to him, as the waitress brought our coffee and cake, joking with him, ready to bring him extra cream and anything else he might demand: "How do you do it, Kroetsch?"

His answer was typically enigmatic. "You just look at them as if you actually see them. You make a connection."

And we watched while she returned, exchanged laughter, bent to ensure he had what he wanted, ignoring us, mere appendages to this compelling older gentleman. There was an invisible current of recognition between him and those who surrounded him, perhaps Hegelian, reality shaking hands with idealism, although without the weight of prior dependencies.

And always, he responded to place with the same intimacy, the intricate variances of place in and of itself, making place a part of his experience and a part of his writing to the extent that place declares itself as character and consequence in all of his writing. The creative place-biography of Robert Kroetsch that I am currently focused on seeks to amplify and challenge approaches to his artistic voice and its engagement with geography, time and locale—although its discoveries are beyond topocentric. The paradoxical aspects of Kroetsch's place-interventions with his writing (enigmatic, distanced, and yet allusively specific and significant) speak powerfully to his engagement with writing's own spatial peregrinations and his intense love of driving as a creative digression and consolation. The solace that he appeared to find in writing suggests the doubtless obvious conclusion that driving was a milieu for him, not an action or a progress, but a setting, of movement, horizon, and possibility. He loved most being driven. And of course, we cannot help but be reminded of the irony of his death: someone else was driving.

The automobile, for Kroetsch, is both escape and refuge, a cocoon space and a wide-open prospect. It recurs as a vehicle of more than vehicle, a moving destination that recites itself as character and aperture in novels and poetry alike. He remembers and remarks on cars precisely, mentioning in "The Cow in the Quicksand and How I(t) Got Out" driving "into Winnipeg from Upstate New York in an aging green four-door Dodge Dart in 1978" (Kroetsch 1995, 65). And how "In 1936 my father bought a new green four-door Ford" (77) in order to "embark on what could only be described as an epic journey—to visit relatives and friends southern Saskatchewan" (78). That early journey provided his first "encounter with abandoned farms" (78) and duplicates itself often, with different destinations and epiphanies, forward and reverse as a multiplication of Kroetsch's own digressionary tactics.

Those old but serviceable and inevitably green cars find their way into his fiction, from his first novel, *But We Are Exiles*.

> Peter's earliest memory was of his father in an old green Graham-Paige, a touring car almost as long as a boxcar with yellowed isinglass windows and a windshield that he would let the boy tip down so the wind would bring tears to their eyes. Unless he put on the old goggles that his father wore around his neck. And there was a worn spare tire on either side of the carefully waxed body, and the cracked leather seats were religiously cleaned. The boy and his father and a Great Dane—all together in the front seat they would explore the dusty country roads, and sometimes the father left them outside an old brick or stone hotel while he went in for a beer, and people would gather to look at the car and the dog and the boy. (Kroetsch 1965, 42)

Those explorations foreshadow Peter's later pell-mell flight north, which begins with his hitchhiking rides in cars of every variety, driven on the wrong side of the road up the Banff-Jasper Highway, driven by an old couple, driven by honeymooners, until he manages to find the airplanes that will enable his escape beyond roads. This follows his initial drive west with Hornyak, an epic road trip only too reminiscent of Kerouac's *On the Road,* the distance they cover compounded by booze and women and speeding tickets until they reach Banff and stop driving, which is when Hornyak betrays Peter with Kettle and initiates Peter's run north. It is a young novel for Kroetsch, but its alienated delays coincide with death, the temptation of eluding responsibility. And it gestures towards how relentlessly driving performs an evasive action for those in search of their own quest, how ongoing motion prolongs delay and initiates death for every one of his characters. How much he loved driving.

In *The Words of My Roaring,* Johnny Backstrom drives his hearse as resolutely as any Rocinante, drives drunk and sober, misses curves and hits a telephone pole, crumpling one fender and breaking his friend Jonah's arm. He bids for a Model A, the prophet's "'chariot of corruption'" (Kroetsch 1966, 69) at auction, the car referred to as "'a headache on four wheels'" (69). Backstrom justifies his extravagant bid "because driving around the country in a hearse wasn't exactly the best thing for [his] electioneering" (70); he persuades himself that the Model A will be "a great automobile for a man with political ambitions" (71). Backstrom's bluster is bigger than his purse, of course, and, unable to pay the price he bids, he must slink off and leave the car. To make himself feel better he tries to fix the damaged fender of his old hearse and hammers both fenders into dented replication. That same hearse, in the rainstorm at the end of the novel, gets stuck, which means that Johnny Backstrom and his political opponent must ride together on the springboard seat of a wagon, as a return to the proto-origins of travel.

Kroetsch's writing returns to the car as a machine for transformation and nostalgia over and over again. He hankered after the imagistic shapes of the Model-T and the Model-A, the T the original Tin Lizzie, widely recognized as the first "affordable" car, now accorded dinosaur or collectable status. In *Badlands,* the Model-T is "converted" into a portable darkroom by Sinnott, the photographer determined to document the "Vanished World" (Kroetsch 1975, 113), who is more interested in taking photographs of the motley crew of bone-hunters than he is in saving his automobile from the flooding river. It is Dawe who is determined to "save the automobile, as if it might be some remnant of a prehistoric existence" (113) (prescient indeed), in the process saving the photographer himself, along with his lust for documentation. While Tune stands beside the seductive car, Sinnott recites a "lechery of names" (130) in an attempt to seduce Tune into joining him and driving away from the river instead of staying with the bonehunters. But Tune stays aboard the raft and ultimately dies. In the end, it is Anna Yellowbird who jumps into the Model-T and vanishes with the photographer. She and Anna Dawe invert this expedition with their later drive in Anna Dawe's Mercedes-Benz to the Badlands, across farmers' fields, back to Drumheller and farther upriver and into the mountains and the dark, looking for the source of the river. *"We drove, one day, and then another, and then, as I recall, another still"* (259). Driving cements the two Annas in their connection; the husk of the car and its movement takes them to their mutual understanding and their wonderful apogee at the end of the novel, when they reject all versions of the male quest.

The desire of *The Studhorse Man,* Hazard Lepage, to propagate the horse attempts to repudiate the fact that the car and Alberta's ready access to gasoline has made that animal obsolete; despite his focus on horses, even Hazard learns to "drive the old Eshpeter car" (Kroetsch 1969, 152) as a replacement for his former means of escape. Perhaps it is that betrayal that ultimately leads to his death by Poseidon.

In *What the Crow Said,* automobiles are moveable sites of seduction; "Bill Morgan and Alphonse Martz and Ken Cruickshank together named thirteen girls who got married because of the back seats of cars" (Kroetsch 1978, 100). While the machismo of that trope cannot go unremarked in our current age, those enumerating men are also counting on their fingers their certain demise as husbands and seducers. The cars that flock to the Lang farm disgorge men from every direction, although they encounter ultimately only frustration, the Lang women the justification-destination for those same men journeying toward the comfort of death and stasis (128). At the end of the schmier game, that disruption of time and temper, the dispossessed men who have lost all wagers scatter: "[T]here were thirteen minor car accidents in the vicinity of Big Indian in less than twenty-four minutes. One driver drove through his own garage wall and into the potato patch behind it. Another, unable to change gears, tried to back all the way home, and two miles south of town, hit a dugout" (115). In *What the Crow Said,* cars are safe only if they serve as dwellings: Joe Lightning lives "in a car body behind Gordie Somer's garage" (83). Joe Lightning is the male reference who concludes the novel, with Kathy hoping he will "fall into her arms" (218). Flight and movement condemn these men to death; only the Lang women's still centres promise respite and a refuge.

Kroetsch was acutely aware of what he called "the temptation of stasis" (Kroetsch 1982, 124) and its dangers, of the essentialism ascribed to one approach to reading or writing, commenting early on "the binary antagonisms that seem to lead to stasis" (124) and declaring his suspicion of the "terrible validation" (127) and immobility of any static image. While his comments are often connected to the photographic, a segue to the irresistible text of motion is almost a given, especially in *Alibi* and *The Puppeteer*, which chronicle driving as impetus, and virtual occupation.

Alibi opens with a drive from Calgary to Banff, once again in an "old green Dodge" (Kroetsch 1983, 9) and driving drives Dorf's peripatetic search for the perfect spa, the one that will provide Deemer with eternal health, if not life. The car's ubiquitous employment and operation throughout *Alibi*—from Dorf's drives to and from the Rockies and his sister's reckless driving in the United Kingdom—ultimately culminates in the "blue Mercedes" that Dorf rents in Portugal, the same blue Mercedes-Benz that Julie Magnuson is found in, "alone and dead" (193) "in the forest at the foot of a cliff, in the hills northwest of Faro, in the south of Portogalia; in the very opposite direction, that is, from the direction we'd planned to drive on our proposed extra day on the Algarve" (194). Which coincides with Dorf's own fall, his violation in the dark orgy at Deadman Spring: "[T]hen the car leapt forward, the blue Mercedes, leapt like a cat, a cougar, over and off the cliff; it fell, the long car, beginning to spin; those broken rocks, those sun-cracked rocks, and the tree, the huge cork oak, like a period, on a blank page" (228). The car acts in conspiracy with death, and the Dorf/Kroetsch duality is left only as a series of fragmented journal entries, possibly edited, possibly unexpurgated.

The urge, then, to drive, to travel, to journey, becomes a chronic itch in the textual presence of a fidgeting writer, his eternal restlessness belied by the silent poet role that he pretended to play. "What one needs for the journey is the journey" (Kroetsch 1999, n.p.) declares the persona in the chapbook poem, *The New World and Finding It*. And experiencing during that drive the eternal and confounding lust that appears to plague the personae of all his poems and fictions: "We are driving, and the road promises a stopping place the way the barker at a sideshow promises naked and hairless sheep and bearded ladies, and upright, noble men" (n.p.). Repeat earlier note on the machismo of this literary world. But wait. To stop, says Kroetsch earlier in the same poem, is to "plant your foreknowledge in the sand" (n.p.). The journey is toward the "New World," but this version of "New World" is an unattainable destination, and the seeds that are carried will not come to fruition. So that the persona's dictum,—"Proceed knowing nothing"— is the answer to the initiating question of all Kroetsch's work: "What is necessary for the journey?" and the further question, "How does one prepare for disorder?" To which no rejoinder is possible, no refuge in discontinuity or disjunction, but instead—to be honest—that fascinating enticement of digression as it veers toward excursus.

Excursus, or excursion, galvanizes Robert Kroetsch's writing, an engagement with side trips and road trips and detours and the escapes and promises provided by that now-geezer machine, the car. In a section entitled "The Frying Pan and How It Was Actually Invented" in *Excerpts from the Real World*, the persona notes on 7/6/85: "We're on the road to Lake Winnipeg. The pelicans are measuring the sky for a new suit of clouds. The gophers measure the width of the road with their lives. You put your left hand on my right thigh. Floor it, you say" (Kroetsch 2000, 224). Earlier in the same poetic sprawl (25/4/85) he refers to "Hammer Happy; the King of Babylon, sells used cars on the Pembina strip, right there in Winnipeg" (222), followed by subsequent references to "transmission problems" and "a four-barrelled carburetor" (222) as well as "shock absorbers" (223). In that poem, parts of the car distribute themselves alongside the persona's articulations of desire, like a vehicle waiting to be assembled.

The car enables the poet's restless digressions, but the car moving toward and through the horizon accompanies a perspective that recurs on the horizon of Kroetsch's writing. In "Late Fall Drive: for Byrna Barclay," the poet imagines a trip he imagines but does not take:

> Early yesterday, driving west alone
> across the prairies, I thought of swinging
> south off Number One to visit shortgrass
>
> country. Down there, everything is real,
> even the emptiness. The buttes are bare.
> Trees are only a memory. But I decided not to
>
> go, mostly because a woman in a parka,
> pumping gas just outside Moose Jaw, asked
> where I was going. (108)

Unnerved by the question—"where are you going?"—the poet resists the impulse to digress and continues westward, toward the "pretentious" (108) mountains, their implacable wall. And so, every drive contains its inverse, the drive not taken, the endless proliferation of possible excursions and their surprises, the road and its history unspooling, often in reverse.

In his 1968 travel meditation on Alberta, Kroetsch drives through the province with a relentless energy, to the extent that he begins to comment on the roads themselves:

> The Banff-Jasper road, for anyone who finds delight in driving an automobile, has little to rival it in all the rest of Alberta. My favourite stretches are the two descents from the Columbia Icefields. Going south I like the beautifully engineered, outflung curve that drops down from the Parker Ridge Trail to the Weeping Wall. The swoop of road is exhilarating, a soaring-hawk experience, and in the evening the eastern cliffs, catching the sun, are yellow and Egyptian, turning rapidly to orange and back again to brown; the mountains in the west are shaded blue then purple, supremely alpine with their fields of protected snow. Anyone who remembers the difficult drive over the old road will especially enjoy this drive. (Kroetsch 1993, 93)

Kroetsch never again sounds so much like an AMA handbook; in the later edition of that book, published twenty-five years later, he rhapsodizes less and travels more, chronicling the province with the infinitive "to drive," but understanding the enigma of finding any right way, his ultimate summary of the quest as "a kind of getting lost" (32). Only at the end of *Alberta,* in a chapter entitled "A Last Word: In Praise of Winter," does he bring together darkness and destination, his secret doppelgänger. "The silence of a winter night drums in from a drifted stubble-field. A car hums in the distance. A faint fall of snow lifts up the glare of headlights like beacons on the sky. An old man slips out once more to read the thermometer, once more to sweep the front steps" (286). The end of all journeys is a cold night in the deep of winter, with the suggestion of travel in the sound of a car humming in the distance.

In "Mile Zero," "being some account of a journey through western Canada in the dead of six nights" (Kroetsch 2000, 118), the trip is defined as "Accidental," with an acceleration of infinity, but also finiteness: "On the third night west / a mountain stopped us. / The mountains were lined up / to dance" (122). That poem contains as well, in its anthemic call and response to "transition," the much-ignored explanation of a line removed from the stanza, but glossed with a more direct narrative than is readily available in any of Kroetsch's work:

> The concern with *nostos* is related to a long family history of losses: *e.g.*, the paternal side of the family landing in New York in June, 1841, aboard the *Pauline,* and the mother of the large Kroetsch family, settled in Waterloo County, Ontario, a few years thereafter widowed, the early death of the poet's mother in Alberta, a century after that first un-homing. Both quest and goal become paradigmatic (RK)" (124).

If *nostos* is primarily the intricate and impossible journey of return, then the desire for return becomes its own destination, and distance the journey's desire. On 12/7/85 in *Excerpts from the Real World,* the persona declares for distance: "West of Outlook, Saskatchewan, you can drive straight into the end of the world. There's a law against shade in that country. Trees are considered improper. Sometimes the cattle graze, for a whole week, in a mirage" (226). The end of the world is a goal, but not necessarily a place to stop.

The connection of the car with a horizon that Kroetsch dispenses as endless and enduring, then becomes the shadow arc of his writing, even comically. When stopping to relieve himself on a seemingly empty road, he is interrupted by other travellers:

29/7/85

> The nearest shadow was four miles away. I had only just begun that which, like falling in love, I cannot control once commenced, when a Greyhound bus, three-half-tons, two galloping horses, a motorcycle gang and a woman in a convertible began to converge on the spot where I was standing with my back to the road. (228)

However much the persona turns his back to the road, its indefatigable vehicles and conveyances will descend on him, his imagination, and even his bodily needs. Converse this reluctance to the photograph of Kroetsch on the cover of *Alberta Views,* December 2010, where he is seated on a folding stool in the middle of a gravel road in Alberta, his cane at the ready, above the title, "Our Odysseus," a title I gave the article as a perfect incarnation of his itinerant association with

Aritha van Herk

movement—as well as his perpetual "return" to Alberta and his fondness for gravel roads.

He was a lover of driving, of "the drive," a now censured activity for its implications of fossil-fuel waste in this post-combustion-engine age of reducing emissions and carbon footprints. And if we have become hyperaware of automobile affection as lechery of the macho-squander variety, there are ever more cars moving on roads around the world. And while we critique such improvident motion, we fail to account for the primal urge of wanderlust that incites so much of imagination and writing.

As I indicated at the beginning of this meditation, Kroetsch's first words were, more often than not: "Let's go for a drive," and his delight in unfolding landscapes and back roads was matched only by his silent interest in what he observed in the ditches. Theoriests would argue that Kroetsch's interest in movement, in the politics and temptations of the open road, in the endlessly enacted journey, is a part of his aesthetics of discontinuity. But I contend that it has less to do with the now overfashionable interest in indeterminacy than with a determined embrace of digression as a means of discovery, an aesthetic, yes, and a practice that might be said to mirror the practice of many writers, from Graham Greene's *Ways of Escape* to my own *Restlessness*. The "escapade" combines with detour and destination in an amplification of digression as a marker of curiosity, albeit a curiosity contradictorily expressed in the "dispatch of silence" (Kroetsch 1982, 111). And there is the real impetus behind the drive and its enactment: it embraces and resists silence.

Indexing Robert Kroetsch's dance with movement is difficult, if not impossible. He was on a quest to outfox quest, the "quest motif" attributed to his work merely a cover for the act itself, as he would have it "meaning that the form itself must violate itself" (Kroetsch 1982, 34). He was fond of these tautologies, their slippage providing him with another means of escape, the sentence without destination except a possible rereading. He argued for the protean temperament of region and location, geography and its mapping: "[T]he notion of place or the notion of geography—geography is also part of text in a strange way, and I think geography is not fixed, it's changing—every journey across it or through it is another reading" (8). Ergo his earnest efforts to get lost, to lose himself in an excursus of avoidance. "The prairies themselves are labyrinthine. They have been mapped like grids, all those roads, but you can get lost in them so easily" (80). And if our "landscape, finally, is our labyrinth. What is a journey in a landscape?" (80), but an exquisite practice of the lost art of getting lost.

Driving toward Digression

Excursus then was his propulsion, an oeuvre of excursion and its inevitable recursion, a *mise en abyme* of journeys toward journeys toward journeys, avoidance of any destination except perhaps the ephemeral inheritance of place and how place shapes the imagination, but only so far as we can all fall "into the chasm between disbelief and longing" (Kroetsch 2000, 233). It is there, in the cleavage between the two that Kroetsch casts a shadow, there that both space and place sculpt an imagination so completely unique that our grief and joy at its rereading can only retrace the journeys that he instigated in his readers, in his friends, and in his words themselves. For him journey and consequence were a dilemma, a conundrum, an invitation to speculation and desire. Excursus was less an embrace of paradox than a test of language and language's own failure to cure disbelief and longing.

Kroetsch's most repeated line: "We were driving."

We were driving up Highway 56 between Stettler and Meeting Creek. I think we were on the way to Calgary, but I could be turned around—if we were driving north we were driving away from Calgary and not toward it. Did we know? Or was that particular excursion an excuse to look at pot-and-kettle country, their lumpy physical reminders of the long-ago retreated glaciers. I had my old Porsche, the fast car, the low-slung beauty that I still miss, every day, bucket seats so beautifully shaped that I could drive for hours without getting stiff.

We were talking about place, Alberta, why we could not leave it alone, this ice-age episode of rank excess and beauty, greed and lust and crazy initiative, how it held us in its imaginative grip so that we could not shake loose. It seems to me it was fall, the landscape slowly fading into that muted green-brown only possible in the palette of the prairie.

I was probably speeding. I have a "lead foot," no explanation necessary, the highways of Alberta are tailored to Porsches. And over one of those kettles, a humpy hill, the surprise of an official car with its flashing lights.

I have been stopped on many a highway, Kroetsch's Banff-Jasper highway, the highway between Calgary and Edmonton, the highway between Calgary and Banff, the highway to Regina. I know what to do. Pull over and stay mum.

The uniformed officer had to bend down to peer into the car's window. He seemed uncertain, as if a white-haired poet and a law-breaking woman were not reconcilable. I expected the speeding question, but he did not haul out that particular lecture. Instead, he asked: "Any guns? Any liquor? Any wild game?"

I had to laugh. I invited him to inspect my hatchback, to check under my bucket seats. We were innocent.

He smiled then, and waved us on, and I pulled around his official flashers and drove more slowly, north—or was it south?

Kroetsch was often silent, so it took a few kilometres before I noticed his silence.

"What?" I asked. "Guns? Liquor? Wild game?"

"I see a cop," he said seriously, "and I'm guilty."

We laughed, both of us innocent.

I extrapolate his comment now to read, "I see a journey and I journey, even if I am innocent of all accusation."

And if, in hindsight, I want to declare him a solivagant, I am still contriving, constructing. Although he always carried his readers with him.

We become the journey we travel. And Robert Kroetsch, in his travelling, became his own endless and incomplete journey.

Works Cited

Kroetsch, Robert. 1965. *But We Are Exiles.* Toronto: Macmillan.

———. [1968] 1993. *Alberta.* Toronto: Macmillan.

———. 1969. *The Studhorse Man.* Edmonton: University of Alberta Press.

———. 1975. *Badlands.* Toronto: General Publishing.

———. 1978. *What the Crow Said.* Edmonton: University of Alberta Press.

———. 1982. *Labyrinths of Voice: Conversations with Robert Kroetsch.* Edited by Shirley Neuman and Robert Wilson. Edmonton: NeWest Press.

———. 1983. *Alibi.* Toronto: Stoddart.

———. 1995. *A Likely Story.* Red Deer, AB: Red Deer Press.

———. 1999. *The New World and Finding It.* Saltspring, BC: Mother Tongue Press.

———. [1989] 2000. *Completed Field Notes.* Edmonton: University of Alberta Press.

van Herk, Aritha. *Restlessness.* Red Deer, AB: Red Deer College Press.

———. 2010. "Our Odysseus." *Alberta Views,* December, 26–31.

Robert Kroetsch:
The Author and the Man
Rudy Wiebe

Winter was ending.
This is what happened:
we were harrowing the garden.
You've got to understand this:
I was sitting on the horse.
The horse was standing still.
I fell off.

    The hired man laughed: how
    in hell did you manage to
    fall off a horse that was
    standing still?

        Bring me the radish seeds,
        my mother whispered. (Kroetsch 1989, 32–33)

Robert Kroetsch created intricate worlds in his novels, his short and long poems, his stories, in his so often slyly self-deprecating essays. The delights, the revelations of his brilliant, questing imagination. I would like to refer to the person I knew: Bob Kroetsch, that immensely complex, imaginative, warm and gentle man.

Rudy Wiebe

Bob and I first met in Edmonton fifty-one years ago—October 1967. My family and I had returned to Alberta after four years of me teaching creative writing in Indiana; he was an English professor in upstate New York, but we were both western Canada farm kids with immigrant forebears whose mother tongue was German; we had both graduated in English from the University of Alberta, and during the later 1950s wrote novels for academic theses—he a PhD at Iowa (1961), I an MA at Alberta (1960). By the time we met, we had each published two novels with large publishers and were furiously working on thirds.

But Bob and I did not become close friends quickly. He was seven years older than me and our differences, both in life experience and philosophy, were many and large. For example: as a growing teenager he was listening to tall tales echoing around the Heisler, Alberta, hotel (which his father had built) and was singing:

> Cigarettes and whiskey and wild, wild women,
> They'll drive you crazy, they'll drive you insane…

At about the same age, I was listening to long German sermons in my Coaldale, Alberta, Mennonite church and singing the tenor arias of Handel's *Messiah*: "Comfort ye, comfort ye my people, saith your God…"

Even a cursory glance at our first two novels—published before either of us knew the other existed (and despite their "biblical" titles!)—reveals the huge difference of our imaginative worlds: my *Peace Shall Destroy Many* (1962) and his *But We Are Exiles* (1965); my *First and Vital Candle* and his *The Words of My Roaring* (both 1966). And, for both of us, the '70s were hugely busy: from 1969 until 1980, Bob published four novels, four major poetry collections, and one non-fiction book, while during the same period I published four novels, two collections of short stories, and one play. We both won GG awards for fiction and with the years became very good friends, but our first published conversation (with Shirley Neuman, 1981) reveals how far apart we were in our thinking. Here is a typical exchange:

> Kroetsch: I believe in longing too, or I would call it desires. I guess what I hear [in your novels] is that the longing for you is for completion, for perfection.

> Wiebe: The apprehension of a perfection. I think man is an animal capable of the apprehension of perfection.
>
> Kroetsch: That's an impossible notion! An impossible notion! I don't know what this longing means. What is this, talk about perfection? You have to stop time to have perfection and the only way to stop time in our world is by death.
>
> Wiebe: But that's why we all want to die anyway. Because we want to get out of this time and what's going to happen after [we are beyond time] is going to be so much more exciting.
>
> Kroetsch: Oh boy, is it going to be exciting!
>
> Wiebe: For me, dying is no end of anything; it's just an opening into another total experience…of which we now keep getting glimmers…and which to me is far more exciting than anything we're living through right now.
>
> Kroetsch: Oh, Rudy, Rudy. (Neuman, 234-35)

Differences indeed—but much more important was what we shared: one was teaching creative writing—we even both attended the University of Iowa's Writing Program, (not at the same time), and in 1967 he visited my University of Alberta writing classes several times. He later wrote me he had "a kind of mad missionary impulse to preach 'writing' to young westerners." That was like Bob—to use my Christian evangelical language on me—but in a private letter, not in public. Above all, during the four months he and his family lived in Edmonton (he was completing the travel book, *Alberta,* in 1968), he and I drove around parkland Alberta, we read each other's books, and we began to talk, talk.

Then, while we did our jobs in Binghamton and Edmonton, we exchanged letters, phone calls, had many encounters at readings and Writers' Union of Canada meetings, and our friendship deepened imaginatively with our third novels. In October 1969, Bob sent me advance uncorrected proofs of *The Studhorse Man* with a signed inscription: "To Rudy Wiebe—in process—the way we must write."

That novel was published in November 1969, and my own *The Blue Mountains of China* ten months later. Those novels, plus my short stories "Where Is the Voice Coming From?" and "The Naming of Albert

Johnson," and his developing poetry ("Old Man Stories," "The Ledger," "Poem for Albert Johnson") gave us mutual inspiration, stimulus. For two summers we were together as visiting writers at the Saskatchewan School of the Arts in the Qu'Appelle Valley. Listening to each other counsel writers, hiking the coulees, eating wild rose petals and saskatoons, driving gravel roads, drinking (he beer, me Tang), and talking. Talking and deepening friendship.

I cannot go into chronological lists. In the '70s, '80s, and '90s many universities and writing groups invited us to festivals and conferences together; we used them as opportunities to drive around every local area—Lethbridge, Edmonton, Kamloops, Calgary, the Mennonite settlements of southern Manitoba and the Icelanders of Lake Winnipeg—eventually even the beauty of Jena and Erfurt and Marburg in Germany, Oviedo and the coast of Spain. And, of course, our home province: again and again. In July 1992, for two whole weeks together we circled Alberta, from Edmonton south through the Medicine Lodge Hills and Calgary and Old Man River Gap, south to the McIntyre Ranch on the Milk River Ridge and then east and on, on to the far north of Zama City in the boreal oil forests of the western corner of the province, over 6,000 kilometers together. What a glorious trip! I have journal notes and many pictures: of Bob everywhere with his spiral notebook—beside the corrals at the Jenner Rodeo interviewing the rodeo clown . . . looking over the South Saskatchewan River to the long spine of Bull's Forehead Hill . . . walking the curve of the Big Horn Highway towards Grande Cache—and always, even when, in the long murmur of the car, he fell asleep for five minutes with his chin sunk on his chest, a notebook filled with his scrawled, unreadable words rested in his hand.

There's a picture I like especially: Bob in a short-sleeved, blue-stripped shirt contemplating the white cross inside the white picket fence surrounding a grave in the Mountain Park Cemetery. His notebook is in his right hand. Beyond the neglected graveyard of that ghost town, you see the open-pit coal mines and their massive slag heaps stretching towards the Rocky Mountain horizon. And I remember, again, his beautiful essay, "Why I Went Up North ..." and the young Métis woman who, in 1948, introduced him to the graveyard at Fitzgerald, a hamlet beside the immense Slave River Rapids: "Every grave... was surrounded by a small picket fence that had once been painted white and . . . at its head a small wooden cross" (Kroetsch 1995, 29–30). He then circumscribes, in his usual elusive manner, while providing not one single detail, how that particular young woman helped him to gain, at the age of twenty-one, the loss of his virginity.

[Let me note here: there is a picket-fence graveyard scene in his posthumous novel manuscript, *The Fence*, to be published by University of Alberta Press. The setting is the thriving Coal Branch town of Mountain Park.]

To return to travelling with Bob: his ever-present notebook [Was he forever trying to complete his field notes?], his steady, contemplative gaze, his curiosity, his easy cameraderie and laughter with everyone he met that could shape-shift into a probing interview without the interviewee ever noticing: what a delightful companion. Disagreements plenty, but quarrels—never. I know, people actually did have quarrels, angers, even rages, with Bob, but I can't remember ever having one myself. He simply never showed me how, he never helped me lose my temper with him.

But we shared much wit and laughter—as did everyone who knew him. Here's a bit from a conversation we had at Canadian Mennonite University, May 2007. [It is not in the text of the printed interview in *Prairie Fire* of October 2008.]

> Audience Member: Let's say a cataclysm occurred and only one of your books survived into the future. Which one would you want it to be?
>
> Kroetsch: What do you mean, just one!
>
> Wiebe: Can we make a deal here? Maybe two books? Okay, I think you're asking: which is our favorite book?
>
> Audience Member: Something like that.
>
> Kroetsch: Well, I have a soft spot in my heart for a novel of mine called *What the Crow Said*. It's very...[well]...reality and imagination flow into each other and there's a talking crow, as you might tell from the title. I kind of like that, but most readers would not agree with me.
>
> Wiebe: Sue Sorensen [director of the Writing School] just read that the other day...the first paragraph.

> Kroetsch: Oh, yeah, the bees…well, this woman gets pregnant by a swarm of bees and some people don't believe me [laughter]. But the community believed her. She said she got pregnant by the bees and the community said, "Fair enough, let's get on with it." That's my answer. (So Rudy—what's yours?)

My answer about my books is irrelevant here: but even as I was talking, I recalled Kroetsch's best-known comment on Canadian writing, made in a conversation with Margaret Laurence. He said: "We want to hear our story…In a sense, we haven't got an identity until somebody tells our story. The fiction makes us real" (Kroetsch 1970, 63).

WHAT THE CROW SAID *real*? Vera Lang's impregnation by bees results in the birth of a son whom, while he is still a baby, Vera throws to a hunting pack of winter wolves, but who nevertheless ten years later returns—because he was "living with a den of coyotes"—and who at age thirteen is elected reeve of the municipality?

That's Western Canada *real*? Where the useless men of Big Indian play a card game called schmier twenty-four hours a day for 151 days? And immediately after start a War with the Sky?

Where a crow does speak: With wise, insightful comments like "Scared shitless?" "Bugger off." "Total asshole."

REAL: where most of the men die grotesquely and all the women, "with no imagination at all," carry the community on, relentlessly.

Such fiction makes us *real*? Come on, Kroetsch, get real!

Bob and I sat in that university, talking to some hundred young people: he was smiling at me. I could read his face:

Ha! Push these pampered middle-class students beyond their acceptable myths and fairy tales, beyond Milton and Bunyan into tall tales, into satire and exploding invective. Push the gossip in their home communities into parody, into confusion and joking and lust and absolutely ludicrous but nevertheless perfectly logical stupidity and burlesque, push them until they, in 2007, are prepared to remember the future of 2017: when an elected president of the United States is convinced he can control the destiny of the entire world with daily 140-character tweets.

O Rudy…Rudy…my fiction is only too real. Ha!

By 2008 Bob was considering, in his gradual way, to return to live in Alberta—as he had not done for over sixty years. But even before he came to settle permanently, he often visited, and one July day he and

I drove out to the parkland, and together contemplated tombstones in the Spring Lake Roman Catholic Cemetery north of Heisler, where his mother's 1903 settler family from Minnesota, the Wellers, are all buried. His mother's mother:

> MARIE MORMANN, Beloved wife of George Weller...
> 1872...1914...Too good for earth, God called her home

Then we drove on through Heisler—no elevators left now, population perhaps a hundred, hotel boarded up—to the Heisler cemetery behind the tall church and a fenceline of trees where his parents are buried side by side. Trails of clouds slid high along the horizon, and we each walked were we wished, reading gravestones. After a time he was beside me. He said, "I think, maybe my ashes should be spread here." For men of our age, body ashes are not a morbid subject. In fact, we talked about dying and death very often.

The piercing cry of a hunting hawk called above us: it was riding the bright air over the wheatfields on motionless wings. Gradually we circled back towards the car. Bob said, "You know, we should try to find that Iron Creek Hill, where that meteorite once was."

"You mean...the Manitou Stone, of the Cree?"

"Yes, that one. Old Man Buffalo."

Some days before we had seen him, Old Man Buffalo, in the Royal Alberta Museum in Edmonton, known to science as one of the earth's largest iron meteorites (175 kg). We were both mesmerized by his shining, pitted shape. "Can you see him?" Bob whispered, and I whispered back, "Yes." The black stone: a jagged human head, gleaming, pockmarked as with smallpox scars, the right side a perfect profile of forehead, eyes, long bent nose, the open—speaking—mouth. As light moved over it, the face moved; talking; neither of us understood.

Now Bob said, "Northeast of here, we could just find Iron Creek, then drive along it, look for a hill." So we drove the gravel grid roads of Flagstaff County looking for Iron Creek, my *Alberta Road Atlas* guiding us, and as we idled through the streets of Sedgewick, Bob noticed— "Hey!"—an Archives and Gallery Museum! A town of 900 with a local archives and open on Friday? Incredible. He talked to the smiling attendant, and in three minutes her copier whirred and she brought us two reports by local historian Allen Ronaghan, with a precise Canada Survey code: NW 17-44-10-West of the 4th Meridian. Well, I could certainly find that. And when we drove east out of town, we soon recognized the distant hill: not high, almost a cone mounded up sharp and solitary beyond the willow twists of the creek. Range Road 105 cut through its base. We parked on the shoulder and climbed, steadily, as we could.

Green grain and dazzling sky…golden miles of canola…the bushy humps of the Wolf Ear Hills. In a notch beyond them, the unnatural white knobs of the Hardisty oil tanks pipelining oil to Oklahoma, USA. And we fumbled through the sad, sad story of this hilltop where we stood: how in 1866 white missionaries came with a cart to this sacred high place of the Indigenous Peoples and stole Old Man Buffalo.

Where are the buffalo? Perhaps the men of the band are hunting along the creek, scouring the ravines of the Wolf Ear Hills for any possible animal. Perhaps, as the moon rises red out of the edge of the earth, a woman stands here on this hill, praying, "O Great Spirit, we are dying. Our children cry for food. O Only One, have pity."

And suddenly: a flash of light splits the sky over her, and out of that exploding light bursts a gigantic ball of fire, a roar such as she has never heard and she collapses in terror as the immense fireball smashes into the valley. The earth shudders as if it were riding a long roll of thunder. A gift from the Great Spirit:

"Here, pray here, and I will always care for you. Here."

How many thousands of human beings saw this unimaginable gift come blazing from the sky? Bob and I stood on the high place where they carried it after they dug it out of the earth, where they prayed and waited to see, anywhere around them, the buffalo herds coming. Their food from the Creator Who Cares. And they came, for generations the animals came, brought by Old Man Buffalo. Torn away now from his place for over 140 years.

Bob said, quietly, "Here I too can have a vision."

A pickup stopped on the road below us, behind our car. A stocky man got out, bent through the fence and climbed toward us. He said he was Bill Paterson, and his family had lived on this land since 1908. What were we doing on the hill?

We told him. We talked as the clouds travelled over us. Then together we gathered and ate purple saskatoons growing down the north slope of the sacred hill.

Bob moved back to Alberta in 2009, to Leduc near his sister Kay, a suite in a seniors' residence. We regularly exchanged visits over coffee; we phoned: his gentle voice, "You have reached Robert. Please leave me a message." At our forest lodge above Strawberry Creek, he could not walk down into the valley, but he sat on the deck, watching the aspen leaves flicker, listening to the birds. When my wife, Tena, and I returned from the funeral of her brother, she talked with him about that grief; he listened intently, as he always did, and then he said to her, slowly, carefully: "I see death as a passing, into the next life."

In May 2007, at the end of Bob's and my conversation in Winnipeg, an audience member asked us:

> ...after spending fifty years writing so many books, how can you feel like you still have some secrets to keep?

Kroetsch: There's some secrets I'll never tell, believe you me!

That response was greeted with much laughter, and then Bob in his usual smooth way evaded the question entirely by shifting it to me— "What do you think?"

And I in turn evaded by talking about "fifty years of story-telling" and how "it takes so unbelievably long to write a novel...that's a real problem as you get older...it can take three, or four, six years to write a novel, I mean—"

And Bob finished the whole conversation with the perfect response: "It takes a lifetime to write a poem."

So here is the end of the Robert Kroetsch lifetime poem, which, as you will remember, began with

> Winter was ending.
> This is what happened:
> we were harrowing the garden.
> You've got to understand this:...

> > Bring me the radish seeds.
> > my mother whispered.

And so in 2011 this is what happened:

Alberta winter finally had ended. On Friday, June 10, Bob and I drove south to Calgary. His body was fragile—his lifelong Mackenzie River back injury was now intensified by Parkinson's—but his mind and spirit were as bright as ever; when we rode up over Antler Hill and there was the staggered line of Rocky Mountains shining along the horizon, he shouted for joy. In Calgary, the Palliser gave us adjacent rooms, and then we joined the Writers' Guild of Alberta (which he helped form in 1980 by giving the Inaugural Address) for its annual meeting. So many friends!

Saturday, June 11: The Writers' Guild honored itself by giving Robert Kroetsch its highest award, the Golden Pen. He was overwhelmed with greetings, friendship, and celebrations till midnight.

Sunday, June 12: Bob and I had breakfast together. He was going to do what he had done all his life: mentor young writers for a week at a mountain retreat in Canmore. We sat long over coffee; finally we hugged each other "Goodbye," and I drove north alone.

Next weekend I call his home three days in a row, but only his quiet machine voice answers. Then Tuesday, June 21, 10 p.m.: I am reading in the evening light when the phone rings. A Royal Canadian Mounted Police voice tells me Robert Kroetsch was killed on Highway 21. The car made a left turn across traffic—he was in the passenger seat—and T-boned. Never regained consciousness.

Tuesday, June 28: My wife, Tena, and I are in the Heisler Cemetery with Bob's two daughters and his three sisters and his son-in-law. Together we murmur the Lord's Prayer, which Bob certainly learned before that bitter winter day when the holy water in the Wanda Church font turned to ice, and thereby transformed—as he himself explained it—his temptation to disbelieve into the larger, lifelong temptation to believe.

But this June Tuesday was warm, the sun brilliant over the great fields around the low hill of the cemetery. His two daughters reluctantly slipped the urn into the earth between the gravestones of Paul Kroetsch and Hildegard (née Weller) Kroetsch. From somewhere nearby, in the bright air meadowlarks were singing.

On Highway 21, Tena and I drove back to Edmonton; the sun was drawing the long summer evening down, north into darkness. We stopped again at the place where it happened. I walked across the highway to the edge of the intersection. A great ragged scar was gouged across the gravel shoulder and into the ditch, and I walked it, down, into the crushed grass. The ugly gash ended abruptly in a sprawl of naked, ashy ground. My foot in the grass stubbed against a splinter of bumper plastic. I bent forward, I hunched down, my hands reached down: Bob had been here, my dearest friend Bob, somehow inside his smashed car when it ripped this earth open. Somehow, I had to feel, to touch, that.

> To write
> a poem
> it takes
> a life
> time.
>
> These are the scars
> that make us whole.
>
> These are the scars
> that empty us
> into our lives.
>
> Hold your horses.
> It was a nice trip
> to heaven. Let us
> now visit the
>
> earth.
> The scarred earth
> is our only
> home.
>
> Mother, where are you?
> (Kroetsch 1989, 218)

What is the answer? Is there an answer? Together with Bob, we long to know.

Works Cited

Kroetsch, Robert. 1970. "A Conversation with Margaret Laurence." In *Creation*, by Robert Kroetsch, James Bacque, and Pierre Cravel; edited by Robert Kroetsch, 53–63. Toronto: New Press.

———. 1989. *Completed Field Notes: The Long Poems of Robert Kroetsch*. Toronto: McClelland & Stewart.

———. 1995. "Why I Went Up North and What I Found When He Got There." In *A Likely Story: the Writing Life*, 13–40. Red Deer, AB: Red Deer College Press.

Neuman, Shirley. 1981. "Unearthing Language: An Interview with Rudy Wiebe and Robert Kroetsch." In *A Voice in the Land: Essays by and about Rudy Wiebe*, edited by W. J. Keith, 226–47. Edmonton, AB: NeWest Press.

Wiebe, Rudy. 2017. "Finding Alberta." *Alberta Views*, January/February 2017, 20 (1): 48.

Contributors

Cameron Anstee, Department of English, University of Ottawa
Jennifer Baker, Department of English, University of Ottawa
Albert Braz, Department of English, University of Alberta
Dennis Cooley, Department of English, University of Manitoba
Tanja Cvetković, Faculty of Philosophy, University of Nis
David Eso, Department of English, University of Victoria
Phil Hall, Perth, Ontario
Wolfgang Klooss, Centre for Canadian Studies, University of Trier
Martin Kuester, Marburg Centre for Canadian Studies, University of Marburg
Nicole Markotić, Department of English, University of Windsor
Laurie Ricou, Department of English, University of British Columbia
Robert David Stacey, Department of English, University of Ottawa
David Staines, Department of English, University of Ottawa
Aritha van Herk, Department of English, University of Calgary
Rudy Wiebe, Department of English, University of Alberta
Jason Wiens, Department of English, University of Calgary

REAPPRAISALS: CANADIAN WRITERS

Series editor: David Staines

Reappraisal: Canadian Writers is the longest-running book series dedicated to the study of Canadian literary subjects. Based on the annual Canadian Literature Symposium, hosted by the Department of English at the University of Ottawa, each volume makes the best of the criticism presented at the symposia available, thereby contributing to a critical body of work on Canadian writers and literary subjects that warrant reconsideration.

Previous titles in this collection

Irena R. Makaryk and Kathryn Prince, eds., *Shakespeare and Canada: Remembrance of Ourselves*, 2017.

Janice Fiamengo and Gerald Lynch, eds., *Alice Munro's Miraculous Art: Critical Essays*, 2017.

David Staines, ed., *The Worlds of Carol Shields*, 2014.

Janice Fiamengo, ed., *Home Ground and Foreign Territory: Essays on Early Canadian Literature*, 2014.

David R. Jarraway, ed., *Double-Takes: Intersections Between Canadian Literature and Film*, 2013.

Robert David Stacey, ed., *RE: Reading the Postmodern: Canadian Literature and Criticism after Modernism*, 2010.

For a complete list of our titles, see:
press.uOttawa.ca

www.ingramcontent.com/pod-product-compliance
Lightning Source LLC
Chambersburg PA
CBHW061345300426
44116CB00011B/2005